Publisher
Jim Scheikofer
The Family Handyman®

Director, Publication Services
Sue Baalman-Pohlman
Home Design Alternatives, Inc.

Editor
Kim Karsanbhai
Home Design Alternatives, Inc.

Newsstand Sales
David Algire
Reader's Digest Association, Inc.

John Crouse
Reader's Digest Association, Inc.

Marketing Manager
Andrea Vecchio
The Family Handyman

Production Manager
Judy Rodriguez
The Family Handyman

Plans Administrator
Curtis Cadenhead
Home Design Alternatives, Inc.

The Family Handyman Contents

Vol. 17, No. 7

Featured Homes

Plan #703-0271 is featured on page 72.

Plan #703-0652 is featured on page 270.

Sections

The Family Handyman magazine and Home Design Alternatives (HDA, Inc.) are pleased to join together to bring you this collection of Home Plans, including Cabins, Cottages and Log Homes, from some of the nation's leading designers and architects.

Technical Specifications - At the time the construction drawings were prepared, every effort was made to ensure that these plan and specifications meet nationally recognized building codes (BOCA, Southern Building Code Congress and others). Because national building codes change or vary from area to area some drawing modifications and/or the assistance of a professional designer or architect may be necessary to comply with your local codes or to accommodate specific building conditions. We advise you to consult with your local building official for information regarding codes governing your area.

On The Cover . . .

Plan #703-JB1010 is featured on page 312.
Photo courtesy of Richard Smithers, Nickolasville, TN;
Jim Barna Log Systems, photographer

Inset Photo . . .

Plan #703-JB1065 is featured on page 310.
Photo courtesy of Cecil Strunk, Oneida, TN;
Jim Barna Log Systems, photographer

Except where noted, all photos on this page are courtesy of Home Design Alternatives, Inc.

Quaint Exterior, Full Front Porch

1,657 total square feet of living area

Price Code B

Special features

- Stylish pass-through between living and dining areas
- Master bedroom is secluded from living area for privacy
- Large windows in breakfast and dining areas
- 3 bedrooms, 2 1/2 baths, 2-car drive under garage
- Basement foundation

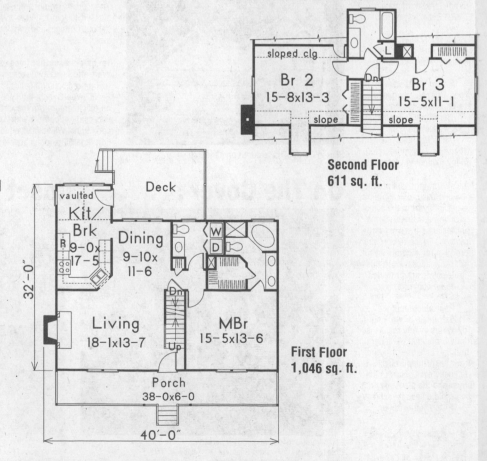

Second Floor
611 sq. ft.

First Floor
1,046 sq. ft.

Terrific Design Loaded With Extras

865 total square feet of living area

Price Code AAA

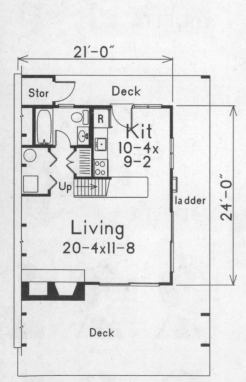

First Floor
495 sq. ft.

Second Floor
370 sq. ft.

Special features

- Central living area provides an enormous amount of space for gathering around the fireplace
- Outdoor ladder on wrap-around deck connects top deck with main deck
- Kitchen is bright and cheerful with lots of windows and access to deck
- 2 bedrooms, 1 bath
- Pier foundation

4

TO ORDER BLUEPRINTS USE THE FORM ON PAGE 15 OR CALL TOLL-FREE 1-877-671-6036
View thousands more home plans online at www.familyhandyman.com/homeplans

Vaulted Second Floor Sitting Area

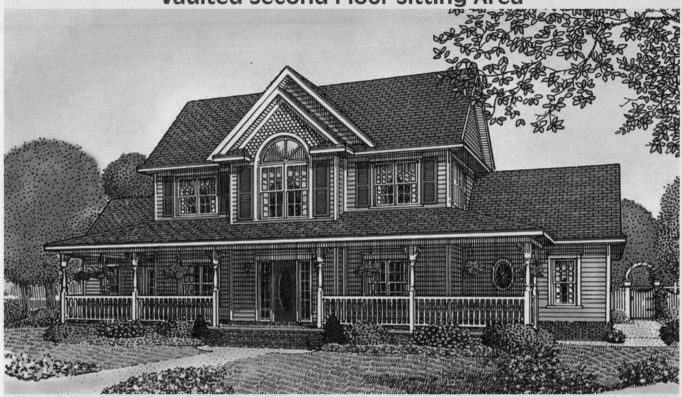

2,433 total square feet of living area

Price Code D

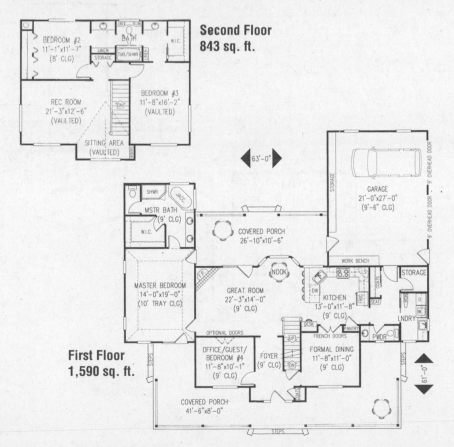

Second Floor
843 sq. ft.

BEDROOM #2
11'-1"x11'-7"
(8' CLG)

BATH

W.I.C.

LINEN

STORAGE

TUB/SHWR

REC ROOM
21'-3"x12'-6"
(VAULTED)

BEDROOM #3
11'-8"x16'-2"
(VAULTED)

DN

SITTING AREA
(VAULTED)

63'-0"

SHWR

JACC

MSTR BATH
(9' CLG)

W.I.C.

MASTER BEDROOM
14'-0"x19'-0"
(10' TRAY CLG)

COVERED PORCH
26'-10"x10'-6"

FP

NOOK

GREAT ROOM
22'-3"x14'-0"
(9' CLG)

KITCHEN
13'-0"x11'-8"
(9' CLG)

DW

PRG

SEAT

STORAGE

GARAGE
21'-0"x27'-0"
(9'-6" CLG)

9' OVERHEAD DOOR

9' OVERHEAD DOOR

STORAGE

WORK BENCH

W

D

LNDRY

PWDR

PANTRY

DESK

FRENCH DOORS

OPTIONAL DOORS

OFFICE/GUEST/
BEDROOM #4
11'-8"x10'-1"
(9' CLG)

FOYER
(9' CLG)

UP

FORMAL DINING
11'-8"x11'-0"
(9' CLG)

61'-0"

First Floor
1,590 sq. ft.

COVERED PORCH
41'-6"x8'-0"

STEPS

STEPS

STEPS

STEPS

Special features

- Two second floor bedrooms share a jack and jill bath
- Terrific covered porch has access into master bedroom or great room
- Snack bar in kitchen provides additional seating for dining
- 3 bedrooms, 2 1/2 baths, 2-car side entry garage
- Basement, crawl space or slab foundation, please specify when ordering

TO ORDER BLUEPRINTS USE THE FORM ON PAGE 15 OR CALL TOLL-FREE 1-877-671-6036
View thousands more home plans online at www.familyhandyman.com/homeplans

5

Spacious A-Frame

1,769 total square feet of living area

Price Code B

Second Floor
463 sq. ft.

Special features

- Living room boasts elegant cathedral ceiling and fireplace
- U-shaped kitchen and dining area combine for easy living
- Secondary bedrooms include double closets
- Secluded master bedroom with sloped ceiling, large walk-in closet and private bath
- 3 bedrooms, 2 baths
- Basement foundation, drawings also include crawl space and slab foundations

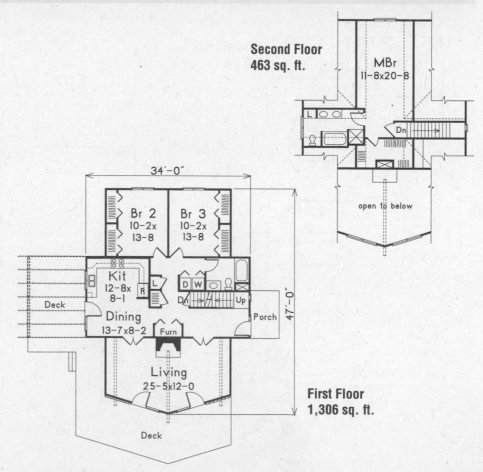

First Floor
1,306 sq. ft.

6

TO ORDER BLUEPRINTS USE THE FORM ON PAGE 15 OR CALL TOLL-FREE 1-877-671-6036
View thousands more home plans online at www.familyhandyman.com/homeplans

Unique Craftsman Style Home

3,246 total square feet of living area

Price Code G

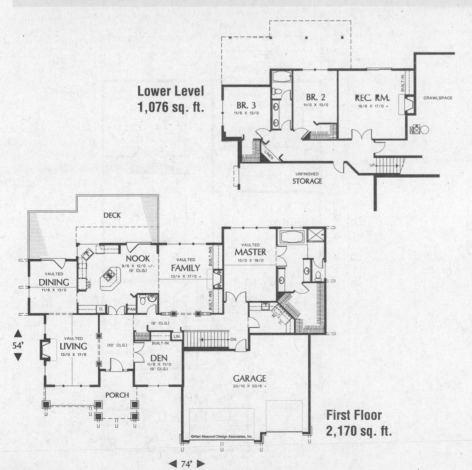

**Lower Level
1,076 sq. ft.**

BR. 3
11/6 X 13/0

BR. 2
11/0 X 13/0

REC. RM.
16/8 X 17/0

CRAWLSPACE

LINEN

UP

UNFINISHED
STORAGE

DECK

NOOK
9/6 X 12/0 +/-
(9' CLG)

VAULTED
FAMILY
13/4 X 17/0

VAULTED
MASTER
13/0 X 18/0

VAULTED
DINING
11/8 X 13/0

REF.

PAN

(9' CLG.)

LIN.

BUILT-IN

DN.

54'

VAULTED
LIVING
13/0 X 17/8

(10' CLG.)

DEN
11/8 X 11/0
(9' CLG.)

GARAGE
30/10 X 20/6

PORCH

©Alan Mascord Design Associates, Inc.

**First Floor
2,170 sq. ft.**

◄ 74' ►

Special features

- Private master bedroom has a sumptuous bath and large walk-in closet
- Second floor recreation room is a great casual family area
- L-shaped kitchen has a large center island with stove top and dining space
- 3 bedrooms, 2 1/2 baths, 3-car garage
- Crawl space foundation

TO ORDER BLUEPRINTS USE THE FORM ON PAGE 15 OR CALL TOLL-FREE 1-877-671-6036
View thousands more home plans online at www.familyhandyman.com/homeplans

7

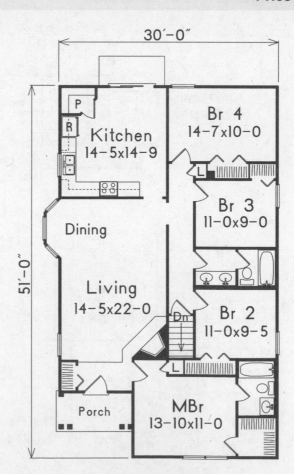

Four Bedroom Living For A Narrow Lot

1,452 total square feet of living area

Price Code A

Special features

- Large living room features cozy corner fireplace, bayed dining area and access from entry with guest closet

- Forward master bedroom suite enjoys having its own bath and linen closet

- Three additional bedrooms share a bath with double-bowl vanity

- 4 bedrooms, 2 baths

- Basement foundation

30'-0"

51'-0"

P

R

Kitchen
14-5x14-9

Br 4
14-7x10-0

Dining

L

Br 3
11-0x9-0

Living
14-5x22-0

Dn

Br 2
11-0x9-5

L

Porch

MBr
13-10x11-0

8

TO ORDER BLUEPRINTS USE THE FORM ON PAGE 15 OR CALL TOLL-FREE 1-877-671-6036
View thousands more home plans online at www.familyhandyman.com/homeplans

Authentic Southern Charm

2,074 total square feet of living area

Price Code C

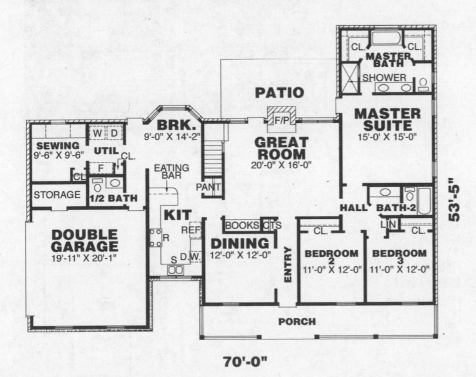

Special features

- Unique sewing room is ideal for hobby enthusiasts and has counterspace for convenience
- Double walk-in closets are located in the luxurious master bath
- A built-in bookcase in the great room adds charm
- 3 bedrooms, 2 baths, 2-car side entry garage
- Slab foundation

Tranquility Of An Atrium Cottage

1,384 total square feet of living area

Price Code A

Special features

- Wrap-around country porch for peaceful evenings

- Vaulted great room enjoys a large bay window, stone fireplace, pass-through kitchen and awesome rear views through atrium window wall

- Master suite features double entry doors, walk-in closet and a fabulous bath

- Atrium open to 611 square feet of optional living area below

- 2 bedrooms, 2 baths, 1-car side entry garage

- Walk-out basement foundation

Rear View

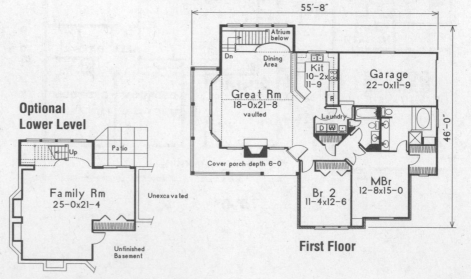

Optional Lower Level

Up

Patio

Family Rm
25-0x21-4

Unexcavated

Unfinished Basement

55'-8"

Atrium below

Dn

Dining Area

Kit
10-2x
11-9

Garage
22-0x11-9

Great Rm
18-0x21-8
vaulted

R

Laundry

D W

Cover porch depth 6-0

46'-0"

Br 2
11-4x12-6

MBr
12-8x15-0

First Floor

TO ORDER BLUEPRINTS USE THE FORM ON PAGE 15 OR CALL TOLL-FREE 1-877-671-6036
View thousands more home plans online at www.familyhandyman.com/homeplans

Vaulted Two-Story Foyer Makes A Grand Entry

2,599 total square feet of living area

Price Code D

Second Floor
997 sq. ft.

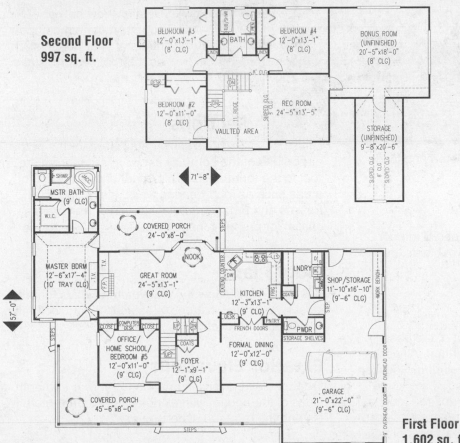

First Floor
1,602 sq. ft.

Special features

- Office/home school room could easily be converted to a fifth bedroom

- Recreation room on the second floor would make a great casual living area or children's play room

- Large shop/storage has an oversized work bench for hobbies or projects

- Bonus room on the second floor has an additional 385 square feet of living area

- 4 bedrooms, 2 1/2 baths, 2-car garage with shop/storage

- Basement, crawl space or slab foundation, please specify when ordering

TO ORDER BLUEPRINTS USE THE FORM ON PAGE 15 OR CALL TOLL-FREE 1-877-671-6036
View thousands more home plans online at www.familyhandyman.com/homeplans

11

Our Blueprint Packages Offer...

Quality plans for building your future, with extras that provide unsurpassed value, ensure good construction and long-term enjoyment.

A quality home - one that looks good, functions well, and provides years of enjoyment - is a product of many things - design, materials, craftsmanship.

But it's also the result of outstanding blueprints - the actual plans and specifications that tell the builder exactly how to build your home.

And with our BLUEPRINT PACKAGES you get the absolute best. A complete set of blueprints is available for every design in this book. These "working drawings," are highly detailed, resulting in two key benefits:

- Better understanding by the contractor of how to build your home and...
- More accurate construction estimates.

When you purchase one of our designs, you'll receive all of the BLUEPRINT components shown here - elevations, foundation plan, floor plans, sections, and/ or details. Other helpful building aids are also available to help make your dream home a reality.

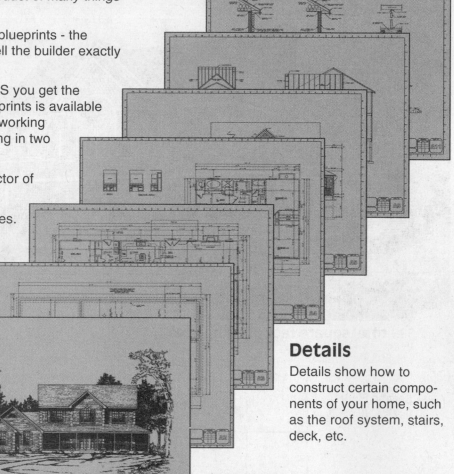

Cover Sheet

The cover sheet is the artist's rendering of the exterior of the home. It will give you an idea of how your home will look when completed and landscaped.

Interior Elevations

Interior elevations provide views of special interior elements such as fireplaces, kitchen cabinets, built-in units and other features of the home.

Foundation Plan

The foundation plan shows the layout of the basement, crawl space, slab or pier foundation. All necessary notations and dimensions are included. See plan page for the foundation types included. If the home plan you choose does not have your desired foundation type, our Customer Service Representatives can advise you on how to customize your foundation to suit your specific needs or site conditions.

Details

Details show how to construct certain components of your home, such as the roof system, stairs, deck, etc.

Sections

Sections show detail views of the home or portions of the home as if it were sliced from the roof to the foundation. This sheet shows important areas such as load-bearing walls, stairs, joists, trusses and other structural elements, which are critical for proper construction.

Floor Plans

The floor plans show the placement of walls, doors, closets, plumbing fixtures, electrical outlets, columns, and beams for each level of the home.

Exterior Elevations

Exterior elevations illustrate the front, rear and both sides of the house, with all details of exterior materials and the required dimensions.

What Kind Of Plan Package Do You Need?

Now that you've found the home you've been looking for, here are some suggestions on how to make your Dream Home a reality. To get started, order the type of plans that fit your particular situation.

YOUR CHOICES

- **THE 1-SET STUDY PACKAGE -** We offer a 1-set plan package so you can study your home in detail. This one set is considered a study set and is marked "not for construction". It is a copyright violation to reproduce blueprints.

- **THE MINIMUM 5-SET PACKAGE -** If you're ready to start the construction process, this 5-set package is the minimum number of blueprint sets you will need. It will require keeping close track of each set so they can be used by multiple subcontractors and tradespeople.

- **THE STANDARD 8-SET PACKAGE -** For best results in terms of cost, schedule and quality of construction, we recommend you order eight (or more) sets of blueprints. Besides one set for yourself, additional sets of blueprints will be required by your mortgage lender, local building department, general contractor and all subcontractors working on foundation, electrical, plumbing, heating/air conditioning, carpentry work, etc.

- **REPRODUCIBLE MASTERS -** If you wish to make some minor design changes, you'll want to order reproducible masters. These drawings contain the same information as the blueprints but are printed on erasable and reproducible paper. This will allow your builder or a local design professional to make the necessary drawing changes without the major expense of redrawing the plans. This package also allows you to print as many copies of the modified plans as you need.

- **MIRROR REVERSE SETS -** Plans can be printed in mirror reverse. These plans are useful when the house would fit your site better if all the rooms were on the opposite side than shown. They are simply a mirror image of the original drawings causing the lettering and dimensions to read backwards. Therefore, when ordering mirror reverse drawings, you must purchase at least one set of right reading plans.

PLAN #703-0151 Pg. 115

Other Helpful Building Aids...

Your Blueprint Package will contain the necessary construction information to build your home. We also offer the following products and services to save you time and money in the building process.

- **MATERIAL LIST -** Material lists are available for many of the plans in this book. Each list gives you the quantity, dimensions and description of the building materials necessary to construct your home. You'll get faster and more accurate bids from your contractor while saving money by paying for only the materials you need. See the Home Plans Index on page 14 for availability. Refer to the order form on page 15 for pricing.

- **DETAIL PLAN PACKAGES:** Framing, Plumbing & Electrical Plan Packages - Three separate packages offer homebuilders details for constructing various foundations; numerous floor, wall and roof framing techniques; simple to complex residential wiring; sump and water softener hookups; plumbing connection methods; installation of septic systems and more. Each package includes three-dimensional illustrations and a glossary of terms. Purchase one or all three. Cost: $20.00 each or all three for $40.00. Note: These drawings do not pertain to a specific home plan.

- **THE LEGAL KIT™ -** Our Legal Kit provides contracts and legal forms to help protect you from the potential pitfalls inherent in the building process. The Kit supplies commonly used forms and contracts suitable for homeowners and builders. It can save you a considerable amount of time and help protect you and your assets during and after construction. Cost: $35.00

- **EXPRESS DELIVERY -** Most orders are processed within 24 hours of receipt. Please allow 7 working days for delivery. If you need to place a rush order, please call us by 11:00 a.m. CST and ask for express service (allow 1-2 business days).

- **TECHNICAL ASSISTANCE-** If you have questions, call our technical support line at 1-314-770-2228 between 8:00 a.m. and 5:00 p.m. CST. Whether it involves design modifications or field assistance, our designers are extremely familiar with all of our designs and will be happy to help you. We want your home to be everything you expect it to be.

HOME DESIGN ALTERNATIVES, INC.

Home Plans Index

Plan Number	Sq. Ft.	Price Code	Page	Mat. List
703-0101	1,039	AA	217	X
703-0102	1,246	A	254	X
703-0104	1,359	A	163	X
703-0105	1,360	A	23	X
703-0106	1,443	A	47	X
703-0108	1,516	B	267	X
703-0109	1,565	B	155	X
703-0111	1,582	B	120	X
703-0112	1,668	C	97	X
703-0118	1,816	C	73	X
703-0143	2,449	E	91	X
703-0151	2,874	E	115	X
703-0161	1,630	B	146	X
703-0163	1,772	C	38	X
703-0173	1,220	A	201	X
703-0174	1,657	B	2	X
703-0190	1,600	C	104	X
703-0192	1,266	A	30	X
703-0196	1,314	A	244	X
703-0198	1,416	A	252	X
703-0201	1,814	D	130	X
703-0203	1,475	B	292	X
703-0207	1,550	B	239	X
703-0209	1,556	B	282	X
703-0212	1,707	C	253	X
703-0213	2,059	C	59	X
703-0216	1,661	B	221	X
703-0217	1,360	A	105	X
703-0221	1,619	B	63	X
703-0237	1,631	B	215	X
703-0239	1,496	A	152	X
703-0241	829	AAA	71	X
703-0242	717	AAA	119	X
703-0243	581	AAA	180	X
703-0246	1,539	B	129	X
703-0249	1,501	B	293	X
703-0265	1,314	A	279	X
703-0270	1,448	A	237	X
703-0271	1,368	A	72	X
703-0272	1,283	A	21	X
703-0273	988	AA	179	X
703-0274	1,020	AA	246	X
703-0277	1,127	AA	67	X
703-0291	1,600	B	238	X
703-0292	1,304	A	65	X
703-0294	1,655	B	148	X
703-0297	1,320	A	177	X
703-0312	1,921	D	94	X
703-0316	1,824	C	209	X
703-0335	1,865	D	171	X
703-0357	1,550	B	17	X
703-0394	1,558	B	113	X
703-0413	2,182	C	236	X
703-0417	2,828	E	114	X
703-0447	1,393	B	36	X
703-0448	1,597	C	100	X
703-0449	2,505	D	103	X
703-0461	828	AAA	234	X
703-0462	1,028	AA	29	X
703-0475	1,711	B	205	X
703-0476	576	AAA	198	X
703-0477	1,140	AA	200	X
703-0479	1,294	A	208	X
703-0484	1,403	A	108	X
703-0485	1,195	AA	229	X
703-0488	2,059	C	122	X
703-0489	1,543	B	175	X
703-0493	976	AA	231	X
703-0494	1,085	AA	53	X
703-0496	977	AA	243	X
703-0502	864	AAA	39	X
703-0503	1,000	AA	81	X
703-0522	1,818	C	158	X
703-0523	1,875	C	223	X
703-0529	1,285	B	57	X
703-0539	1,769	B	6	X
703-0547	720	AAA	49	X
703-0549	1,230	A	268	X
703-0651	962	AA	90	X
703-0652	1,524	B	270	X
703-0653	1,563	B	196	X
703-0657	914	AA	204	X
703-0658	647	AAA	298	X
703-0660	1,321	A	277	X
703-0670	1,170	AA	50	X
703-0676	1,367	A	117	X
703-0690	1,400	A	18	X
703-0692	1,339	A	68	X
703-0694	1,285	A	257	X
703-0696	676	AAA	294	X
703-0698	1,143	AA	48	X
703-0700	416	AAA	296	X
703-0705	2,758	E	295	X
703-0712	2,029	C	45	X
703-0717	1,268	A	194	X
703-0726	1,428	A	230	X
703-0732	1,384	A	10	X
703-0739	1,684	B	109	X
703-0749	2,727	E	86	X
703-0751	1,278	A	37	X
703-0765	1,000	AA	190	X
703-0766	990	AA	127	X
703-0767	990	AA	184	X
703-0768	1,879	C	251	X
703-0769	1,440	A	249	X
703-0779	1,277	A	173	X
703-0795	1,399	A	140	X
703-0806	1,452	A	8	X
703-0807	1,231	A	197	X
703-0808	969	AA	85	X
703-0809	1,084	AA	112	X
703-0810	1,200	A	139	X
703-0811	1,161	AA	291	X
703-0813	888	AAA	41	X
703-0814	1,169	AA	291	X
703-1120	1,232	A	162	X
703-1233	1,948	C	281	X
703-1293	1,200	A	156	X
703-1297	1,922	C	131	X
703-1305	2,009	C	101	X
703-1329	1,364	A	166	X
703-1336	1,364	A	76	X
703-1347	1,948	C	19	X
703-1413	1,400	A	273	
703-AMD-1307B	3,246	G	7	X
703-AMD-2163	1,978	C	118	X
703-AMD-2229	2,287	D	87	X
703-AP-1002	1,050	AA	102	X
703-AP-1410	1,496	A	220	X
703-AP-1612	1,643	B	43	X
703-AX-301	1,783	D	203	X
703-AX-1140	1,207	A	213	X
703-AX-7944	1,648	B	95	X
703-AX-8382	1,563	B	138	X
703-AX-91316	1,097	AA	83	X
703-AX-91317	1,419	A	144	
703-AX-93308	1,793	B	77	X
703-AX-97359	1,380	A	226	X
703-BF-1314	1,375	A	40	X
703-BF-3007	3,012	E	272	X
703-BF-DR1108	1,150	AA	245	X
703-BF-DR1109	1,191	AA	124	X
703-CHD-14-18	1,429	A	207	X
703-CHD-15-54	1,612	B	261	X
703-CHD-16-8	1,609	B	290	X
703-CHD-16-60	1,686	B	248	X
703-CHD-20-09	2,074	C	9	X
703-CHD-20-51	2,084	C	66	X
703-CHP-1432-A-142	1,405	A	84	X
703-CHP-1532A1	1,520	B	157	X
703-CHP-1632A	1,649	B	167	X
703-CHP-1633-A-18	1,618	C	241	X
703-CHP-1642-A-10	1,650	B	199	X
703-CHP-1733-A-7	1,737	B	145	X
703-DBI-8077	1,858	C	225	X
703-DBI-8095	1,694	B	280	X
703-DBI-24035-9P	1,395	A	135	X
703-DBI-24038-9P	2,126	C	20	X
703-DBI-24045-9P	1,263	A	60	
703-DDI-95-234	1,649	B	52	
703-DDI-100213	2,202	D	92	
703-DDI-100214	2,104	C	181	
703-DDI-100-215	1,757	B	121	
703-DDI-101-301	1,224	A	284	
703-DH-864G	864	AAA	132	
703-DH-1377	1,377	A	178	
703-DH-1786	1,785	B	98	
703-DH-2005	1,700	B	44	
703-DH-2189	2,189	C	278	
703-DH-2313J	2,123	C	189	
703-DL-17353L1	1,735	B	88	
703-DL-21644L1	2,164	C	170	
703-DL-25454L1	2,545	D	185	
703-DR-2290	1,124	AA	110	X
703-DR-2916	1,484	A	111	X
703-DR-2929	1,285	A	297	X
703-DR-2936	1,056	AA	202	X
703-DR-2939	1,480	A	195	X
703-FB-282	1,425	A	22	
703-FB-489	1,215	A	172	
703-FB-894	1,124	AA	250	X
703-FB-902	1,856	C	169	X
703-FB-1148	1,491	A	42	X
703-FDG-4044	1,577	B	227	
703-FDG-7913	1,702	B	274	
703-FDG-7963-L	1,830	C	56	X
703-FDG-8729-L	2,529	D	126	X
703-GH-10785	1,907	C	299	X
703-GH-20198	1,792	B	143	X
703-GH-24705	1,562	B	263	X
703-GH-24706	1,470	A	46	X
703-GH-24711	1,434	A	64	X
703-GH-24721	1,539	B	247	X
703-GH-24724	1,982	C	218	X
703-GH-34043	1,583	B	256	X
703-GM-1253	1,253	A	82	X
703-GM-1333	1,333	A	219	X
703-GM-1406	1,406	A	159	X
703-GM-1474	1,474	A	285	X
703-GM-1550	1,550	B	116	X
703-GM-1780	1,780	B	32	X
703-GM-1815	1,815	C	191	X
703-GM-1966	1,966	C	188	X
703-GSD-1123	1,734	B	134	X
703-GSD-1748	1,496	A	70	X
703-HDG-97006	1,042	AA	79	X
703-HDG-99004	1,231	A	233	X
703-HDS-1167	1,167	AA	27	X
703-HDS-1442-2	1,442	A	176	X
703-HDS-1558-2	1,885	C	28	X
703-HDS-1668	1,668	B	255	X
703-HDS-1993	1,993	C	240	X
703-HP-C316	1,997	C	154	X
703-HP-C460	1,389	A	78	X
703-HP-C619	1,771	B	183	X
703-HP-C659	1,118	AA	141	X
703-HP-C675	1,673	B	165	X
703-HP-C689	1,295	A	264	X
703-JA-50294	1,430	A	160	X
703-JA-62995	1,342	A	74	X
703-JA-65996	1,962	C	228	X
703-JB-1003	1,477	A	311	X
703-JB-1004	1,382	A	307	X
703-JB-1005	1,616	B	302	X
703-JB-1007	1,449	A	300	X
703-JB-1010	3,341	F	312	X
703-JB-1013	2,137	C	313	X
703-JB-1014	2,206	D	317	X
703-JB-1015	1,725	B	315	X
703-JB-1018	1,684	B	315	X
703-JB-1023	1,492	A	318	X
703-JB-1016	3,098	E	319	X
703-JB-1027	2,064	C	309	X
703-JB-1028	1,122	AA	318	X
703-JB-1029	1,591	B	303	X
703-JB-1030	1,940	C	316	X
703-JB-1031	1,769	B	301	
703-JB-1039	1,810	C	308	
703-JB-1043	1,665	B	305	
703-JB-1046	1,743	B	306	
703-JB-1048	2,301	D	304	
703-JB-1050	2,821	E	320	
703-JB-1065	1,658	B	310	
703-JB-1060	1,480	A	307	
703-JB-1064	4,885	G	314	
703-JFD-20-1887-1	1,887	C	242	
703-JFD-20-2097-1	2,097	C	96	
703-JFD-20-2643-2	2,643	E	258	
703-JV-1325-B	1,325	A	164	X
703-JV-1735A	1,735	B	24	X
703-JV-1765-A-SJ	1,765	B	51	X
703-JV-1870-A	1,870	C	210	X
703-JV-2008-B	2,008	C	151	
703-JV-2091-A	2,475	D	192	X
703-LBD-10-1B	1,087	AA	287	
703-LBD-13-1A	1,310	A	259	
703-LBD-15-2A	1,553	B	186	
703-LBD-17-14A	1,725	B	26	
703-LBD-19-16A	1,993	C	150	
703-MG-01240	2,272	G	106	
703-MG-96132	2,450	D	80	
703-MG-97099	1,093	AA	136	
703-N006	1,209	A	35	X
703-N010	624	AAA	61	X
703-N015	1,275	A	193	X
703-N026	1,106	AA	214	X
703-N027	1,312	A	232	X
703-N042	1,280	A	75	X
703-N048	1,272	A	54	X
703-N061	1,224	A	265	X
703-N063	1,299	A	275	X
703-N064	1,176	AA	283	X
703-N065	1,750	B	69	X
703-N085	1,316	A	216	X
703-N087	784	AAA	212	X
703-N107	1,680	B	289	X
703-N114	792	AAA	211	X
703-N118	527	AAA	125	X
703-N119	1,200	A	153	X
703-N127	1,344	A	187	X
703-N130	1,584	B	235	X
703-N142	1,354	A	276	X
703-N145	618	AAA	286	X
703-N147	865	AAA	4	X
703-NDG-415	1,544	B	142	X
703-NDG-416	1,397	A	182	X
703-NDG-418	1,472	A	34	X
703-NDG-623	1,294	A	147	X
703-NDG-624	1,903	C	161	X
703-RDD-1374-9	1,374	A	123	
703-RDD-1753-9	1,753	B	25	
703-RDD-1815-8	1,815	C	55	
703-RDD-1895-9	1,895	C	262	
703-RJ-A921	977	AA	271	
703-RJ-A1079	1,021	AA	137	
703-RJ-A1369A	1,398	A	224	
703-RJ-B123	1,270	A	58	
703-RJ-B1416	1,455	A	174	
703-SH-SEA-001	1,735	B	266	
703-SH-SEA-008	1,073	AA	269	X
703-SH-SEA-100	2,582	D	288	
703-SH-SEA-226	1,543	B	99	
703-SH-SEA-245	1,578	B	93	
703-SH-SEA-400	1,568	B	107	
703-SRD-241	1,315	A	149	
703-SRD-279	1,611	B	260	
703-SRD-317	2,764	E	62	
703-SRD-335	1,544	B	222	
703-SRD-348	1,648	B	33	
703-SRD-352	1,509	B	133	
703-UD-D167	2,433	D	5	
703-UD-E162	2,599	D	11	
703-VL947	947	AA	31	X
703-VL2069	2,069	C	128	X
703-VL2888	2,888	E	89	X
703-VL3011	3,011	E	168	X

IMPORTANT INFORMATION TO KNOW BEFORE YOU ORDER

◆ **Exchange Policies -** Since blueprints are printed in response to your order, we cannot honor requests for refunds. However, if for some reason you find that the plan you have purchased does not meet your requirements, you may exchange that plan for another plan in our collection. At the time of the exchange, you will be charged a processing fee of 25% of your original plan package price, plus the difference in price between the plan packages (if applicable) and the cost to ship the new plans to you.

◆ **Building Codes & Requirements -** At the time the construction drawings were prepared, every effort was made to ensure that these plans and specifications meet nationally recognized codes. Our plans conform to most national building codes. Because building codes vary from area to area, some drawing modifications and/or the assistance of a professional designer or architect may be necessary to comply with your local codes or to accommodate specific building site conditions. We advise you to consult with your local building official for information regarding codes governing your area.

Please note: Reproducible drawings can only be exchanged if the package is unopened, and exchanges are allowed only within 90 days of purchase.

Questions? Call Our Customer Service Number
1-877-671-6036

BLUEPRINT PRICE SCHEDULE — BEST VALUE

Price Code	1-Set	SAVE $110 5-Sets	SAVE $200 8-Sets	Material List*	Reproducible Masters
AAA	$225	$295	$340	$50	$440
AA	$275	$345	$390	$55	$490
A	$325	$395	$440	$60	$540
B	$375	$445	$490	$60	$590
C	$425	$495	$540	$65	$640
D	$475	$545	$590	$65	$690
E	$525	$595	$640	$70	$740
F	$575	$645	$690	$70	$790
G	$650	$720	$765	$75	$865
H	$755	$825	$870	$80	$970

Plan prices guaranteed through June 30, 2004.
Please note that plans are not refundable.

◆ **Additional Sets* -** Additional sets of the plan ordered are available for $45.00 each. Five-set, eight-set, and reproducible packages offer considerable savings.

◆ **Mirror Reverse Plans* -** Available for an additional $5.00 per set, these plans are simply a mirror image of the original drawings causing the dimensions & lettering to read backwards. Therefore, when ordering mirror reverse plans, you must purchase at least one set of right reading plans.

◆ **One-Set Study Package -** We offer a one-set plan package so you can study your home in detail. This one set is considered a study set and is marked "not for construction". It is a copyright violation to reproduce blueprints.

*Available only within 90 days after purchase of plan package or reproducible masters of same plan.

SHIPPING & HANDLING CHARGES

U.S. SHIPPING	1-4 Sets	5-7 Sets	8 Sets or Reproducibles
Regular *(allow 7-10 business days)*	$15.00	$17.50	$25.00
Priority *(allow 3-5 business days)*	$25.00	$30.00	$35.00
Express* *(allow 1-2 business days)*	$35.00	$40.00	$45.00

CANADA SHIPPING (to/from) - Plans with suffix DR & SH	1-4 Sets	5-7 Sets	8 Sets or Reproducibles
Standard *(allow 8-12 business days)*	$25.00	$30.00	$35.00
Express* *(allow 3-5 business days)*	$40.00	$40.00	$45.00

Overseas Shipping/International - Call, fax, or e-mail (plans@hdainc.com) for shipping costs.

* For express delivery please call us by 11:00 a.m. CST

How To Order

For fastest service, Call Toll-Free
1-877-671-6036
24 HOURS A DAY

Three Easy Ways To Order

1. CALL toll-free 1-877-671-6036 for credit card orders. MasterCard, Visa, Discover and American Express are accepted.

2. FAX your order to 1-314-770-2226.

3. MAIL the Order Form to:

   HDA, Inc.
   4390 Green Ash Drive
   St. Louis, MO 63045

ORDER FORM

Please send me -
PLAN NUMBER 703BT - _____

PRICE CODE _____ (see Plan Index)

Specify Foundation Type - see plan page for availability
☐ Slab   ☐ Crawl space   ☐ Pier
☐ Basement   ☐ Walk-out basement

☐ Reproducible Masters .... $ _____
☐ Eight-Set Plan Package .... $ _____
☐ Five-Set Plan Package .... $ _____
☐ One-Set Study Package (no mirror reverse) $ _____
☐ Additional Plan Sets
   _____ (Qty.) at $45.00 each .... $ _____
☐ Print in Mirror Reverse
   _____ (Qty.) add $5.00 per set .... $ _____
☐ Material List .... $ _____
☐ Legal Kit (see page 13) .... $ _____
Detail Plan Packages: (see page 13)
   ☐ Framing ☐ Electrical ☐ Plumbing $ _____
                          SUBTOTAL $ _____
SALES TAX (MO residents add 7%) .... $ _____
☐ Shipping / Handling (see chart at left) $ _____
   TOTAL ENCLOSED (US funds only) $ _____
   (Sorry no CODs)

I hereby authorize HDA, Inc. to charge this purchase to my credit card account (check one):

☐ MasterCard   ☐ VISA   ☐ DISCOVER NOVUS   ☐ AMERICAN EXPRESS Cards

Credit Card number _____

Expiration date _____

Signature _____

Name _____
          (Please print or type)

Street Address _____
          (Please do not use PO Box)

City _____

State _____   Zip _____

Daytime phone number (____) - _____

I'm a ☐ Builder/Contractor   I ☐ have
      ☐ Homeowner   ☐ have not
      ☐ Renter   selected my
                                general contractor

Thank you for your order!

15

QUICK AND EASY CUSTOMIZING
MAKE CHANGES TO YOUR HOME PLAN IN 4 STEPS

HERE'S AN AFFORDABLE AND EFFICIENT WAY TO MAKE CHANGES TO YOUR PLAN.

1 Select the house plan that most closely meets your needs. Purchase of a reproducible master is necessary in order to make changes to a plan.

2 Call 1-877-671-6036 to place your order. Tell the sales representative you're interested in customizing a plan. A $50 refundable consultation fee will be charged. You will then be instructed to complete a customization checklist indicating all the changes you wish to make to your plan. You may attach sketches if necessary. If you proceed with the custom changes the $50 will be credited to the total amount charged.

3 FAX the completed customization checklist to our design consultant at 1-866-477-5173 or e-mail custom@drummonddesigns.com. Within *24-48 business hours you will be provided with a written cost estimate to modify your plan. Our design consultant will contact you by phone if you wish to discuss any of your changes in greater detail.

4 Once you approve the estimate, a 75% retainer fee is collected and customization work gets underway. Preliminary drawings can usually be completed within *5-10 business days. Following approval of the preliminary drawings your design changes are completed within *5-10 business days. Your remaining 25% balance due is collected prior to shipment of your completed drawings. You will be shipped five sets of revised blueprints or a reproducible master, plus a customized materials list if required.

*Terms are subject to change without notice.

BEFORE
Plan 2829

Customized Version of Plan 2829

AFTER

MODIFICATION PRICING GUIDE

CATEGORIES	Average Cost from…	to
Adding or removing living space (square footage)	Quote required	
Adding or removing a garage	$400	$680
Garage: Front entry to side load or vice versa	Starting at $300	
Adding a screened porch	$280	$600
Adding a bonus room in the attic	$450	$780
Changing full basement to crawl space or vice versa	Starting at $220	
Changing full basement to slab or vice versa	Starting at $260	
Changing exterior building material	Starting at $200	
Changing roof lines	$360	$630
Adjusting ceiling height	$280	$500
Adding, moving or removing an exterior opening	$55 per opening	
Adding or removing a fireplace	$90	$200
Modifying a non-bearing wall or room	$55 per rooom	
Changing exterior walls from 2"x4" to 2"x6"	Starting at $200	
Redesigning a bathroom or a kitchen	$120	$280
Reverse plan right reading	Quote required	
Adapting plans for local building code requirements	Quote required	
Engineering stamping only	$450 / any state	
Any other engineering services	Quote required	
Adjust plan for handicapped accessibility	Quote required	
Interactive illustrations (choices of exterior materials)	Quote required	
Metric conversion of home plan	$400	

Note: Any home plan can be customized to accommodate your desired changes. The average prices specifed above are provided only as examples for the most commonly requested changes, and are subject to change without notice. Prices for changes will vary according to the number of modifications requested, plan size, style, and metod of design used by the original designer. To obtain a detailed cost estimate, please contact us.

16

Vaulted Ceilings Add Dimension

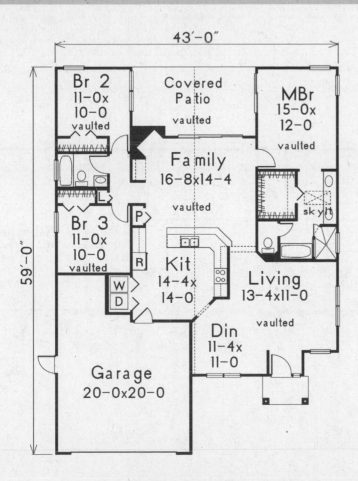

1,550 total square feet of living area

Price Code B

Special features

- Cozy corner fireplace provides focal point in family room
- Master bedroom features large walk-in closet, skylight and separate tub and shower
- Convenient laundry closet
- Kitchen with pantry and breakfast bar connects to family room
- Family room and master bedroom access covered patio
- 3 bedrooms, 2 baths, 2-car garage
- Slab foundation

Classic Ranch Has Grand Appeal With Expansive Porch

1,400 total square feet of living area   **Price Code A**

Special features

- Master bedroom is secluded for privacy
- Large utility room with additional cabinet space
- Covered porch provides an outdoor seating area
- Roof dormers add great curb appeal
- Vaulted ceilings in living room and master bedroom
- Oversized two-car garage with storage
- 3 bedrooms, 2 baths, 2-car garage
- Basement foundation, drawings also include crawl space foundation

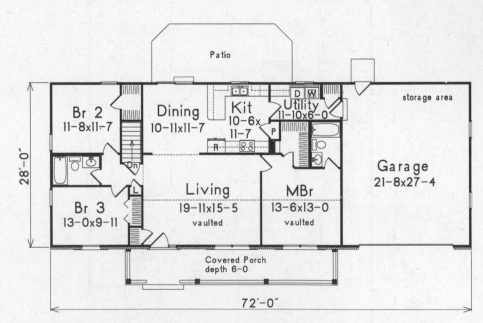

Patio

Br 2
11-8x11-7

Dining
10-11x11-7

Kit
10-6x
11-7

Utility
11-10x6-0

storage area

28'-0"

Br 3
13-0x9-11

Living
19-11x15-5
vaulted

MBr
13-6x13-0
vaulted

Garage
21-8x27-4

Covered Porch
depth 6-0

72'-0"

Inviting Home With Country Flavor

1,948 total square feet of living area

Price Code C

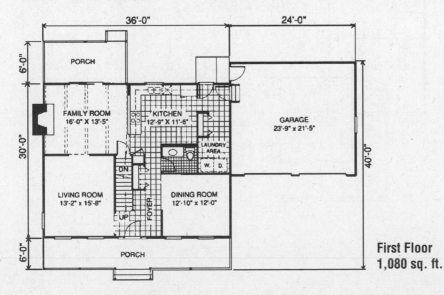

MASTER BEDROOM 13'-4" x 15'-0"

BEDROOM 12'-6" x 12'-10"

BEDROOM 15'-2" x 11'-7"

DN

Second Floor 868 sq. ft.

36'-0"   24'-0"

6'-0"

PORCH

FAMILY ROOM 16'-0" X 13'-5"

KITCHEN 12'-9" X 11'-6"

GARAGE 23'-9" x 21'-5"

30'-0"

40'-0"

LAUNDRY AREA   W. D.

DN

LIVING ROOM 13'-2" x 15'-8"

FOYER

UP

DINING ROOM 12'-10" x 12'-0"

6'-0"

PORCH

First Floor 1,080 sq. ft.

Special features

- Large elongated porch for moonlit evenings
- Stylish family room features beamed ceiling
- Skillfully designed kitchen convenient to an oversized laundry area
- Second floor bedrooms all generously sized
- 3 bedrooms, 2 1/2 baths, 2-car garage
- Basement foundation, drawings also include crawl space foundation

Unique Three-Way Fireplace

2,126 total square feet of living area

Price Code C

Special features

- Elegant bay windows in master bedroom welcome the sun
- Double vanities in master bath separated by large whirlpool tub
- 3 bedrooms, 2 baths, 2-car side entry garage
- Slab foundation

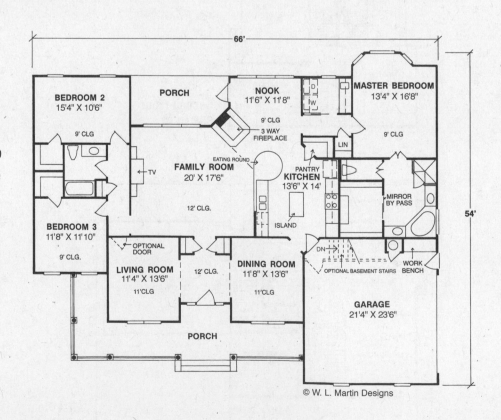

© W. L. Martin Designs

Large Corner Deck

1,283 total square feet of living area

Price Code A

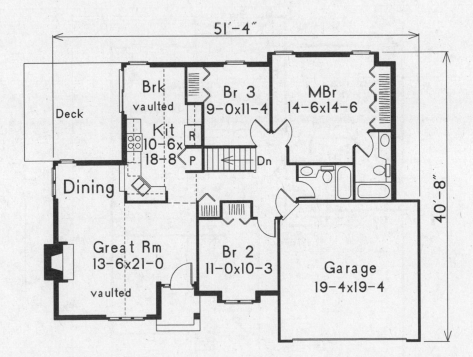

51'-4"

40'-8"

Deck

Brk
vaulted

Br 3
9-0x11-4

MBr
14-6x14-6

Kit
10-6x
18-8

R

P

Dn

Dining

Great Rm
13-6x21-0
vaulted

Br 2
11-0x10-3

Garage
19-4x19-4

Special features

- Vaulted breakfast room with sliding doors that open onto deck

- Kitchen features convenient corner sink and pass-through to dining room

- Open living atmosphere in dining area and great room

- Vaulted great room features a fireplace

- 3 bedrooms, 2 baths, 2-car garage

- Basement foundation

Traditional Ranch With Extras

1,425 total square feet of living area

Price Code A

Special features

- Kitchen and vaulted breakfast room are the center of activity
- Corner fireplace warms spacious family room
- Oversized serving bar extends seating in dining room
- 3 bedrooms, 2 baths, 2-car garage
- Crawl space, slab or walk-out basement foundation, please specify when ordering

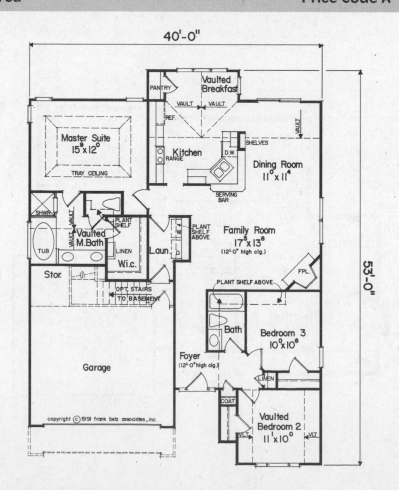

Distinctive Ranch Has A Larger Look

1,360 total square feet of living area

Price Code A

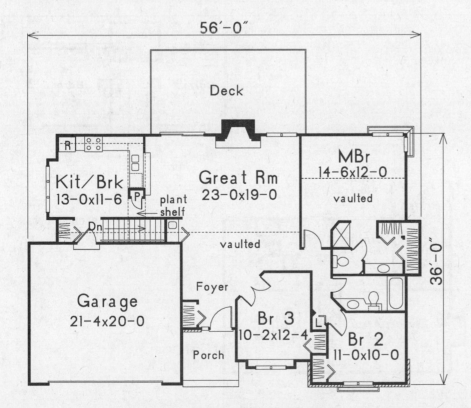

Special features

- Double-gabled front facade frames large windows
- Entry area is open to vaulted great room, fireplace and rear deck creating an open feel
- Vaulted ceiling and large windows add openness to kitchen/breakfast room
- Bedroom #3 easily converts to a den
- Plan easily adapts to crawl space or slab construction, with the utilities replacing the stairs
- 3 bedrooms, 2 baths, 2-car garage
- Basement foundation

Quaint Porch Adds Charm

1,735 total square feet of living area

Price Code B

Special features

- Angled kitchen wall expands space into the dining room
- Second floor has cozy sitting area with cheerful window
- Two spacious bedrooms on second floor share a bath
- 3 bedrooms, 2 1/2 baths, 2-car drive under garage
- Basement foundation

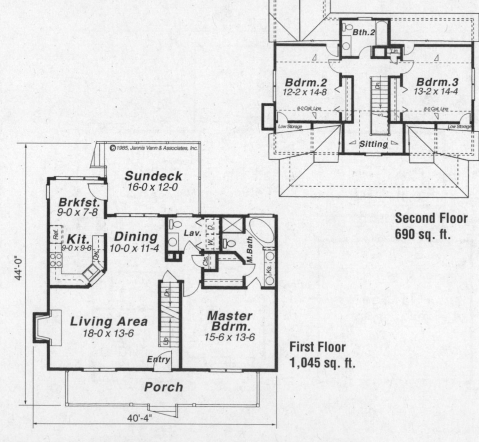

Second Floor 690 sq. ft.

First Floor 1,045 sq. ft.

Easy Living

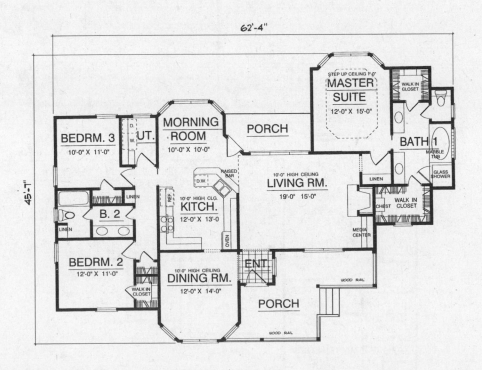

1,753 total square feet of living area

Price Code B

Special features

- Large front porch has charming appeal

- Kitchen with breakfast bar overlooks morning room and accesses covered porch

- Master suite with amenities like private bath, spacious closets and sunny bay window

- 3 bedrooms, 2 baths

- Slab or crawl space foundation, please specify when ordering

Covered Porches All Around

1,725 total square feet of living area

Price Code B

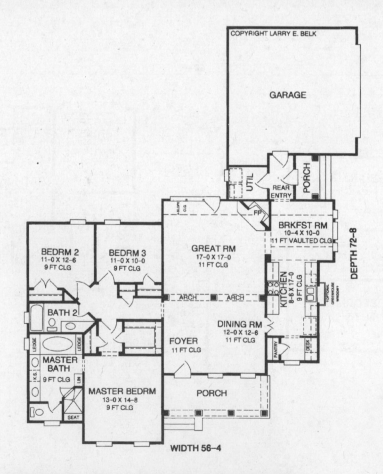

Special features

- Spectacular arches when entering the foyer
- Dining room has double-doors leading to the kitchen
- Unique desk area off kitchen is ideal for computer work station
- 3 bedrooms, 2 baths, 2-car side entry garage
- Slab or crawl space foundation, please specify when ordering

COPYRIGHT LARRY E. BELK

GARAGE

UTIL

REAR ENTRY

PORCH

BRKFST RM
10-4 X 10-0
11 FT VAULTED CLG

DEPTH 72-8

BEDRM 2
11-0 X 12-6
9 FT CLG

BEDRM 3
11-0 X 10-0
9 FT CLG

GREAT RM
17-0 X 17-0
11 FT CLG

KITCHEN
8-6 X 17-0
9 FT CLG

BATH 2

ARCH   ARCH

MASTER BATH
9 FT CLG

FOYER
11 FT CLG

DINING RM
12-0 X 12-6
11 FT CLG

DESK

PANTRY

MASTER BEDRM
13-0 X 14-8
9 FT CLG

PORCH

SEAT

WIDTH 56-4

TO ORDER BLUEPRINTS USE THE FORM ON PAGE 15 OR CALL TOLL-FREE 1-877-671-6036
View thousands more home plans online at www.familyhandyman.com/homeplans

Traditional Ranch Styling

1,167 total square feet of living area

Price Code AA

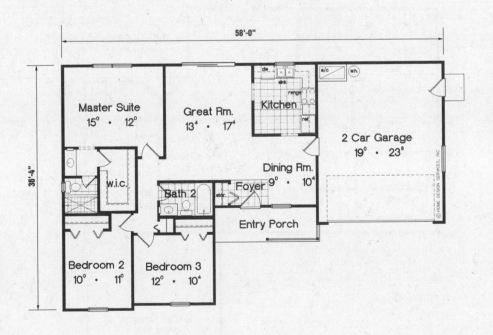

Special features

- Master suite has a private bath
- Handy coat closet in foyer
- Lots of storage space through-out
- 3 bedrooms, 2 baths, 2-car garage
- Slab foundation

TO ORDER BLUEPRINTS USE THE FORM ON PAGE 15 OR CALL TOLL-FREE 1-877-671-6036
View thousands more home plans online at www.familyhandyman.com/homeplans

27

Rustic Styling With All The Comforts

1,885 total square feet of living area

Price Code C

Special features

- Enormous covered patio creates a nice outdoor living area
- Dining and great rooms combine to create one large and versatile living area
- Utility room directly off kitchen for convenience
- 3 bedrooms, 2 baths, 2-car side entry garage
- Basement foundation

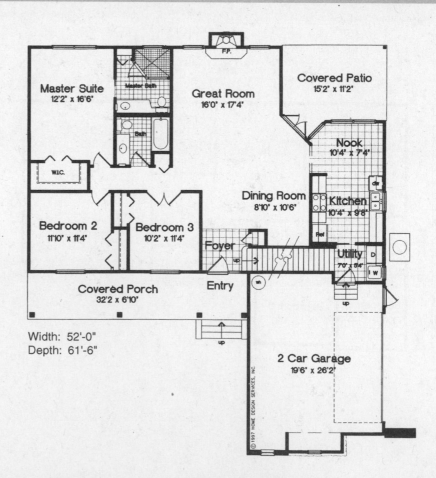

Width: 52'-0"
Depth: 61'-6"

Quaint Country Home Is Ideal

1,028 total square feet of living area

Price Code AA

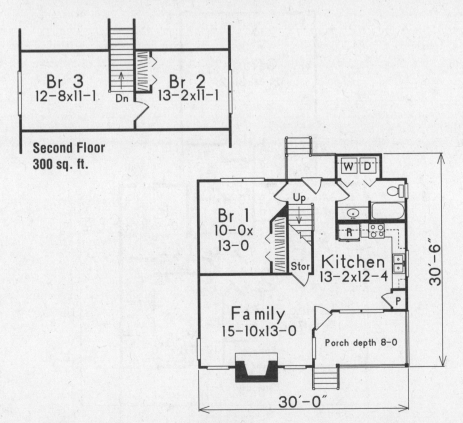

Br 3
12-8x11-1

Dn

Br 2
13-2x11-1

Second Floor
300 sq. ft.

W D

Up

Br 1
10-0x
13-0

Stor

R

Kitchen
13-2x12-4

P

Family
15-10x13-0

Porch depth 8-0

30'-6"

30'-0"

First Floor
728 sq. ft.

Special features

- Master bedroom conveniently located on first floor
- Well-designed bath contains laundry facilities
- L-shaped kitchen has a handy pantry
- Tall windows flank family room fireplace
- Cozy covered porch provides unique angled entry into home
- 3 bedrooms, 1 bath
- Crawl space foundation

Compact, Convenient And Charming

1,266 total square feet of living area

Price Code A

Special features

- Narrow frontage is perfect for small lots

- Energy efficient home with 2" x 6" exterior walls

- Prominent central hall provides a convenient connection for all main rooms

- Design incorporates full-size master bedroom complete with dressing room, bath and walk-in closet

- Angled kitchen includes handy laundry facilities and is adjacent to an oversized storage area

- 3 bedrooms, 2 baths, 2-car rear entry garage

- Crawl space foundation, drawings also include slab foundation

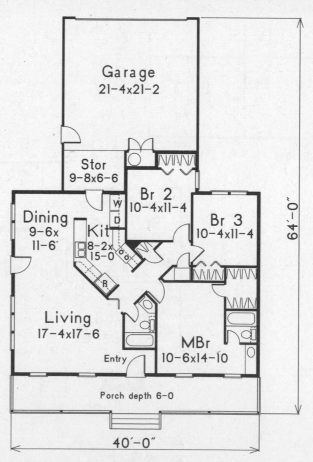

Garage
21-4x21-2

Stor
9-8x6-6

Br 2
10-4x11-4

Br 3
10-4x11-4

Dining
9-6x
11-6

Kit
8-2x
15-0

Living
17-4x17-6

MBr
10-6x14-10

Entry

Porch depth 6-0

64'-0"

40'-0"

Inviting Victorian Details

947 total square feet of living area

Price Code AA

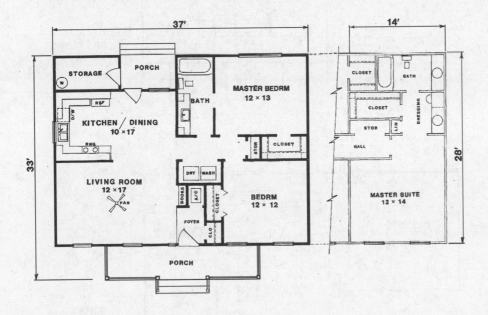

Special features

- Efficiently designed kitchen/dining area accesses the outdoors onto a rear porch
- Future expansion plans included which allow the home to become 392 square feet larger with 3 bedrooms and 2 baths
- 2 bedrooms, 1 bath
- Crawl space or slab foundation, please specify when ordering

Trio Of Dormers Adds Light

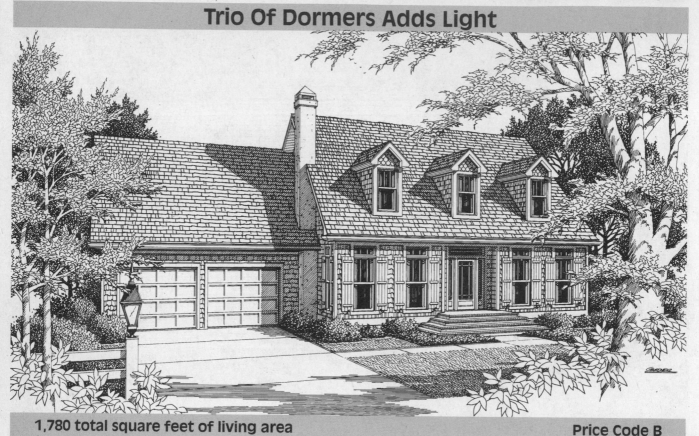

1,780 total square feet of living area

Price Code B

Special features

- Traditional styling with the comforts of home

- First floor master bedroom has walk-in closet and bath

- Large kitchen and dining area open to deck

- 3 bedrooms, 2 1/2 baths, 2-car garage

- Basement, crawl space or slab foundation, please specify when ordering

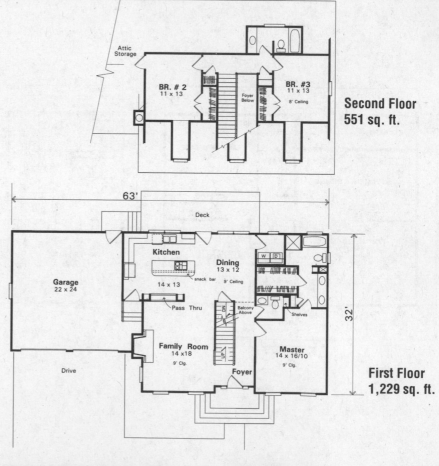

Second Floor 551 sq. ft.

First Floor 1,229 sq. ft.

Plan #703-SRD-348

Appealing Multiple Gables

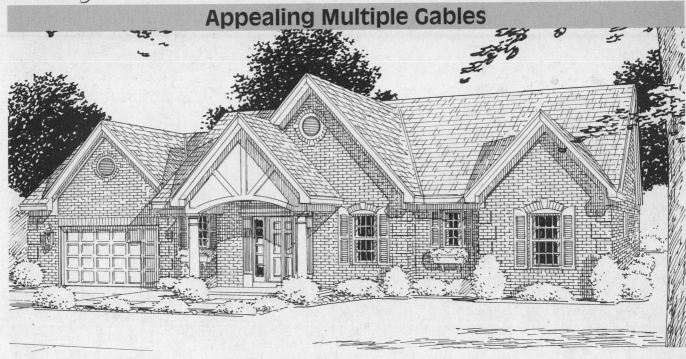

1,648 total square feet of living area   **Price Code B**

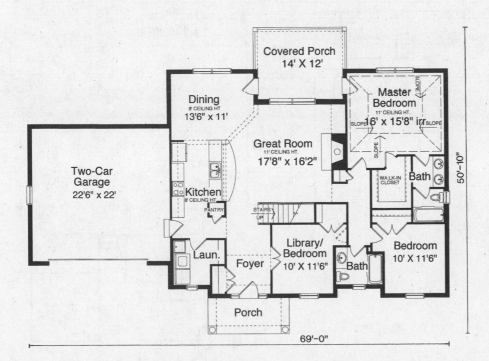

Special features

- A large master bedroom, with 11' ceiling and access to the covered porch adds elegance
- Open floor plan with varied ceiling heights
- Dining area accesses covered porch
- 3 bedrooms, 2 baths, 2-car garage
- Basement foundation

Comfortable Sports Cabin

1,472 total square feet of living area

Price Code A

Special features

- 8' wrap-around porch entry is inviting and creates an outdoor living area

- Great room has a rock hearth fireplace and is open to the second floor above

- Side grilling porch has a cleaning sink for fish or game

- Optional bonus room on the second floor has an additional 199 square feet of living area

- 3 bedrooms, 2 baths

- Crawl space or slab foundation, please specify when ordering

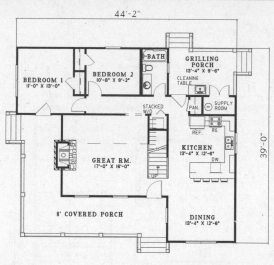

First Floor
1,140 sq. ft.

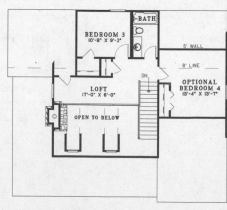

Second Floor
332 sq. ft.

Mountain Retreat

1,209 total square feet of living area

Price Code A

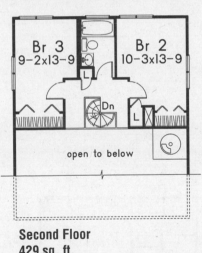

Second Floor
429 sq. ft.

Br 3
9-2x13-9

Br 2
10-3x13-9

Dn

open to below

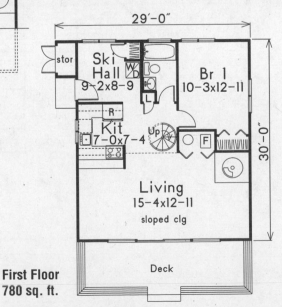

29'-0"

stor

Ski
Hall
9-2x8-9

W
D

Br 1
10-3x12-11

30'-0"

R

Kit
7-0x7-4

Up

F

Living
15-4x12-11
sloped clg

First Floor
780 sq. ft.

Deck

Special features

- Bracketed shed roof and ski storage add charm to vacation home
- Living and dining rooms enjoy a sloped ceiling, second floor balcony overlook and view to a large deck
- Kitchen features snack bar and access to second floor via circular stair
- Second floor includes two bedrooms with sizable closets, center hall bath and balcony overlooking rooms below
- 3 bedrooms, 2 baths
- Crawl space foundation

TO ORDER BLUEPRINTS USE THE FORM ON PAGE 15 OR CALL TOLL-FREE 1-877-671-6036
View thousands more home plans online at www.familyhandyman.com/homeplans

35

Cozy Front Porch Welcomes Guests

1,393 total square feet of living area

Price Code B

Special features

- L-shaped kitchen features walk-in pantry, island cooktop and is convenient to laundry room and dining area

- Master bedroom features large walk-in closet and private bath with separate tub and shower

- Convenient storage/coat closet in hall

- View to the patio from the dining area

- 3 bedrooms, 2 baths, 2-car detached garage

- Crawl space foundation, drawings also include slab foundation

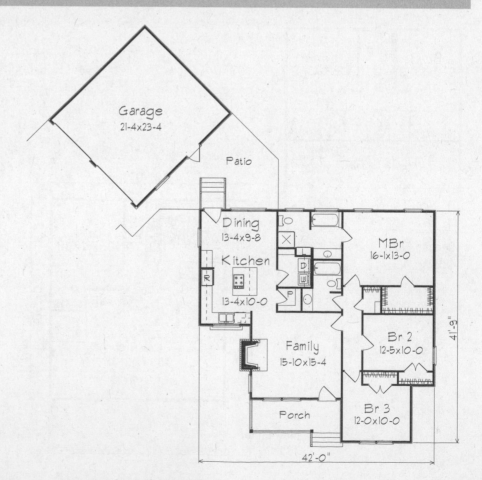

Garage
21-4x23-4

Patio

Dining
13-4x9-8

Kitchen
13-4x10-0

MBr
16-1x13-0

Family
15-10x15-4

Br 2
12-5x10-0

Porch

Br 3
12-0x10-0

41'-9"

42'-0"

36

TO ORDER BLUEPRINTS USE THE FORM ON PAGE 15 OR CALL TOLL-FREE 1-877-671-6036
View thousands more home plans online at www.familyhandyman.com/homeplans

Grandscale Great Room In A Country Ranch

1,278 total square feet of living area

Price Code A

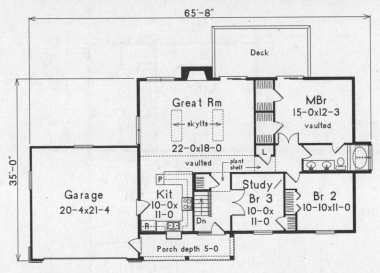

First Floor
1,278 sq. ft.

Deck

Great Rm
skylts
22-0x18-0
vaulted

MBr
15-0x12-3
vaulted

Garage
20-4x21-4

Kit
10-0x
11-0

plant shelf

Study/
Br 3
10-0x
11-0

Br 2
10-10x11-0

Porch depth 5-0

65'-8"

35'-0"

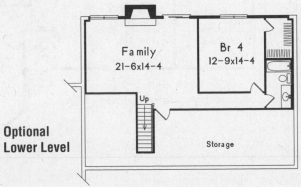

Optional
Lower Level

Family
21-6x14-4

Br 4
12-9x14-4

Storage

Up

Special features

- Excellent U-shaped kitchen with garden window opens to an enormous great room with vaulted ceiling, fireplace and two skylights

- Vaulted master bedroom offers double entry doors, access to a deck and bath and two walk-in closets

- The bath has a double-bowl vanity and dramatic step-up garden tub with a lean-to greenhouse window

- 805 square feet of optional living area on the lower level with family room, bedroom #4 and bath

- 3 bedrooms, 1 bath, 2-car garage

- Walk-out basement foundation

Old-Fashioned Comfort And Privacy

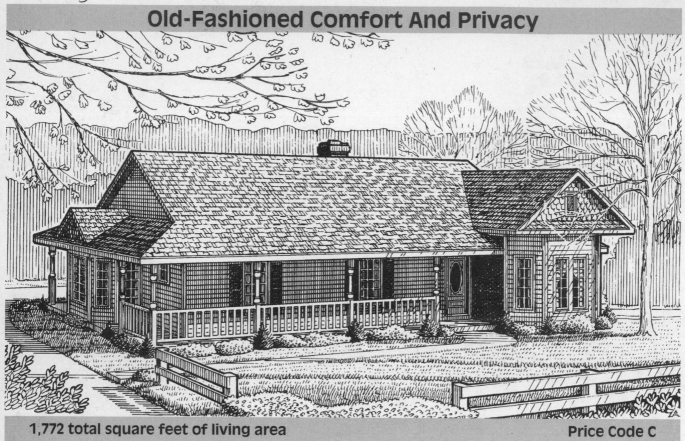

1,772 total square feet of living area

Price Code C

Special features

- Extended porches in front and rear provide a charming touch
- Large bay windows lend distinction to dining room and bedroom #3
- Efficient U-shaped kitchen
- Master bedroom includes two walk-in closets
- Full corner fireplace in family room
- 3 bedrooms, 2 baths, 2-car detached garage
- Slab foundation, drawings also include crawl space foundation

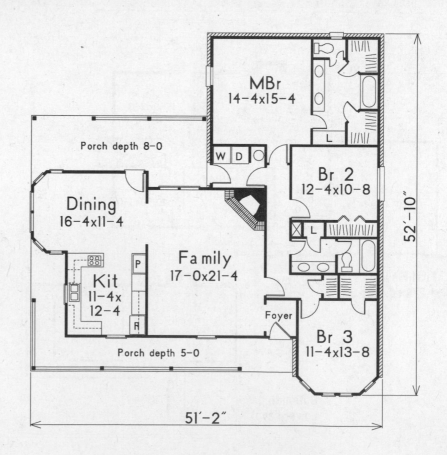

Porch depth 8-0

MBr
14-4x15-4

W D

Dining
16-4x11-4

Br 2
12-4x10-8

Family
17-0x21-4

Kit
11-4x
12-4

P

R

Foyer

Br 3
11-4x13-8

Porch depth 5-0

52'-10"

51'-2"

Perfect Home For A Small Family

864 total square feet of living area

Price Code AAA

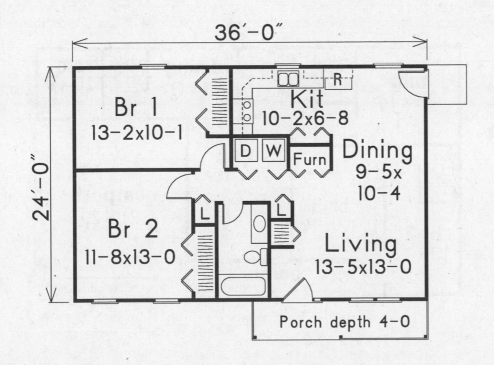

36'-0"

24'-0"

Br 1
13-2x10-1

Kit
10-2x6-8

Dining
9-5x
10-4

D W Furn

Br 2
11-8x13-0

L L

Living
13-5x13-0

Porch depth 4-0

R

Special features

- L-shaped kitchen with convenient pantry is adjacent to dining area
- Easy access to laundry area, linen closet and storage closet
- Both bedrooms include ample closet space
- 2 bedrooms, 1 bath
- Crawl space foundation, drawings also include basement and slab foundations

Gable Roof And Large Porch Create A Cozy Feel

1,375 total square feet of living area

Price Code A

Special features

- Master bedroom has private bath and walk-in closet

- Kitchen and dining room located conveniently near utility and living rooms

- Cathedral ceiling in living room adds spaciousness

- 3 bedrooms, 2 baths, 2-car carport

- Slab foundation

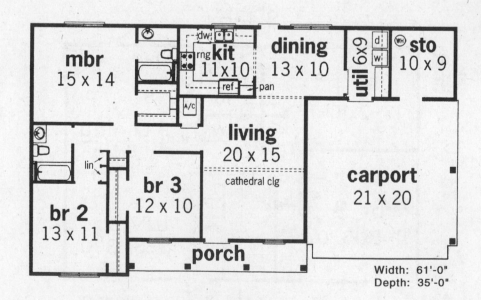

Elegance In A Starter Or Retirement Home

888 total square feet of living area

Price Code AAA

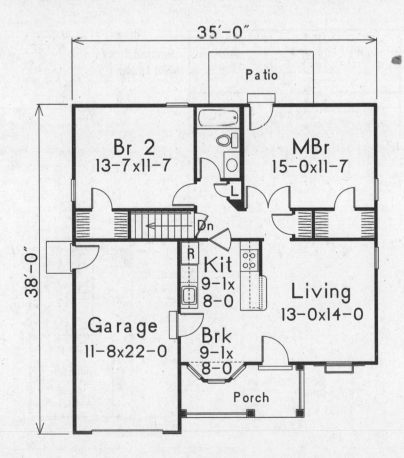

35'-0"

38'-0"

Patio

Br 2
13-7x11-7

MBr
15-0x11-7

Dn

Kit
9-1x
8-0

Living
13-0x14-0

Garage
11-8x22-0

Brk
9-1x
8-0

Porch

Special features

- Home features an eye-catching exterior and includes a spacious porch
- The breakfast room with bay window is open to living room and adjoins kitchen with pass-through snack bar
- The bedrooms are quite roomy and feature walk-in closets and the master bedroom has double entry doors and access to rear patio
- The master bedroom has double entry doors and access to rear patio
- 2 bedrooms, 1 bath, 1-car garage
- Basement foundation

Southern Styling With Covered Porch

1,491 total square feet of living area

Price Code A

Special features

- Two-story family room has vaulted ceiling

- Well-organized kitchen has serving bar which overlooks family and dining rooms

- First floor master suite has tray ceiling, walk-in closet and master bath

- 3 bedrooms, 2 1/2 baths, 2-car drive under garage

- Walk-out basement foundation

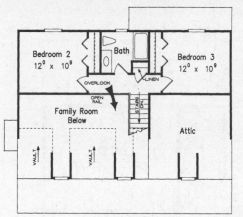

Second Floor 430 sq. ft.

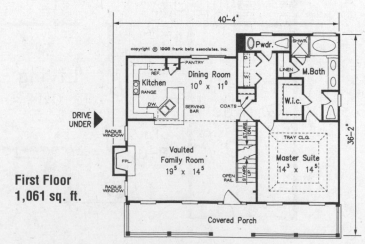

First Floor 1,061 sq. ft.

Appealing Charming Porch

1,643 total square feet of living area

Price Code B

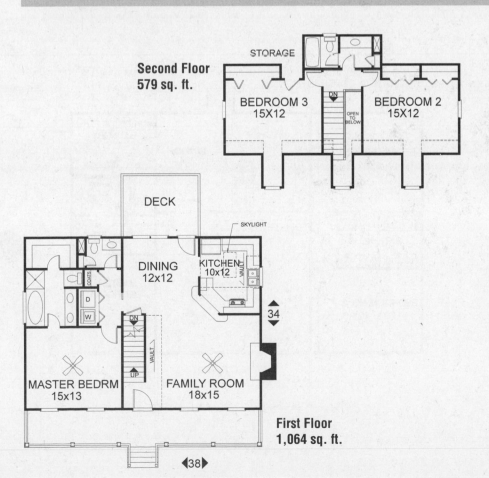

Second Floor
579 sq. ft.

STORAGE

BEDROOM 3
15X12

OPEN TO BELOW

BEDROOM 2
15X12

DN

DECK

DINING
12x12

SKYLIGHT

KITCHEN
10x12

VAULT

34

DN

VAULT

MASTER BEDRM
15X13

UP

FAMILY ROOM
18x15

First Floor
1,064 sq. ft.

◄38►

Special features

- First floor master bedroom has private bath, walk-in closet and easy access to laundry closet

- Comfortable family room features a vaulted ceiling and a cozy fireplace

- Two bedrooms on the second floor share a bath

- 3 bedrooms, 2 1/2 baths, 2-car drive under garage

- Basement or crawl space foundation, please specify when ordering

TO ORDER BLUEPRINTS USE THE FORM ON PAGE 15 OR CALL TOLL-FREE 1-877-671-6036

View thousands more home plans online at www.familyhandyman.com/homeplans

Plan #703-DH-2005

Perfect Home For Family Living

1,700 total square feet of living area

Price Code B

Special features

- Oversized laundry room has large pantry and storage area as well as access to the outdoors

- Master bedroom separated from other bedrooms for privacy

- Raised snack bar in kitchen allows extra seating for dining

- 3 bedrooms, 2 baths

- Crawl space foundation

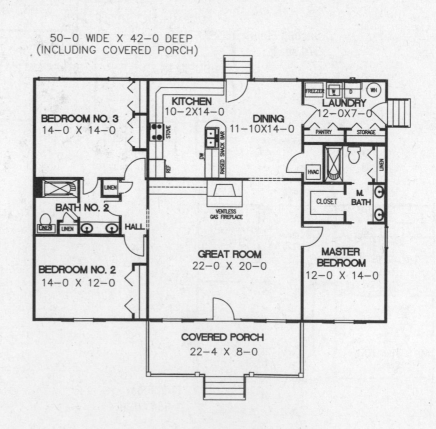

50–0 WIDE X 42–0 DEEP
(INCLUDING COVERED PORCH)

BEDROOM NO. 3
14–0 X 14–0

KITCHEN
10–2X14–0

DINING
11–10X14–0

LAUNDRY
12–0X7–0

FREEZER

PANTRY   STORAGE

REF   DW   RAISED SNACK BAR

HVAC

LINEN

BATH NO. 2

LINEN   LINEN

HALL

VENTLESS GAS FIREPLACE

CLOSET

M. BATH

BEDROOM NO. 2
14–0 X 12–0

GREAT ROOM
22–0 X 20–0

MASTER BEDROOM
12–0 X 14–0

COVERED PORCH
22–4 X 8–0

Country Home With Front Orientation

2,029 total square feet of living area

Price Code C

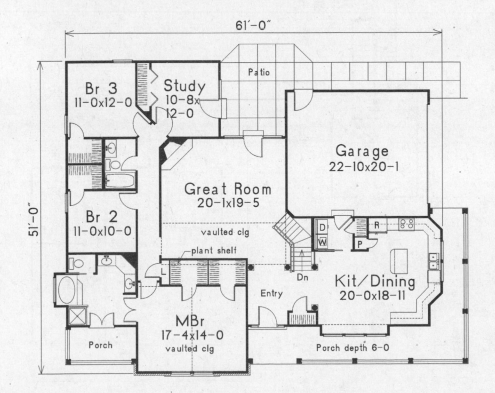

Special features

- Stonework, gables, roof dormer and double porches create a country flavor

- Kitchen enjoys extravagant cabinetry and counterspace in a bay, island snack bar, built-in pantry and cheery dining area with multiple tall windows

- Angled stair descends from large entry with wood columns and is open to vaulted great room with corner fireplace

- Master bedroom boasts his and hers walk-in closets, double-doors leading to an opulent master bath and private porch

- 4 bedrooms, 2 baths, 2-car side entry garage

- Basement foundation

An Open Feel With Vaulted Ceilings

1,470 total square feet of living area

Price Code A

Special features

- Vaulted breakfast room is cheerful and sunny
- Private second floor master bedroom with bath and walk-in closet
- Large utility room has access to the outdoors
- 3 bedrooms, 2 baths
- Basement, crawl space or slab foundation, please specify when ordering

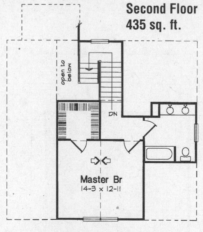

Second Floor
435 sq. ft.

open to below

DN

Master Br
14-3 x 12-11

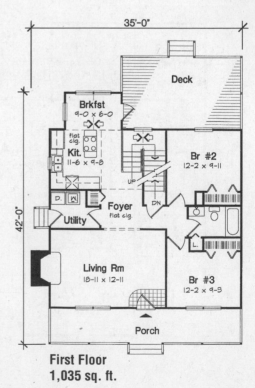

35'-0"

42'-0"

Deck

Brkfst
9-0 x 6-0
flat clg.

Kit.
11-6 x 9-8

Br #2
12-2 x 9-11

UP

D.

Utility

Foyer
flat clg.

DN

Living Rm
18-11 x 12-11

Br #3
12-2 x 9-3

Porch

First Floor
1,035 sq. ft.

Rear View

TO ORDER BLUEPRINTS USE THE FORM ON PAGE 15 OR CALL TOLL-FREE 1-877-671-6036
View thousands more home plans online at www.familyhandyman.com/homeplans

Gabled Front Porch Adds Charm And Value

1,443 total square feet of living area   **Price Code A**

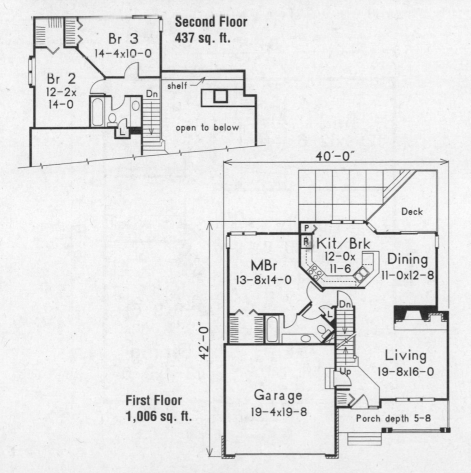

Second Floor
437 sq. ft.

Br 3
14-4x10-0

Br 2
12-2x
14-0

shelf

Dn

open to below

L

First Floor
1,006 sq. ft.

40'-0"

42'-0"

Deck

P
R

Kit/Brk
12-0x
11-6

Dining
11-0x12-8

MBr
13-8x14-0

Dn

L

Up

Living
19-8x16-0

Garage
19-4x19-8

Porch depth 5-8

Special features

- Raised foyer and cathedral ceiling in living room
- Impressive tall-wall fireplace between living and dining rooms
- Open U-shaped kitchen with breakfast bay
- Angular side deck accentuates patio and garden
- First floor master bedroom suite has a walk-in closet and a corner window
- 3 bedrooms, 2 baths, 2-car garage
- Basement foundation

TO ORDER BLUEPRINTS USE THE FORM ON PAGE 15 OR CALL TOLL-FREE 1-877-671-6036
View thousands more home plans online at www.familyhandyman.com/homeplans

47

Flexible Layout For Various Uses

1,143 total square feet of living area

Price Code AA

Special features

- Enormous stone fireplace in family room adds warmth and character
- Spacious kitchen with breakfast bar overlooks family room
- Separate dining area great for entertaining
- Vaulted family room and kitchen create an open atmosphere
- 2 bedrooms, 1 bath
- Crawl space foundation

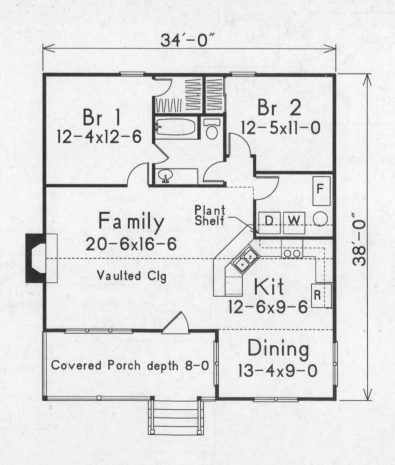

34'-0"

38'-0"

Br 1
12-4x12-6

Br 2
12-5x11-0

Family
20-6x16-6

Vaulted Clg

Plant Shelf

F

D W

Kit
12-6x9-6

R

Covered Porch depth 8-0

Dining
13-4x9-0

Designed For Comfort And Utility

720 total square feet of living area   **Price Code AAA**

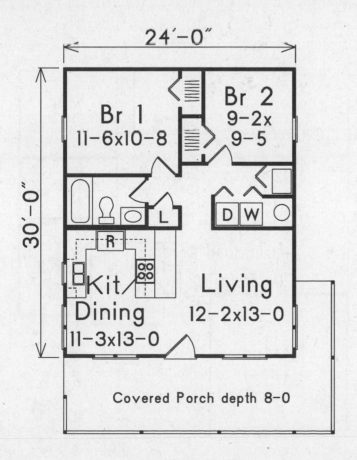

24'-0"

30'-0"

Br 1
11-6x10-8

Br 2
9-2x
9-5

L

D W

R

Kit
Dining
11-3x13-0

Living
12-2x13-0

Covered Porch depth 8-0

Special features

- Abundant windows in living and dining rooms provide generous sunlight
- Secluded laundry area with handy storage closet
- U-shaped kitchen with large breakfast bar opens into living area
- Large covered deck offers plenty of outdoor living space
- 2 bedrooms, 1 bath
- Crawl space foundation, drawings also include slab foundation

TO ORDER BLUEPRINTS USE THE FORM ON PAGE 15 OR CALL TOLL-FREE 1-877-671-6036
View thousands more home plans online at www.familyhandyman.com/homeplans

49

Brick And Siding Enhance This Traditional Home

1,170 total square feet of living area

Price Code AA

Special features

- Master bedroom enjoys privacy at the rear of this home
- Kitchen has angled bar that overlooks great room and breakfast area
- Living areas combine to create a greater sense of spaciousness
- Great room has a cozy fireplace
- 3 bedrooms, 2 baths, 2-car garage
- Slab foundation

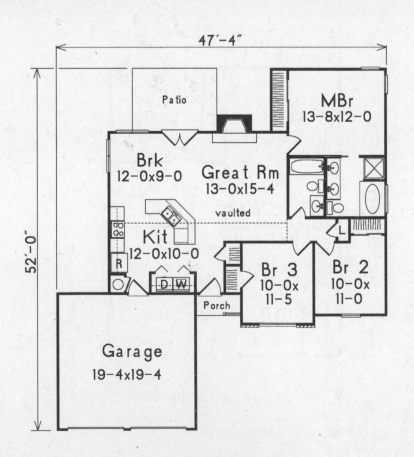

47'-4"

52'-0"

Patio

MBr
13-8x12-0

Brk
12-0x9-0

Great Rm
13-0x15-4
vaulted

Kit
12-0x10-0

R

D W

L

Br 3
10-0x
11-5

Br 2
10-0x
11-0

Porch

Garage
19-4x19-4

Country Cottage

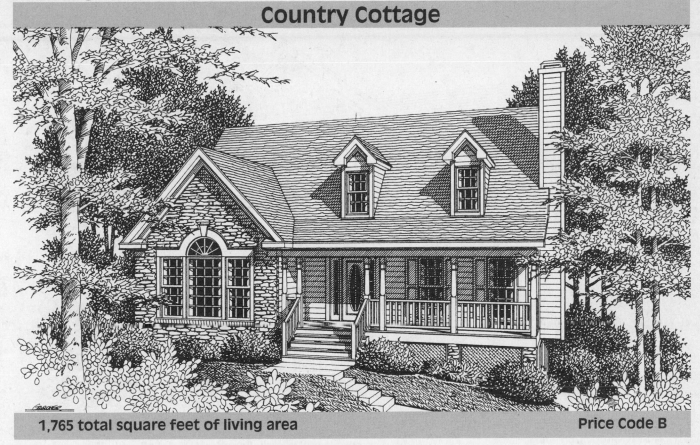

1,765 total square feet of living area

Price Code B

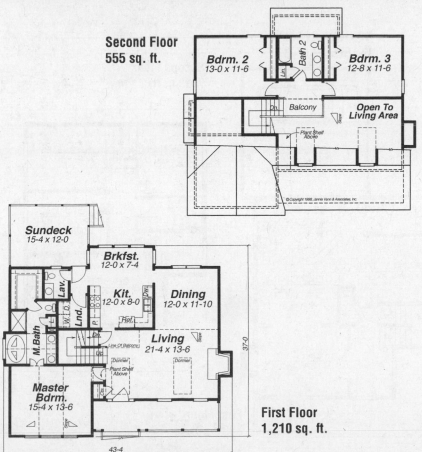

Second Floor
555 sq. ft.

Bdrm. 2
13-0 x 11-6

Bath 2

Bdrm. 3
12-8 x 11-6

Dn.

Balcony

Open To Living Area

Plant Shelf Above

©Copyright 1996 Jannie Vann & Associates, Inc.

Sundeck
15-4 x 12-0

Brkfst.
12-0 x 7-4

Kit.
12-0 x 8-0

Dining
12-0 x 11-10

Lav.

W.D.

Lnd.

M. Bath

Dn.

Up.

Ref.

Line Of Balcony

Living
21-4 x 13-6

Plant Shelf Above

Dormer

Dormer

Master Bdrm.
15-4 x 13-6

37-0

43-4

First Floor
1,210 sq. ft.

Special features

■ Palladian window accenting stone gable adds new look to a popular cottage design

■ Dormers open into vaulted area inside

■ Kitchen extends to breakfast room with access to sun deck

■ 3 bedrooms, 2 1/2 baths, 2-car drive under garage

■ Basement foundation

Craftsman Cottage

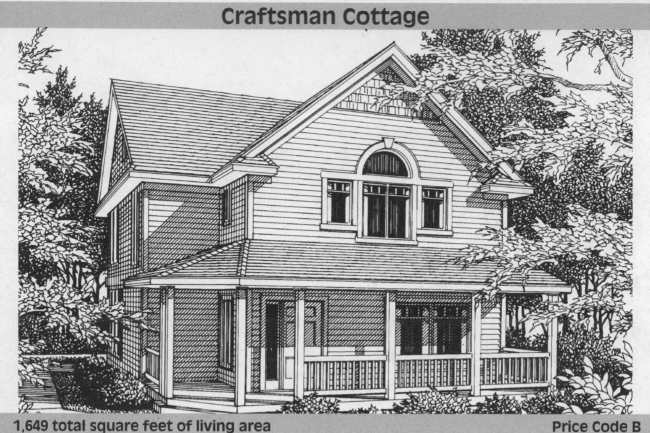

1,649 total square feet of living area

Price Code B

Special features

- Energy efficient home with 2" x 6" exterior walls

- Ideal design for a narrow lot

- Country kitchen includes an island and eating bar

- Master bedroom has 12' vaulted ceiling and a charming arched window

- 4 bedrooms, 2 1/2 baths, 2-car side entry garage

- Basement or crawl space foundation, please specify when ordering

Width: 30'-0"
Depth: 52'-0"

Second Floor
791 sq. ft.

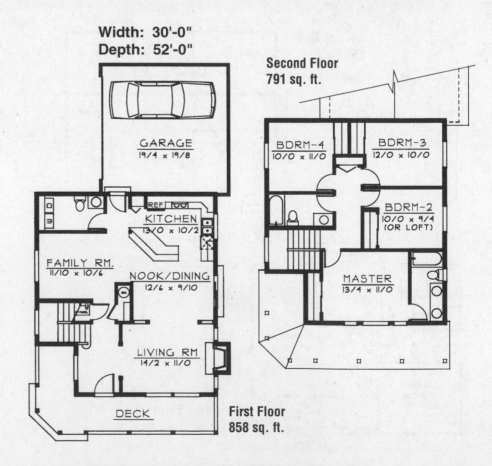

First Floor
858 sq. ft.

52

TO ORDER BLUEPRINTS USE THE FORM ON PAGE 15 OR CALL TOLL-FREE 1-877-671-6036
View thousands more home plans online at www.familyhandyman.com/homeplans

1,085 total square feet of living area

Price Code AA

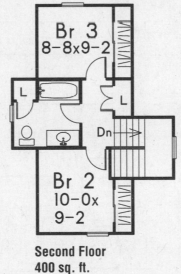

Br 3
8-8x9-2

L   L

Dn

Br 2
10-0x
9-2

Second Floor
400 sq. ft.

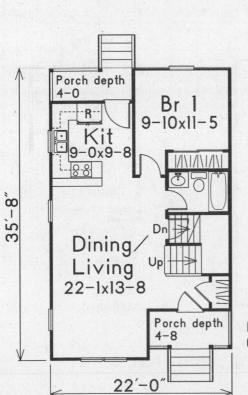

Porch depth 4-0

R

Kit
9-0x9-8

Br 1
9-10x11-5

Dn

Up

Dining/ Living
22-1x13-8

Porch depth 4-8

First Floor
685 sq. ft.

35'-8"

22'-0"

Special features

- Rear porch is a handy access through the kitchen
- Convenient hall linen closet located on the second floor
- Breakfast bar in kitchen offers additional counterspace
- Living and dining rooms combine for an open living atmosphere
- 3 bedrooms, 2 baths
- Basement foundation

TO ORDER BLUEPRINTS USE THE FORM ON PAGE 15 OR CALL TOLL-FREE 1-877-671-6036
View thousands more home plans online at www.familyhandyman.com/homeplans

53

Unique A-Frame Detailing Has Appeal

1,272 total square feet of living area

Price Code A

Special features

- Stone fireplace accents living room
- Spacious kitchen includes snack bar overlooking living room
- First floor bedroom roomy and secluded
- Plenty of closet space for second floor bedrooms plus a generous balcony which wraps around second floor
- 3 bedrooms, 1 1/2 baths
- Crawl space foundation

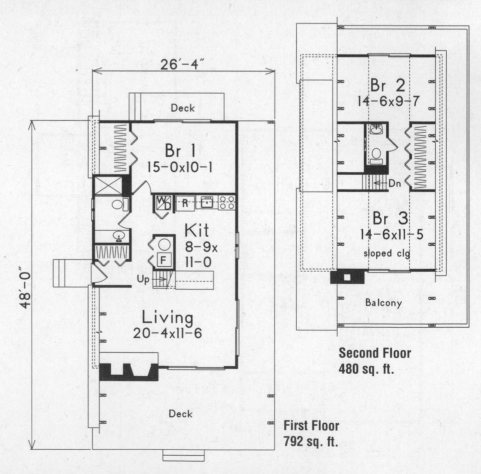

26'-4"

Deck

Br 1
15-0x10-1

W D   R

Kit
8-9x
11-0

F

Up

Living
20-4x11-6

48'-0"

Deck

First Floor
792 sq. ft.

Br 2
14-6x9-7

Dn

Br 3
14-6x11-5
sloped clg

Balcony

Second Floor
480 sq. ft.

TO ORDER BLUEPRINTS USE THE FORM ON PAGE 15 OR CALL TOLL-FREE 1-877-671-6036
View thousands more home plans online at www.familyhandyman.com/homeplans

Plan #703-RDD-1815-8

Kitchen Overlooks Living Area

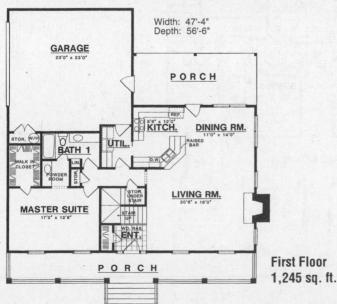

1,815 total square feet of living area

Price Code C

Second Floor
570 sq. ft.

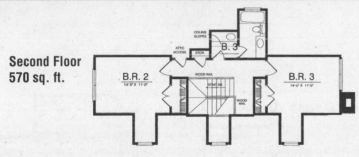

Width: 47'-4"
Depth: 56'-6"

First Floor
1,245 sq. ft.

Special features

- Well-designed kitchen opens to dining room and features raised breakfast bar

- First floor master suite has walk-in closet

- Front and back porches unite this home with the outdoors

- 3 bedrooms, 2 baths, 2-car side entry garage

- Basement, crawl space or slab foundation, please specify when ordering

Inviting Covered Verandas

1,830 total square feet of living area

Price Code C

Special features

- Inviting covered verandas in the front and rear of the home

- Great room has fireplace and cathedral ceiling

- Handy service porch allows easy access

- Master suite has vaulted ceiling and private bath

- 3 bedrooms, 2 baths, 3-car side entry garage

- Basement, crawl space or slab foundation, please specify when ordering

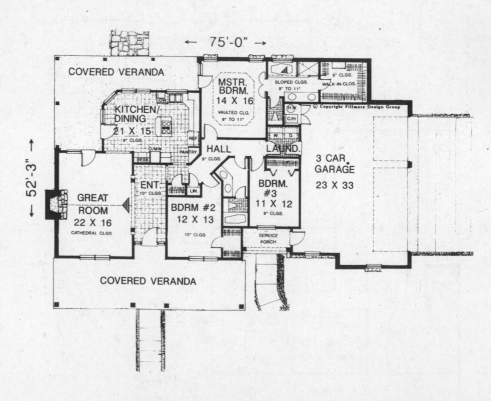

Layout Creates Large Open Living Area

1,285 total square feet of living area

Price Code B

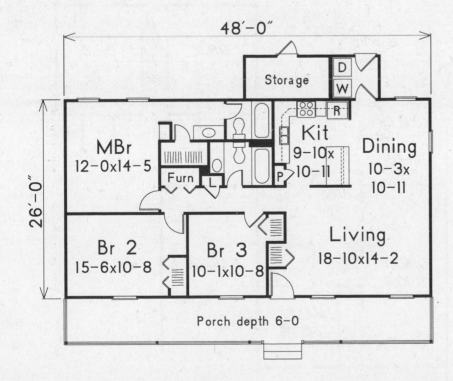

48'-0"

26'-0"

Storage

D
W
R

MBr
12-0x14-5

Furn L

Kit
9-10x
10-11

P

Dining
10-3x
10-11

Br 2
15-6x10-8

Br 3
10-1x10-8

Living
18-10x14-2

Porch depth 6-0

Special features

- Accommodating home with ranch-style porch
- Large storage area on back of home
- Master bedroom includes dressing area, private bath and built-in bookcase
- Kitchen features pantry, breakfast bar and complete view to dining room
- 3 bedrooms, 2 baths
- Crawl space foundation, drawings also include basement and slab foundations

TO ORDER BLUEPRINTS USE THE FORM ON PAGE 15 OR CALL TOLL-FREE 1-877-671-6036
View thousands more home plans online at www.familyhandyman.com/homeplans

57

Lovely Front Dormers

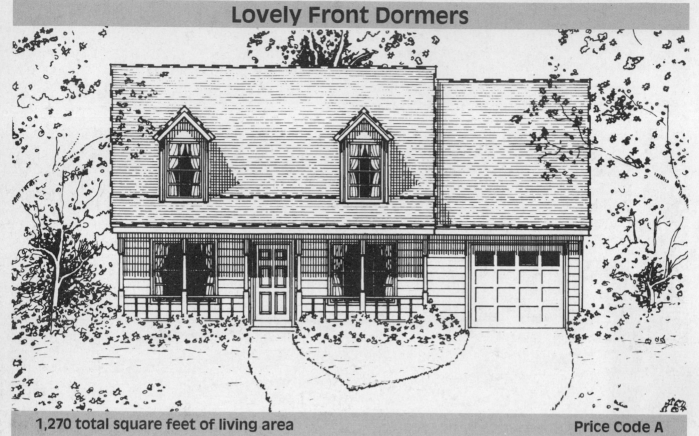

1,270 total square feet of living area

Price Code A

Special features

- Convenient master suite on first floor

- Two secondary bedrooms on second floor each have a large walk-in closet and share a full bath

- Sunny breakfast room has lots of sunlight and easy access to great room and kitchen

- 3 bedrooms, 2 baths, 1-car garage

- Slab or crawl space foundation, please specify when ordering

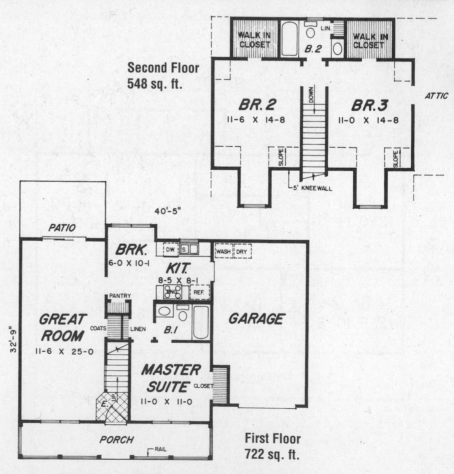

Second Floor 548 sq. ft.

WALK IN CLOSET   LIN.   WALK IN CLOSET
B.2

BR. 2   DOWN   BR. 3   ATTIC
11-6 X 14-8   11-0 X 14-8

SLOPE   SLOPE
5' KNEE WALL

40'-5"

PATIO

BRK.   DW. S.   WASH DRY
6-0 X 10-1

KIT.
8-5 X 8-1
REF.

PANTRY

32'-9"   GREAT ROOM   COATS   LINEN   GARAGE
11-6 X 25-0   B.1

MASTER SUITE   CLOSET
11-0 X 11-0

PORCH   RAIL

First Floor 722 sq. ft.

Country Charm Wrapped In A Veranda

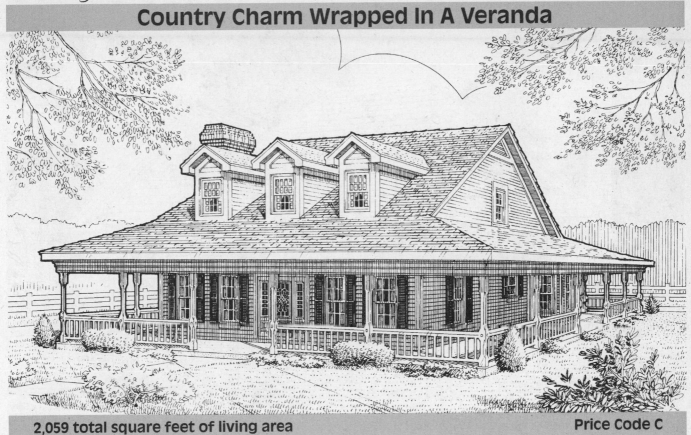

2,059 total square feet of living area

Price Code C

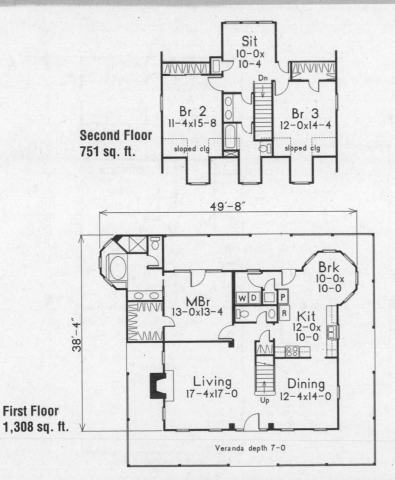

Second Floor
751 sq. ft.

Sit
10-0x
10-4

Dn

Br 2
11-4x15-8

Br 3
12-0x14-4

sloped clg

sloped clg

49'-8"

38'-4"

Brk
10-0x
10-0

MBr
13-0x13-4

W D P

R

Kit
12-0x
10-0

Living
17-4x17-0

Dining
12-4x14-0

Up

First Floor
1,308 sq. ft.

Veranda depth 7-0

Special features

- Octagon-shaped breakfast room offers plenty of windows and creates a view to the veranda

- First floor master bedroom has large walk-in closet and deluxe bath

- 9' ceilings throughout the home

- Secondary bedrooms and bath feature dormers and are adjacent to cozy sitting area

- 3 bedrooms, 2 1/2 baths, 2-car detached garage

- Slab foundation, drawings also include basement and crawl space foundations

TO ORDER BLUEPRINTS USE THE FORM ON PAGE 15 OR CALL TOLL-FREE 1-877-671-6036
View thousands more home plans online at www.familyhandyman.com/homeplans

59

Arched Entry Adds Appeal

1,263 total square feet of living area

Price Code A

Special features

- 9' ceilings throughout most of this home

- Kitchen features large island eating bar ideal for extra seating when entertaining

- 3 bedrooms, 2 baths, 2-car side entry garage

- Basement foundation

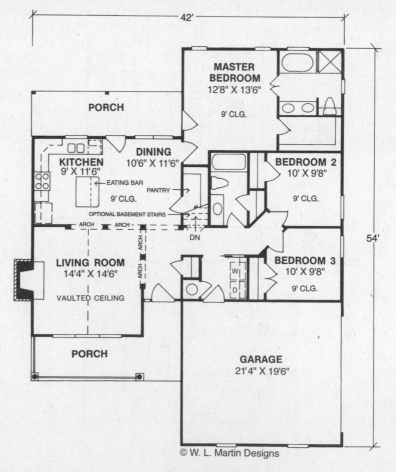

© W. L. Martin Designs

60

TO ORDER BLUEPRINTS USE THE FORM ON PAGE 15 OR CALL TOLL-FREE 1-877-671-6036
View thousands more home plans online at www.familyhandyman.com/homeplans

Designed For Seclusion

624 total square feet of living area

Price Code AAA

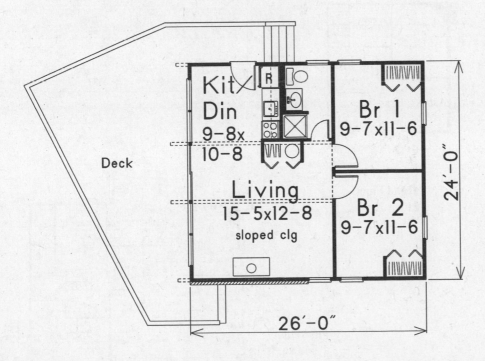

Kit
Din
9-8x
10-8

Br 1
9-7x11-6

Deck

Living
15-5x12-8
sloped clg

Br 2
9-7x11-6

24'-0"

26'-0"

Special features

- The combination of stone, vertical siding, lots of glass and a low roof line creates a cozy retreat

- Vaulted living area features free-standing fireplace that heats adjacent stone wall for warmth

- Efficient kitchen includes dining area and view to angular deck

- Two bedrooms share a hall bath with shower

- 2 bedrooms, 1 bath

- Pier foundation

Wrap-Around Porch Offers A Warm Welcome

2,764 total square feet of living area

Price Code E

Special features

- A balcony leads to a small study area while offering a dramatic view to the family room and fireplace below

- Master bedroom provides convenience and comfort with its whirlpool tub, double-bowl vanity, shower and large walk-in closet

- Delightful library is a nice quiet place to relax

- 4 bedrooms, 2 1/2 baths, 2-car side entry garage

- Basement foundation

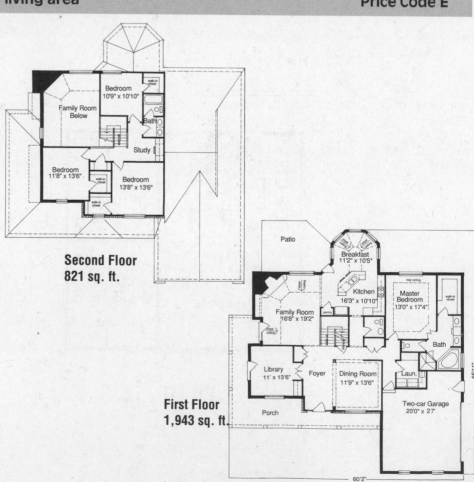

**Second Floor
821 sq. ft.**

Bedroom 10'9" x 10'10"
Family Room Below
Bath
Study
Bedroom 11'8" x 13'6"
walk-in closet
Bedroom 13'8" x 13'6"
walk-in closet

**First Floor
1,943 sq. ft.**

Patio
Breakfast 11'2" x 10'5"
Kitchen 16'3" x 10'10"
Master Bedroom 13'0" x 17'4"
walk-in closet
Family Room 16'8" x 19'2"
Bath
Library 11' x 13'6"
Foyer
Dining Room 11'9" x 13'6"
Laun.
Porch
Two-car Garage 20'0" x 27'
65'11"
60'2"

Wrap-Around Porch Adds Country Charm

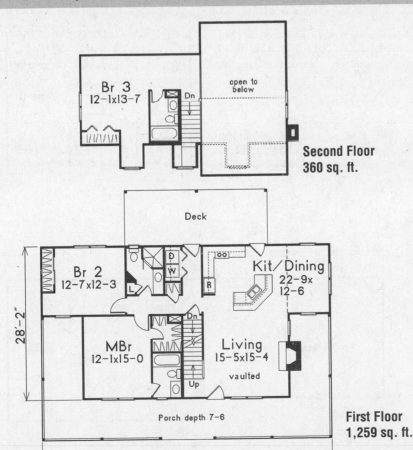

1,619 total square feet of living area

Price Code B

Second Floor
360 sq. ft.

Br 3
12-1x13-7

open to below

Dn

First Floor
1,259 sq. ft.

Deck

Br 2
12-7x12-3

Kit/Dining
22-9x 12-6

MBr
12-1x15-0

Living
15-5x15-4
vaulted

Dn

Up

28'-2"

52'-6"

Porch depth 7-6

Special features

■ Private second floor bedroom and bath

■ Kitchen features a snack bar and adjacent dining area

■ Master bedroom has a private bath

■ Centrally located washer and dryer

■ 3 bedrooms, 3 baths

■ Basement foundation, drawings also include crawl space and slab foundations

Screened Area Makes A Great Place To Relax

1,434 total square feet of living area

Price Code A

Special features

- Private second floor master bedroom features a private bath and a roomy walk-in closet

- A country kitchen with peninsula counter adjoins the living room creating a larger living area

- The living room has a warm fireplace and a volume ceiling

- 3 bedrooms, 2 baths, 2-car garage

- Basement, crawl space or slab foundation, please specify when ordering

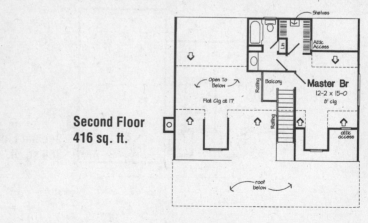

Second Floor
416 sq. ft.

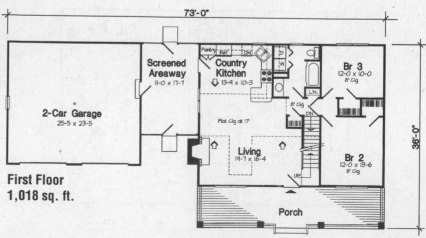

First Floor
1,018 sq. ft.

TO ORDER BLUEPRINTS USE THE FORM ON PAGE 15 OR CALL TOLL-FREE 1-877-671-6036
View thousands more home plans online at www.familyhandyman.com/homeplans

Gable Facade Adds Appeal To This Ranch

1,304 total square feet of living area

Price Code A

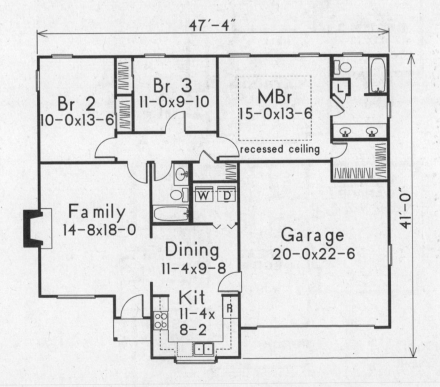

47'-4"

Br 2
10-0x13-6

Br 3
11-0x9-10

MBr
15-0x13-6
recessed ceiling

Family
14-8x18-0

Dining
11-4x9-8

Garage
20-0x22-6

Kit
11-4x
8-2

W D

41'-0"

Special features

- Covered entrance leads into family room with 10' ceiling and fireplace
- 10' ceilings in kitchen, dining and family rooms
- Master bedroom features coffered ceiling, walk-in closet and private bath
- Efficient kitchen includes large window over the sink
- 3 bedrooms, 2 baths, 2-car garage
- Slab foundation

Victorian Styled Gazebo Enhances Front Porch

2,084 total square feet of living area

Price Code C

Special features

- Charming bay window in master suite allows sunlight in as well as style
- Great room accesses front covered porch extending the living area to the outdoors
- Large playroom on second floor is ideal for family living
- 3 bedrooms, 2 1/2 baths, 2-car side entry garage
- Slab, crawl space or basement foundation, please specify when ordering

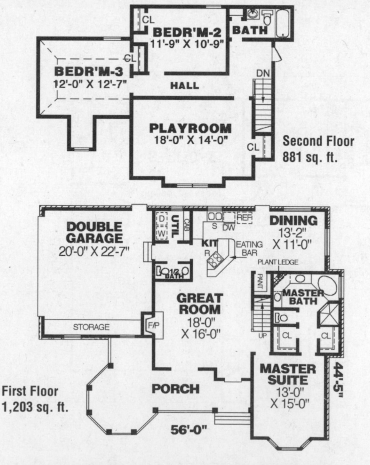

Charming Exterior And Cozy Interior

1,127 total square feet of living area

Price Code AA

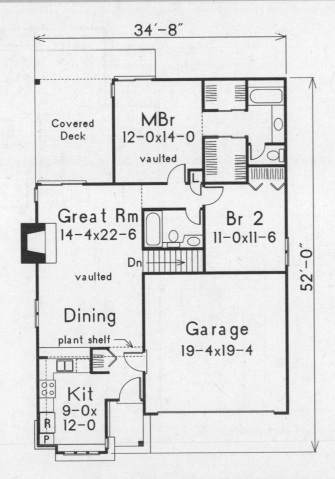

Special features

- Plant shelf joins kitchen and dining room
- Vaulted master suite has double walk-in closets, deck access and private bath
- Great room features vaulted ceiling, fireplace and sliding doors to covered deck
- Ideal home for a narrow lot
- 2 bedrooms, 2 baths, 2-car garage
- Basement foundation

Year-Round Or Weekend Getaway Home

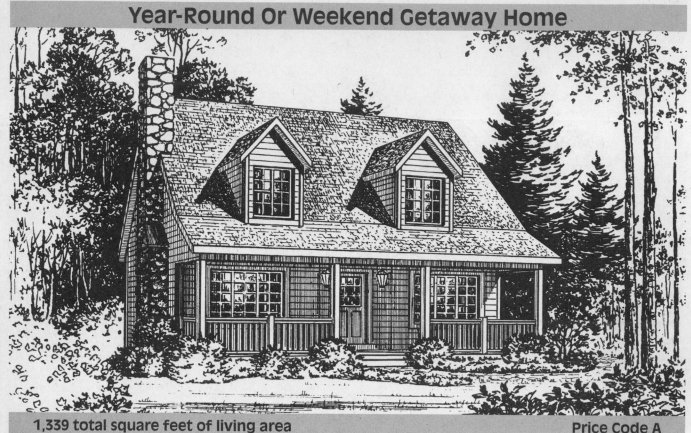

1,339 total square feet of living area

Price Code A

Second Floor
415 sq. ft.

Loft/Br 3
10-7x11-11

Open To Below

Dn

L

Br 2
12-8x10-0

Special features

- Full-length covered porch enhances front facade
- Vaulted ceiling and stone fireplace add drama to family room
- Walk-in closets in bedrooms provide ample storage space
- Combined kitchen/dining area adjoins family room for perfect entertaining space
- 3 bedrooms, 2 1/2 baths
- Crawl space foundation

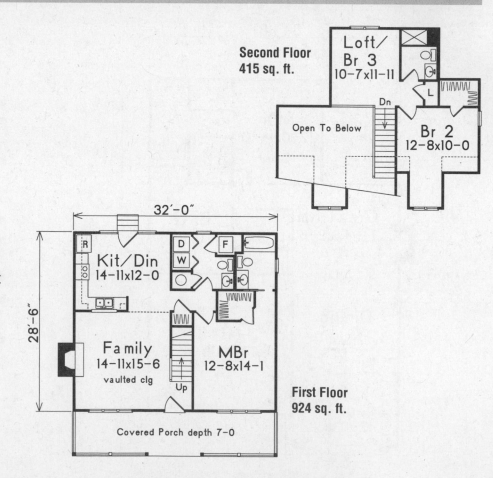

32'-0"

28'-6"

R

Kit/Din
14-11x12-0

D   F
W

Family
14-11x15-6
vaulted clg

Up

MBr
12-8x14-1

Covered Porch depth 7-0

First Floor
924 sq. ft.

Dramatic Look For Quiet Hideaway

1,750 total square feet of living area

Price Code B

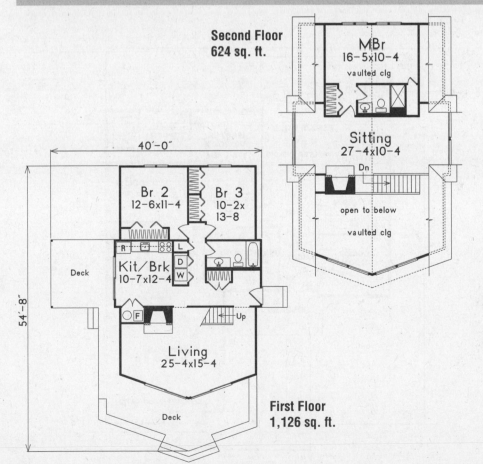

Second Floor 624 sq. ft.

MBr
16-5x10-4
vaulted clg

Sitting
27-4x10-4

Dn

open to below

vaulted clg

40'-0"

Br 2
12-6x11-4

Br 3
10-2x
13-8

Kit/Brk
10-7x12-4

Deck

54'-8"

Up

Living
25-4x15-4

Deck

First Floor 1,126 sq. ft.

Special features

- Family room brightened by floor-to-ceiling windows and sliding doors providing access to large deck

- Second floor sitting area perfect for game room or entertaining

- Kitchen includes eat-in dining area plus outdoor dining patio as a bonus

- Plenty of closet and storage space throughout

- 3 bedrooms, 2 baths

- Basement foundation, drawings also include crawl space and slab foundations

TO ORDER BLUEPRINTS USE THE FORM ON PAGE 15 OR CALL TOLL-FREE 1-877-671-6036
View thousands more home plans online at www.familyhandyman.com/homeplans

69

Cottage-Style Adds Charm

1,496 total square feet of living area

Price Code A

Special features

- Large utility room with sink and extra counterspace

- Covered patio off breakfast nook extends dining to the outdoors

- Eating counter in kitchen overlooks vaulted family room

- 3 bedrooms, 2 baths, 2-car side entry garage

- Crawl space foundation

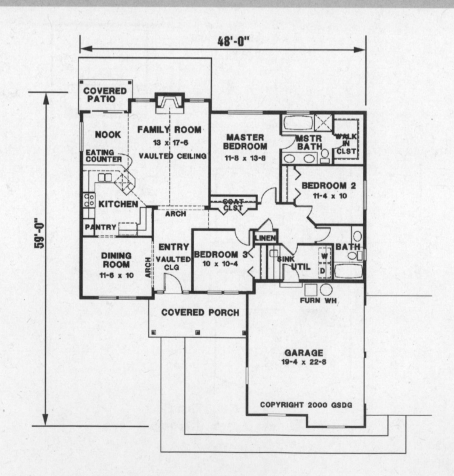

Large Front Porch Adds Welcoming Appeal

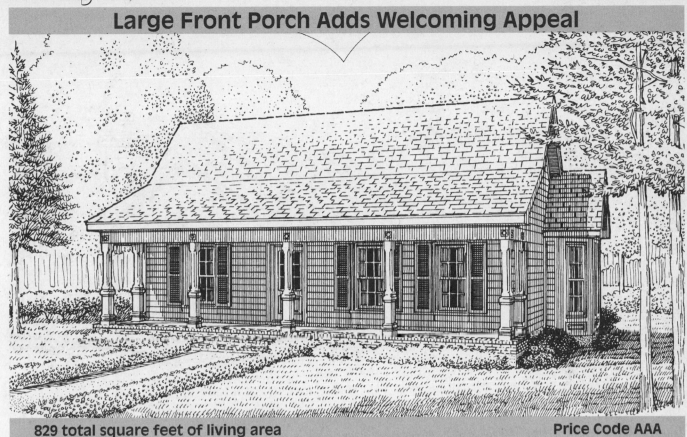

829 total square feet of living area

Price Code AAA

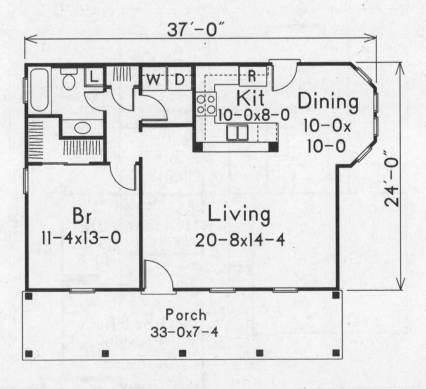

37'-0"

24'-0"

Kit
10-0x8-0

Dining
10-0x
10-0

Br
11-4x13-0

Living
20-8x14-4

Porch
33-0x7-4

L W D R

Special features

- U-shaped kitchen opens into living area by a 42" high counter
- Oversized bay window and French door accent dining room
- Gathering space is created by the large living room
- Convenient utility room and linen closet
- 1 bedroom, 1 bath
- Slab foundation

Great Room Window Adds Character Inside And Out

1,368 total square feet of living area

Price Code A

Special features

- Entry foyer steps down to open living area which combines great room and formal dining area
- Vaulted master suite includes box bay window, large vanity, separate tub and shower
- Cozy breakfast area features direct access to the patio and pass-through kitchen
- Handy linen closet located in hall
- 3 bedrooms, 2 baths, 2-car garage
- Basement foundation

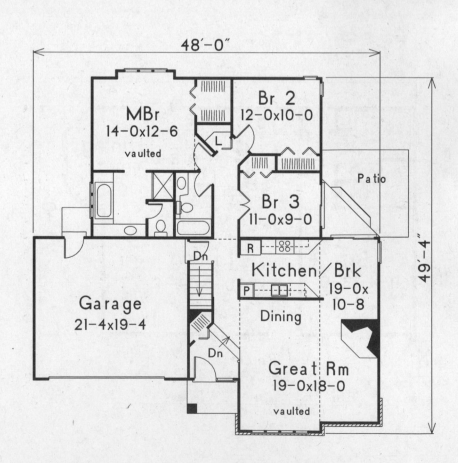

TO ORDER BLUEPRINTS USE THE FORM ON PAGE 15 OR CALL TOLL-FREE 1-877-671-6036
View thousands more home plans online at www.familyhandyman.com/homeplans

English Cottage With Modern Amenities

1,816 total square feet of living area

Price Code C

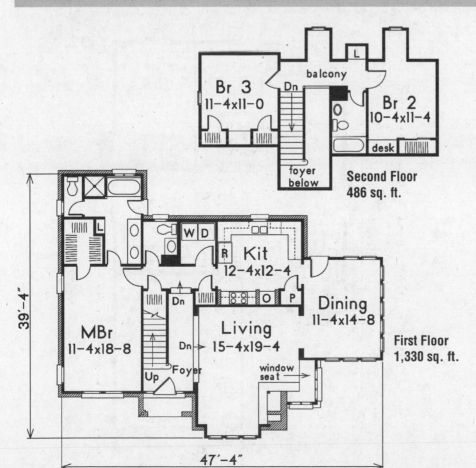

Br 3
11-4x11-0

balcony

Dn

Br 2
10-4x11-4

desk

foyer below

Second Floor 486 sq. ft.

L

W D

R

Kit
12-4x12-4

O

P

Dn

Dining
11-4x14-8

MBr
11-4x18-8

Dn

Living
15-4x19-4

Up   Foyer

window seat

First Floor 1,330 sq. ft.

39'-4"

47'-4"

Special features

- Two-way living room fireplace with large nearby window seat
- Wrap-around dining room windows create sunroom appearance
- Master bedroom has abundant closet and storage space
- Rear dormers, closets and desk areas create interesting and functional second floor
- 3 bedrooms, 2 1/2 baths, 2-car detached garage
- Slab foundation, drawings also include crawl space foundation

TO ORDER BLUEPRINTS USE THE FORM ON PAGE 15 OR CALL TOLL-FREE 1-877-671-6036
View thousands more home plans online at www.familyhandyman.com/homeplans

73

Attractive Gabled Front Window

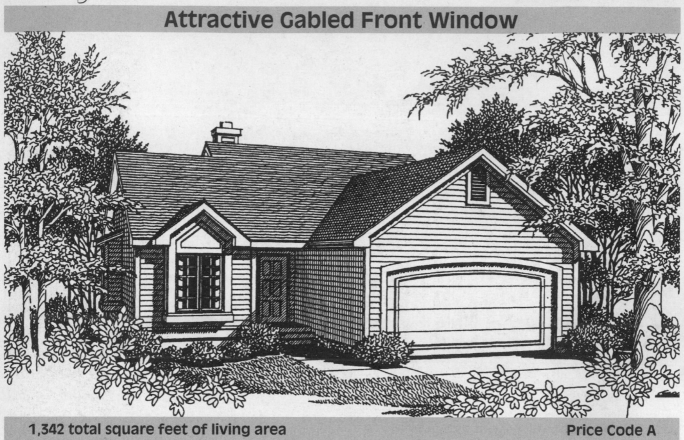

1,342 total square feet of living area   **Price Code A**

Special features

- Open living and dining rooms enjoy the warmth of a fireplace
- Compact yet efficient kitchen has everything within reach
- Centrally located laundry room
- 3 bedrooms, 2 baths, 2-car garage
- Basement foundation

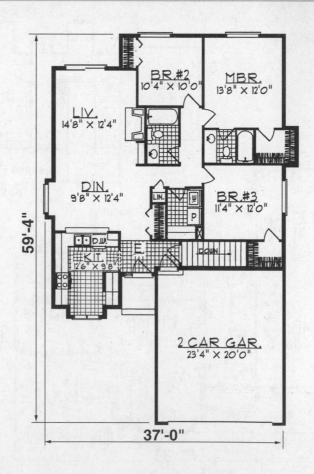

Plan #703-N042

A Chalet For Lakeside Living

1,280 total square feet of living area

Price Code A

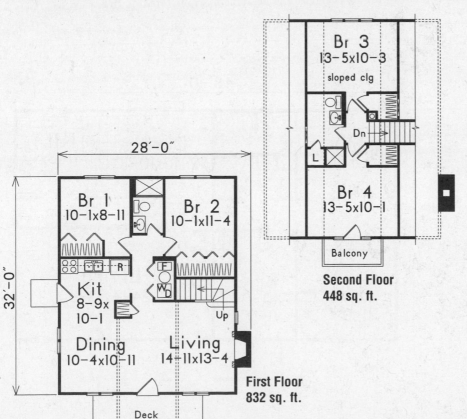

Br 3
13-5x10-3
sloped clg

Dn

L

Br 4
13-5x10-1

Balcony

Second Floor
448 sq. ft.

28'-0"

Br 1
10-1x8-11

Br 2
10-1x11-4

32'-0"

Kit
8-9x
10-1

F W D

Up

Dining
10-4x10-11

Living
14-11x13-4

First Floor
832 sq. ft.

Deck

Special features

- Attention to architectural detail has created the look of an authentic Swiss cottage

- Spacious living room including adjacent kitchenette and dining area, enjoy views to the front deck

- Hall bath shared by two sizable bedrooms is included on first and second floors

- 4 bedrooms, 2 baths

- Crawl space foundation, drawings also include basement and slab foundations

TO ORDER BLUEPRINTS USE THE FORM ON PAGE 15 OR CALL TOLL-FREE 1-877-671-6036
View thousands more home plans online at www.familyhandyman.com/homeplans

75

Efficient Ranch With Country Charm

1,364 total square feet of living area

Price Code A

Special features

- Master suite features spacious walk-in closet and private bath

- Great room highlighted with several windows

- Kitchen with snack bar adjacent to dining area

- Plenty of storage space throughout

- 3 bedrooms, 2 baths, optional 2-car garage

- Basement foundation, drawings also include crawl space foundation

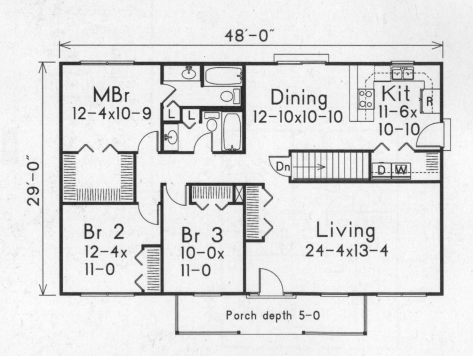

Wrap-Around Porch Adds To Farmhouse Style

1,793 total square feet of living area   **Price Code B**

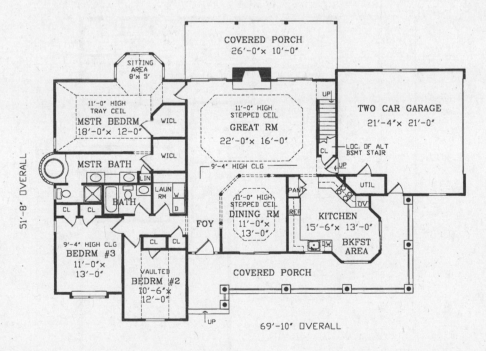

Special features

- A beautiful foyer leads into the great room which has a fireplace flanked by two sets of beautifully transomed doors both leading to a large covered porch

- Dramatic eat-in kitchen includes an abundance of cabinets and workspace in an exciting angled shape

- Delightful master suite has many amenities

- Optional bonus room has an additional 779 square feet of living area

- 3 bedrooms, 2 baths, 2-car side entry garage

- Basement, crawl space or slab foundation, please specify when ordering

TO ORDER BLUEPRINTS USE THE FORM ON PAGE 15 OR CALL TOLL-FREE 1-877-671-6036
View thousands more home plans online at www.familyhandyman.com/homeplans

77

Simple Rooflines And Inviting Porch

1,389 total square feet of living area   **Price Code A**

Special features

- Formal living room has warming fireplace and a delightful bay window

- U-shaped kitchen shares a snack bar with the bayed family room

- Lovely master suite has its own private bath

- 3 bedrooms, 2 baths, 2-car garage

- Slab foundation

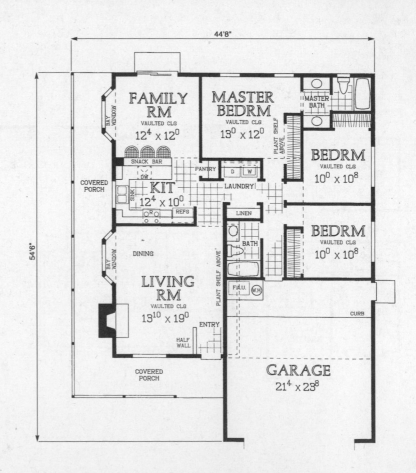

Perfect For A Narrow Lot

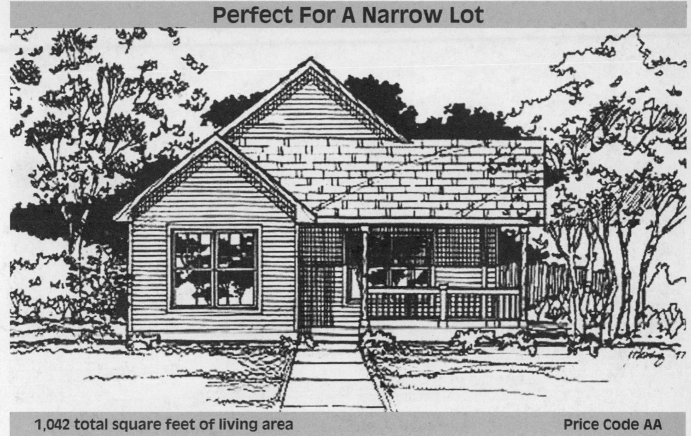

1,042 total square feet of living area | Price Code AA

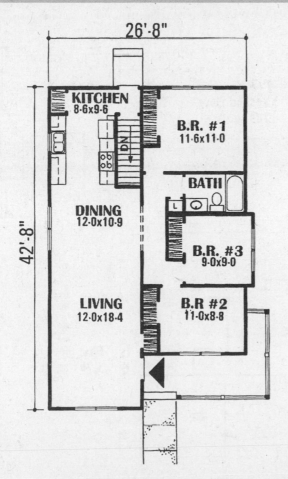

26'-8"

42'-8"

KITCHEN
8-6x9-6

B.R. #1
11-6x11-0

DN

BATH

DINING
12-0x10-9

B.R. #3
9-0x9-0

LIVING
12-0x18-4

B.R #2
11-0x8-8

Special features

■ Dining and living areas combine for added space

■ Cozy covered front porch

■ Plenty of closet space through-out

■ 3 bedrooms, 1 bath

■ Basement foundation

TO ORDER BLUEPRINTS USE THE FORM ON PAGE 15 OR CALL TOLL-FREE 1-877-671-6036
View thousands more home plans online at www.familyhandyman.com/homeplans

79

Windows Add Plenty Of Light

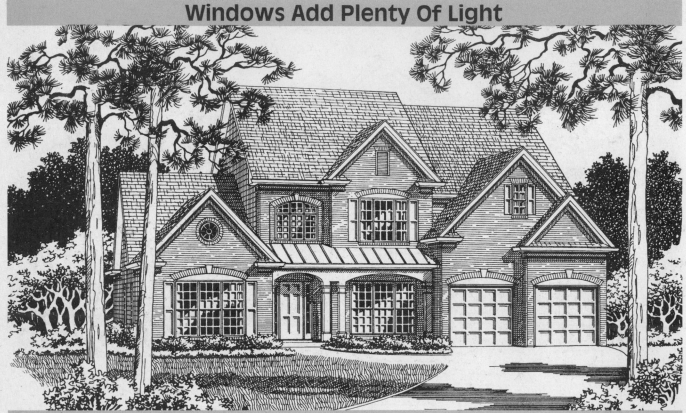

2,450 total square feet of living area

Price Code D

Special features

- Convenient first floor master bedroom has double walk-in closets and an optional sitting area/study

- Two-story breakfast and grand room are open and airy

- Laundry room has a sink and overhead cabinets for convenience

- 4 bedrooms, 2 1/2 baths, 2-car garage

- Basement or slab foundation, please specify when ordering

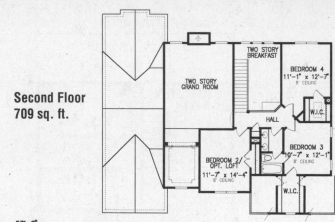

Second Floor 709 sq. ft.

TWO STORY GRAND ROOM

TWO STORY BREAKFAST

BEDROOM 4
11'-1" x 12'-7"
8' CEILING

W.I.C.

HALL

BEDROOM 2/ OPT. LOFT
11'-7" x 14'-4"
8' CEILING

BEDROOM 3
10'-7" x 12'-1"
8' CEILING

W.I.C.

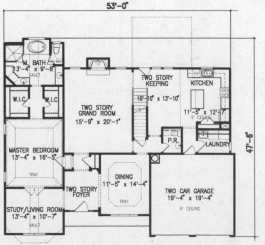

53'-0"

47'-6"

M. BATH
13'-4" x 9'-8"
VAULT

W.I.C.

W.I.C.

TWO STORY GRAND ROOM
15'-9" x 20'-1"

TWO STORY KEEPING
10'-10" x 13'-10"

KITCHEN
11'-5" x 12'-7"
9' CEILING

P.R.

LAUNDRY

MASTER BEDROOM
13'-4" x 16'-5"
TRAY

TWO STORY FOYER

DINING
11'-5" x 14'-4"
TRAY

TWO CAR GARAGE
19'-4" x 19'-4"
9' CEILING

STUDY/LIVING ROOM
13'-4" x 10'-7"
VAULT

First Floor 1,751 sq. ft.

TO ORDER BLUEPRINTS USE THE FORM ON PAGE 15 OR CALL TOLL-FREE 1-877-671-6036
View thousands more home plans online at www.familyhandyman.com/homeplans

Open Living Spaces

1,000 total square feet of living area   **Price Code AA**

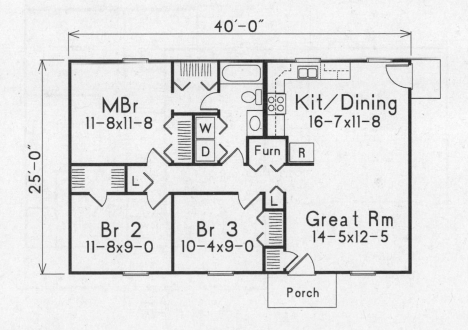

Special features

- Bath includes convenient closeted laundry area
- Master bedroom includes double closets and private access to bath
- Foyer features handy coat closet
- L-shaped kitchen provides easy access outdoors
- 3 bedrooms, 1 bath
- Crawl space foundation, drawings also include basement and slab foundations

Covered Rear Porch

1,253 total square feet of living area

Price Code A

Special features

- Sloped ceiling and fireplace in family room add drama
- U-shaped kitchen is efficiently designed
- Large walk-in closets are found in all the bedrooms
- 3 bedrooms, 2 baths, 2-car garage
- Crawl space or slab foundation, please specify when ordering

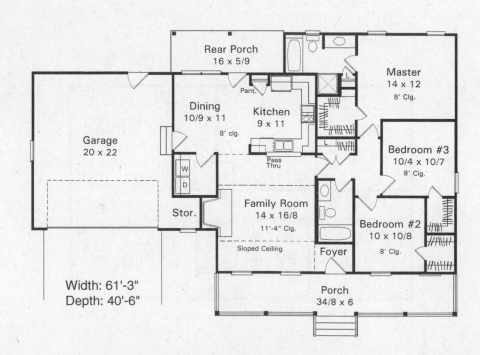

Width: 61'-3"
Depth: 40'-6"

TO ORDER BLUEPRINTS USE THE FORM ON PAGE 15 OR CALL TOLL-FREE 1-877-671-6036
View thousands more home plans online at www.familyhandyman.com/homeplans

1,097 total square feet of living area

Price Code AA

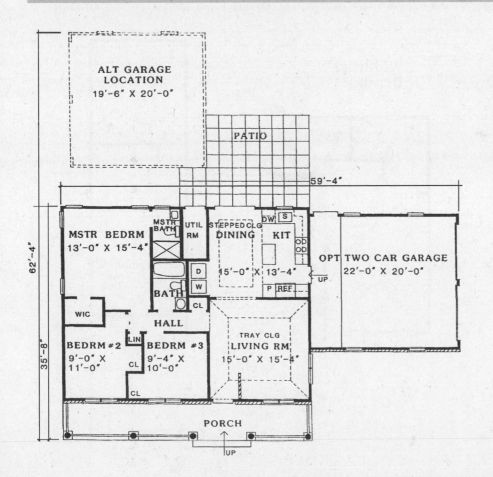

Special features

- U-shaped kitchen wraps around center island
- Master suite includes its own private bath and walk-in closet
- Living room provides expansive view to the rear
- 3 bedrooms, 2 baths, optional 2-car side entry garage
- Basement, crawl space or slab foundation, please specify when ordering

TO ORDER BLUEPRINTS USE THE FORM ON PAGE 15 OR CALL TOLL-FREE 1-877-671-6036
View thousands more home plans online at www.familyhandyman.com/homeplans

83

Central Living Room Great For Gathering

1,405 total square feet of living area

Price Code A

Special features

- Compact design has all the luxuries of a larger home
- Master bedroom has its privacy away from other bedrooms
- Living room has corner fireplace, access to the outdoors and easy access to the dining area and kitchen
- Large utility room with access outdoors
- 3 bedrooms, 2 baths
- Slab foundation

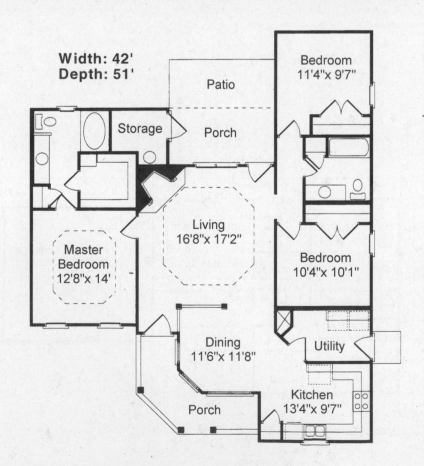

Width: 42'
Depth: 51'

Patio

Storage

Porch

Bedroom
11'4"x 9'7"

Living
16'8"x 17'2"

Master
Bedroom
12'8"x 14'

Bedroom
10'4"x 10'1"

Dining
11'6"x 11'8"

Utility

Porch

Kitchen
13'4"x 9'7"

Cottage With Atrium

969 total square feet of living area

Price Code AA

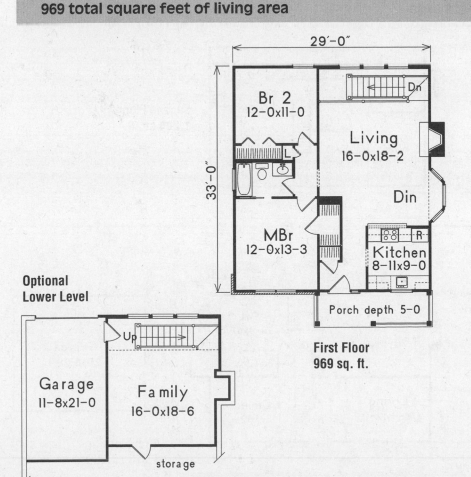

29'-0"

33'-0"

Br 2
12-0x11-0

Dn

Living
16-0x18-2

Din

MBr
12-0x13-3

Kitchen
8-11x9-0

R

Porch depth 5-0

First Floor
969 sq. ft.

Optional
Lower Level

Up

Garage
11-8x21-0

Family
16-0x18-6

storage

Special features

- Eye-pleasing facade enjoys stone accents with country porch for quiet evenings

- A bayed dining area, cozy fireplace and atrium with sunny two-story windows are the many features of the living room

- Step-saver kitchen includes a pass-through snack bar

- 325 square feet of optional living area on the lower level

- 2 bedrooms, 1 bath, 1-car rear entry garage

- Walk-out basement foundation

TO ORDER BLUEPRINTS USE THE FORM ON PAGE 15 OR CALL TOLL-FREE 1-877-671-6036
View thousands more home plans online at www.familyhandyman.com/homeplans

85

Stately Country Home For The "Spacious Age"

2,727 total square feet of living area

Price Code E

Special features

- Wrap-around porch and large foyer create impressive entrance

- A state-of-the-art vaulted kitchen has walk-in pantry and is open to the breakfast room and adjoining screened porch

- A walk-in wet bar, fireplace bay window and deck access are features of the family room

- Vaulted master bedroom suite enjoys a luxurious bath with skylight and an enormous 13' deep walk-in closet

- 4 bedrooms, 2 1/2 baths, 2-car side entry garage

- Walk-out basement foundation

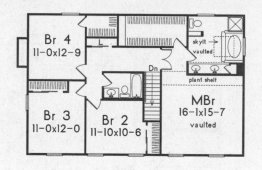

**Second Floor
1,204 sq. ft.**

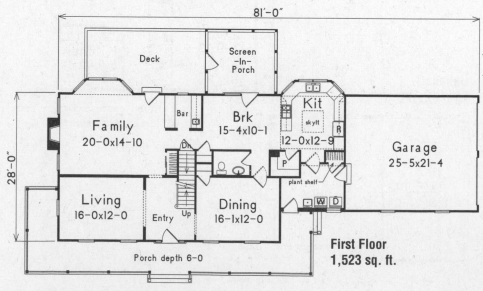

**First Floor
1,523 sq. ft.**

TO ORDER BLUEPRINTS USE THE FORM ON PAGE 15 OR CALL TOLL-FREE 1-877-671-6036
View thousands more home plans online at www.familyhandyman.com/homeplans

Dramatic U-Shaped Stairs

2,287 total square feet of living area

Price Code D

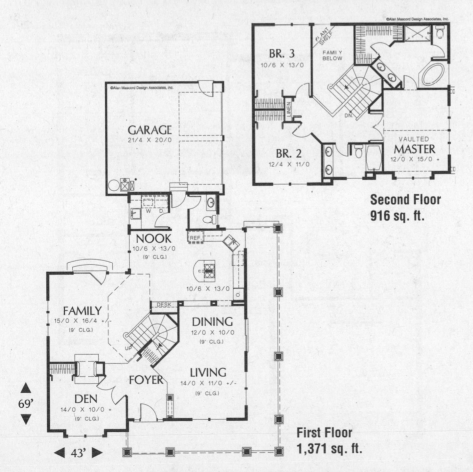

©Alan Mascord Design Associates, Inc.

**Second Floor
916 sq. ft.**

BR. 3
10/6 X 13/0

FAMILY BELOW

PLANT SHELF

LINEN

DN.

BR. 2
12/4 X 11/0

VAULTED
MASTER
12/0 X 15/0 +

©Alan Mascord Design Associates, Inc.

GARAGE
21/4 X 20/0

W   D

NOOK
10/6 X 13/0
(9' CLG.)

REF.

10/6 X 13/0

DESK

FAMILY
15/0 X 16/4 +
(9' CLG.)

DINING
12/0 X 10/0
(9' CLG.)

UP

FOYER

LIVING
14/0 X 11/0 +/-
(9' CLG.)

DEN
14/0 X 10/0 +
(9' CLG.)

69'

43'

**First Floor
1,371 sq. ft.**

Special features

- Wrap-around porch creates inviting feeling
- First floor windows have transom windows above
- Den has see-through fireplace into the family area
- 4 bedrooms, 2 1/2 baths, 2-car side entry garage
- Crawl space foundation

Sunny Dining Room

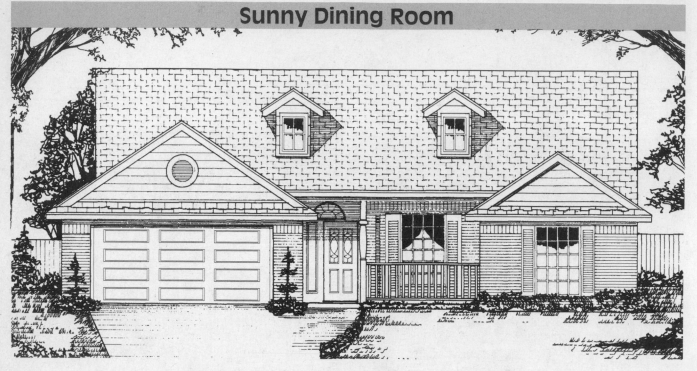

1,735 total square feet of living area

Price Code B

Special features

- Luxurious master bath has spa tub, shower, double vanity and large walk-in closet
- Peninsula in kitchen has sink and dishwasher
- Massive master bedroom has step up ceiling and private location
- 3 bedrooms, 2 baths, 2-car garage
- Slab foundation

Width: 50'-0"
Depth: 55'-0"

Cheerful And Bright Great Room

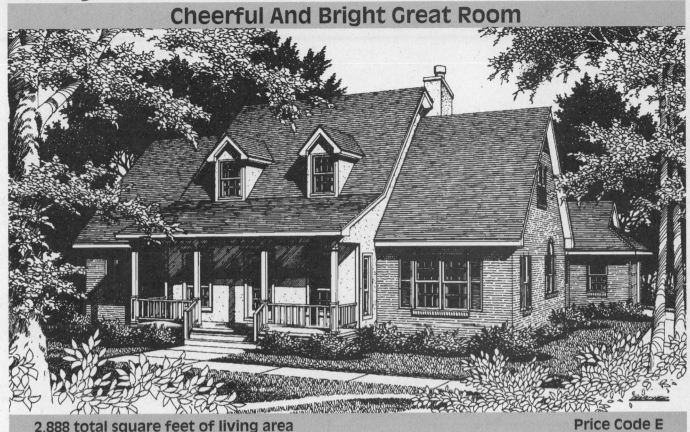

2,888 total square feet of living area

Price Code E

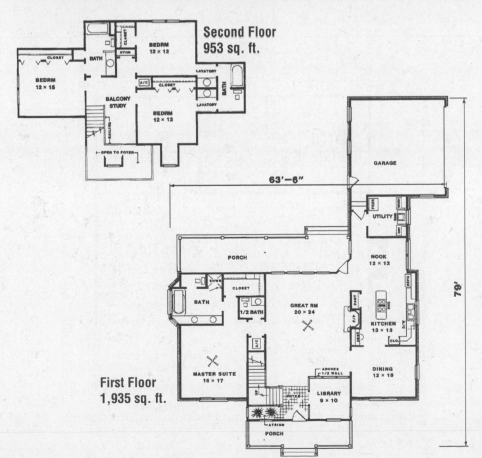

Second Floor 953 sq. ft.

BEDRM 12 × 12

CLOSET

BATH

CLOSET

BEDRM 12 × 15

BALCONY STUDY

BEDRM 12 × 12

LAVATORY

A/C CLOSET

LAVATORY

BATH

OPEN TO FOYER

First Floor 1,935 sq. ft.

63'-6"

78'

GARAGE

PORCH

UTILITY

NOOK 12 × 12

KITCHEN 13 × 13

SHWR

CLOSET

BATH

1/2 BATH

GREAT RM 20 × 24

PANT

MASTER SUITE 15 × 17

A/C

ARCHED 1/2 WALL

LIBRARY 9 × 10

DINING 12 × 15

ATRIUM PORCH

Special features

- An arched half-wall accents secluded library
- First floor master suite has a spacious bath with tub-in-a-bay
- Kitchen has center island with cooktop for convenience
- 9' ceilings on the first floor
- 4 bedrooms, 3 1/2 baths, 2-car side entry garage
- Slab or crawl space foundation, please specify when ordering

Country Cottage Has Vaulted Ceiling

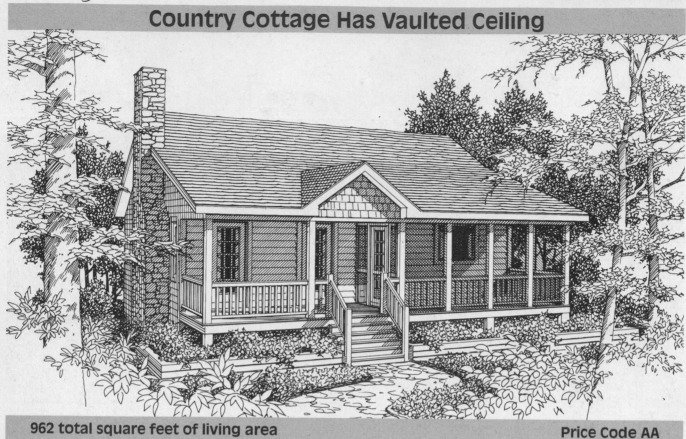

962 total square feet of living area

Price Code AA

Special features

- Both the kitchen and family room share warmth from the fireplace
- Charming facade features covered porch on one side, screened porch on the other and attractive planter boxes
- L-shaped kitchen boasts convenient pantry
- 2 bedrooms, 1 bath
- Crawl space foundation

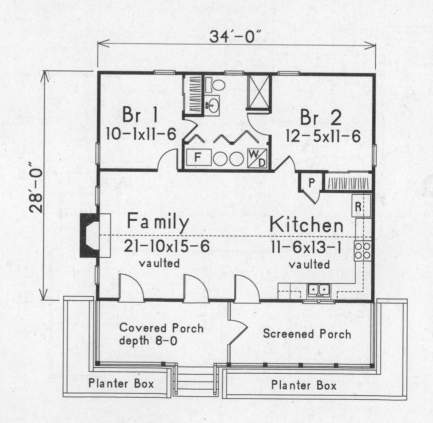

TO ORDER BLUEPRINTS USE THE FORM ON PAGE 15 OR CALL TOLL-FREE 1-877-671-6036

View thousands more home plans online at www.familyhandyman.com/homeplans

Wrap-Around Veranda Softens Country-Style Home

2,449 total square feet of living area

Price Code E

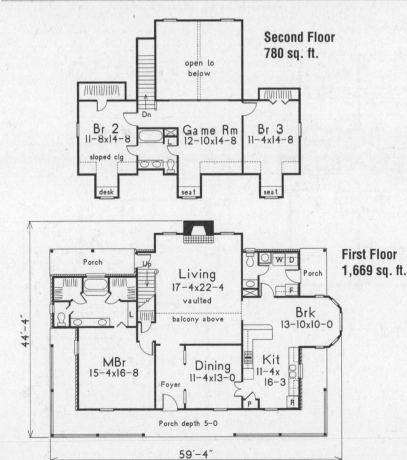

Second Floor
780 sq. ft.

open to below

Dn

Br 2
11-8x14-8

sloped clg

desk

Game Rm
12-10x14-8

seat

Br 3
11-4x14-8

seat

First Floor
1,669 sq. ft.

Porch

Up

Living
17-4x22-4
vaulted

balcony above

W D

F

Porch

Brk
13-10x10-0

44'-4"

MBr
15-4x16-8

Foyer

Dining
11-4x13-0

P

Kit
11-4x
16-3

R

Porch depth 5-0

59'-4"

Special features

- Striking living area features fireplace flanked with windows, cathedral ceiling and balcony
- First floor master bedroom with twin walk-in closets and large linen storage
- Dormers add space for desks or seats
- 3 bedrooms, 2 1/2 baths, 2-car detached garage
- Slab foundation, drawings also include crawl space foundation

TO ORDER BLUEPRINTS USE THE FORM ON PAGE 15 OR CALL TOLL-FREE 1-877-671-6036
View thousands more home plans online at www.familyhandyman.com/homeplans

91

Warm And Cozy Feeling

2,202 total square feet of living area

Price Code D

Special features

- 9' ceilings on first floor
- Guest bedroom located on the first floor for convenience could easily be converted to an office area
- Large kitchen with oversized island overlooks dining area
- 5 bedrooms, 4 full baths, 2 half baths, 2-car drive under garage
- Basement or walk-out basement foundation, please specify when ordering

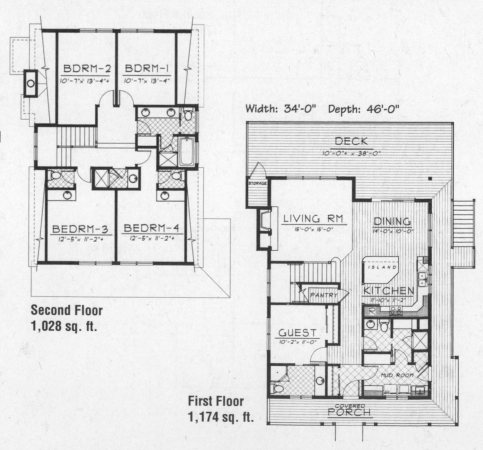

Second Floor
1,028 sq. ft.

Width: 34'-0"   Depth: 46'-0"

First Floor
1,174 sq. ft.

Quaint Home Made For Country Living

1,578 total square feet of living area

Price Code B

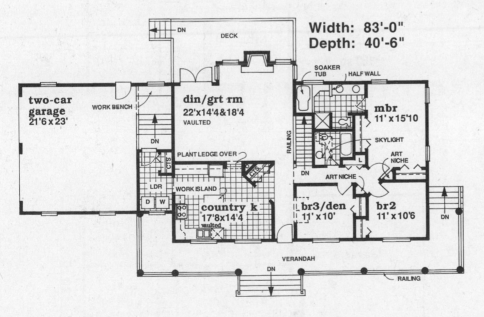

Width: 83'-0"
Depth: 40'-6"

DECK

DN

two-car garage 21'6 x 23'

WORK BENCH

din/grt rm 22'x14'4 &18'4 VAULTED

DN

PLANT LEDGE OVER

RAILING

SOAKER TUB   HALF WALL

mbr 11' x 15'10

SKYLIGHT

ART NICHE

LDR

WORK ISLAND

D W

country k 17'8x14'4 vaulted

FRS

DN

ART NICHE

br3/den 11' x 10'

br2 11' x 10'6

DN

VERANDAH

DN

RAILING

Special features

- A fireplace warms the great room and is flanked by windows overlooking the rear deck

- Bedrooms are clustered on one side of the home for privacy from living areas

- Master bedroom has unique art niche at its entry and a private bath with separate tub and shower

- 3 bedrooms, 2 baths, 2-car side entry garage

- Basement or crawl space foundation, please specify when ordering

TO ORDER BLUEPRINTS USE THE FORM ON PAGE 15 OR CALL TOLL-FREE 1-877-671-6036
View thousands more home plans online at www.familyhandyman.com/homeplans

93

Country Classic With Modern Floor Plan

1,921 total square feet of living area

Price Code D

Special features

- Energy efficient home with 2" x 6" exterior walls

- Sunken family room includes a built-in entertainment center and coffered ceiling

- Sunken formal living room features a coffered ceiling

- Dressing area has double sinks, spa tub, shower and French door to private deck

- Large front porch adds to home's appeal

- 3 bedrooms, 2 1/2 baths, 2-car garage

- Basement foundation

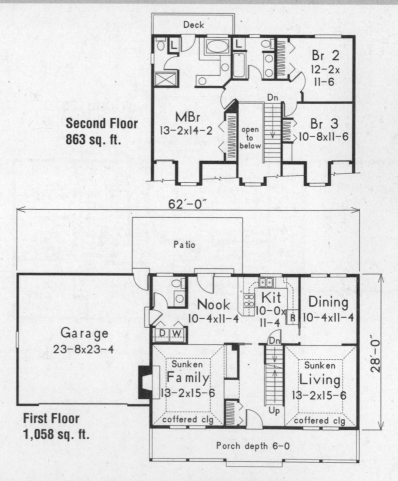

Second Floor 863 sq. ft.

Deck

Br 2 12-2x 11-6

MBr 13-2x14-2

open to below

Dn

Br 3 10-8x11-6

62'-0"

Patio

Garage 23-8x23-4

Nook 10-4x11-4

Kit 10-0x 11-4

Dining 10-4x11-4

D.W.

Dn

Sunken Family 13-2x15-6

coffered clg

Up

Sunken Living 13-2x15-6

coffered clg

28'-0"

First Floor 1,058 sq. ft.

Porch depth 6-0

Rustic Feel With Stone Accent

1,648 total square feet of living area

Price Code B

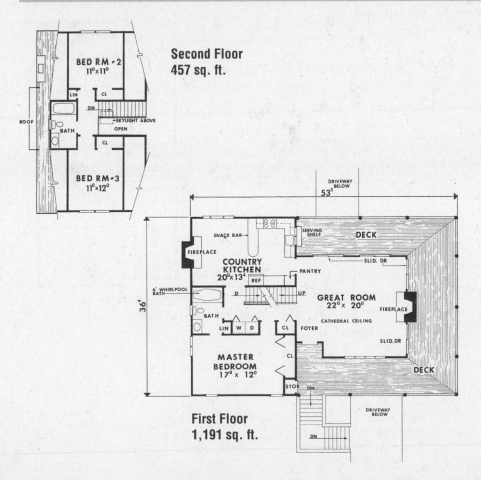

Second Floor
457 sq. ft.

BED RM #2
11⁰ x 11⁰

BED RM #3
11⁰ x 12⁰

First Floor
1,191 sq. ft.

Special features

- Enormous country kitchen has fireplace and a snack bar
- Four sets of sliding glass doors fill this home full of light and make the deck convenient from any room
- Secondary bedrooms both located on second floor along with a full bath
- 3 bedrooms, 2 baths, 2-car drive under garage
- Basement, crawl space or slab foundation, please specify when ordering

Comfortable Family Living

2,097 total square feet of living area

Price Code C

Special features

- Formal living room connects with dining room, perfect for entertaining
- Elegant two-story foyer
- Spacious entry off garage near bath and laundry area
- Family room has cozy fireplace
- 4 bedrooms, 2 1/2 baths, 2-car side entry garage
- Basement foundation

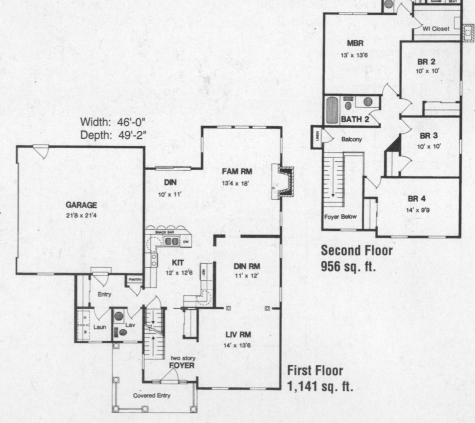

Width: 46'-0"
Depth: 49'-2"

GARAGE 21'8 x 21'4

DIN 10' x 11'

FAM RM 13'4 x 18'

SNACK BAR

DW

KIT 12' x 12'6

PANTRY

Entry

DIN RM 11' x 12'

Laun

Lav

LIV RM 14' x 13'6

two story FOYER

Covered Entry

First Floor 1,141 sq. ft.

MBATH

MBR 13' x 13'6

WI Closet

BR 2 10' x 10'

BATH 2

Balcony

BR 3 10' x 10'

Foyer Below

BR 4 14' x 9'9

Second Floor 956 sq. ft.

TO ORDER BLUEPRINTS USE THE FORM ON PAGE 15 OR CALL TOLL-FREE 1-877-671-6036
View thousands more home plans online at www.familyhandyman.com/homeplans

Bay Window Graces Luxury Master Bedroom

1,668 total square feet of living area

Price Code C

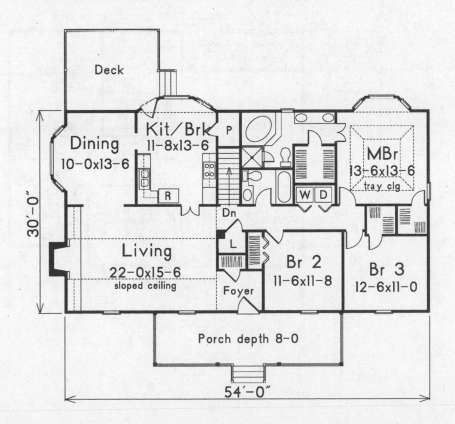

Special features

- Large bay windows in breakfast area, master bedroom and dining room
- Extensive walk-in closets and storage spaces throughout the home
- Handy entry covered porch
- Large living room has fireplace, built-in bookshelves and sloped ceiling
- 3 bedrooms, 2 baths, 2-car drive under garage
- Basement foundation

Traditional Southern Style Home

1,785 total square feet of living area

Price Code B

Special features

- 9' ceilings throughout home
- Luxurious master bath includes whirlpool tub and separate shower
- Cozy breakfast area is convenient to kitchen
- 3 bedrooms, 3 baths, 2-car detached garage
- Basement, crawl space or slab foundation, please specify when ordering

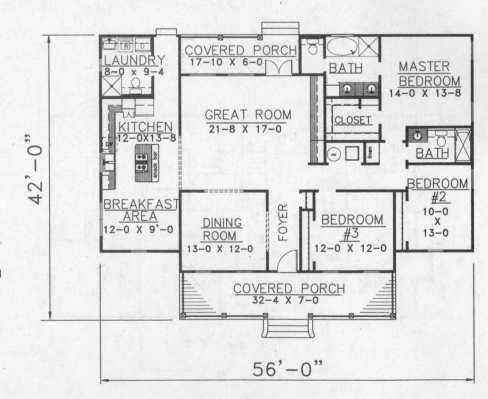

Expansive Glass Wall In Living Areas

1,543 total square feet of living area

Price Code B

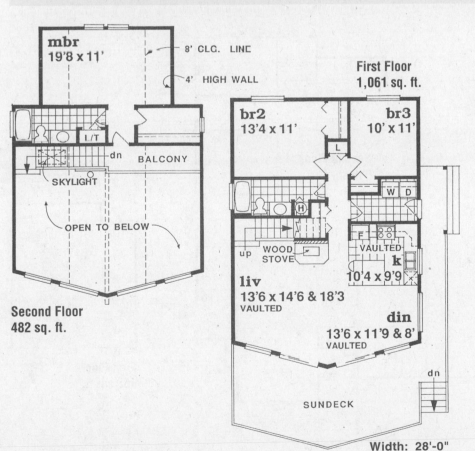

mbr
19'8 x 11'

8' CLG. LINE

4' HIGH WALL

dn BALCONY

SKYLIGHT

OPEN TO BELOW

Second Floor
482 sq. ft.

First Floor
1,061 sq. ft.

br2
13'4 x 11'

br3
10' x 11'

L

W D

up WOOD STOVE

F

VAULTED

k
10'4 x 9'9

liv
13'6 x 14'6 & 18'3
VAULTED

din
13'6 x 11'9 & 8'
VAULTED

dn

SUNDECK

Width: 28'-0"
Depth: 39'-9"

Special features

- Enormous sundeck makes this a popular vacation style
- A woodstove warms the vaulted living and dining rooms
- A vaulted kitchen has a prep island and breakfast bar
- Second floor vaulted master bedroom has private bath and walk-in closet
- 3 bedrooms, 2 baths
- Crawl space foundation

TO ORDER BLUEPRINTS USE THE FORM ON PAGE 15 OR CALL TOLL-FREE 1-877-671-6036
View thousands more home plans online at www.familyhandyman.com/homeplans

99

Country-Style With Wrap-Around Porch

1,597 total square feet of living area

Price Code C

Special features

- Spacious family room includes fireplace and coat closet
- Open kitchen and dining room provides breakfast bar and access to the outdoors
- Convenient laundry area located near kitchen
- Secluded master suite with walk-in closet and private bath
- 4 bedrooms, 2 1/2 baths, 2-car detached garage
- Basement foundation

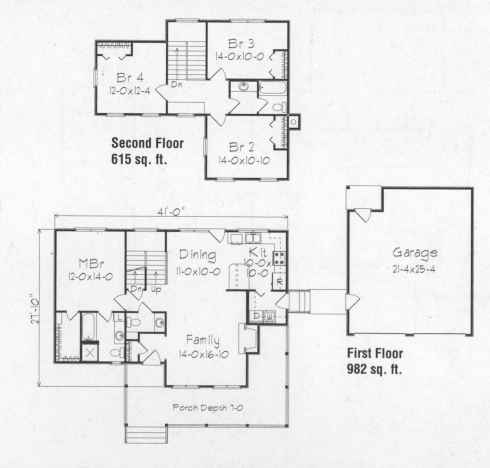

Second Floor 615 sq. ft.

Br 4 12-0x12-4
Br 3 14-0x10-0
Br 2 14-0x10-10

First Floor 982 sq. ft.

41'-0"
27'-10"
MBr 12-0x14-0
Dining 11-0x10-0
Kit 10-0x10-0
Family 14-0x16-10
Garage 21-4x25-4
Porch Depth 7-0

Extra Amenities Enhance Living

2,009 total square feet of living area

Price Code C

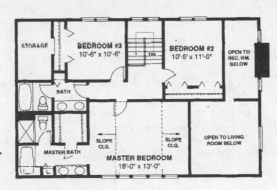

Second Floor
847 sq. ft.

STORAGE

BEDROOM #3
10'-6" x 10'-6"

DN.

BEDROOM #2
10'-6' x 11'-6"

OPEN TO
REC. RM.
BELOW

BATH

MASTER BATH

SLOPE CLG.

SLOPE CLG.

OPEN TO LIVING ROOM BELOW

MASTER BEDROOM
18'-0" x 13'-0"

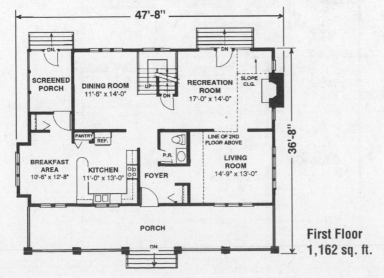

47'-8"

36'-8"

SCREENED PORCH

DINING ROOM
11'-6" x 14'-0"

UP
DN.

RECREATION ROOM
17'-0" x 14'-0"

SLOPE CLG.

PANTRY

REF.

LINE OF 2ND FLOOR ABOVE

P.R.

BREAKFAST AREA
10'-6" x 12'-8"

KITCHEN
11'-0" x 13'-0"

FOYER

LIVING ROOM
14'-9" x 13'-0"

PORCH

DN.

First Floor
1,162 sq. ft.

Special features

- Spacious master bedroom has dramatic sloped ceiling and private bath with double sinks and walk-in closet

- Bedroom #3 has extra storage inside closet

- Versatile screened porch is ideal for entertaining year-round

- Sunny breakfast area located near kitchen and screened porch for convenience

- 3 bedrooms, 2 1/2 baths

- Basement foundation

Open Living Spaces

1,050 total square feet of living area

Price Code AA

Special features

- Master bedroom features a private bath and access outdoors onto a private patio
- A vaulted ceiling in the living and dining areas creates a feeling of spaciousness
- Laundry closet is convenient to all bedrooms
- Efficient U-shaped kitchen
- 3 bedrooms, 2 baths, 1-car garage
- Basement or slab foundation, please specify when ordering

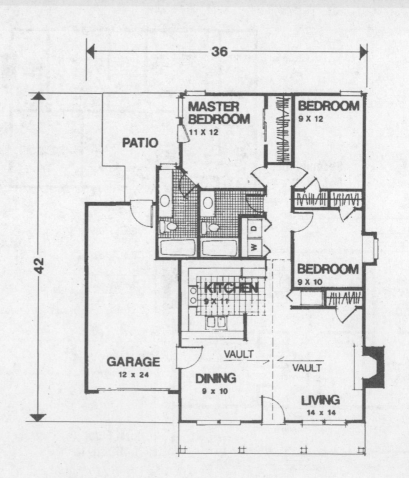

Charming House, Spacious And Functional

2,505 total square feet of living area

Price Code D

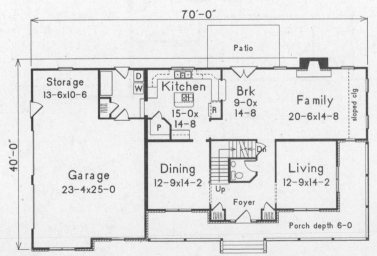

Second Floor
1,069 sq. ft.

Br 2
12-6x11-6

MBr
12-9x18-0

Dn

Br 3
12-9x12-0

open to below

70'-0"

Patio

Storage
13-6x10-6

D/W

Kitchen
15-0x
14-8

P

R

Brk
9-0x
14-8

Family
20-6x14-8

40'-0"

Garage
23-4x25-0

Dining
12-9x14-2

Up

Dn

Living
12-9x14-2

Foyer

Porch depth 6-0

First Floor
1,436 sq. ft.

Special features

- The garage features extra storage area and ample work space
- Laundry room accessible from the garage and the outdoors
- Deluxe raised tub and immense walk-in closet grace master bath
- 3 bedrooms, 2 1/2 baths, 2-car side entry garage
- Basement foundation, drawings also include crawl space foundation

TO ORDER BLUEPRINTS USE THE FORM ON PAGE 15 OR CALL TOLL-FREE 1-877-671-6036
View thousands more home plans online at www.familyhandyman.com/homeplans

103

Charming Country Styling In This Ranch

1,600 total square feet of living area

Price Code C

Special features

- Energy efficient home with 2" x 6" exterior walls

- Impressive sunken living room has massive stone fireplace and 16' vaulted ceilings

- Dining room conveniently located next to kitchen and divided for privacy

- Special amenities include sewing room, glass shelves in kitchen and master bath and a large utility area

- Sunken master bedroom features a distinctive sitting room

- 3 bedrooms, 2 baths, 2-car side entry garage

- Slab foundation, drawings also include crawl space and basement foundations

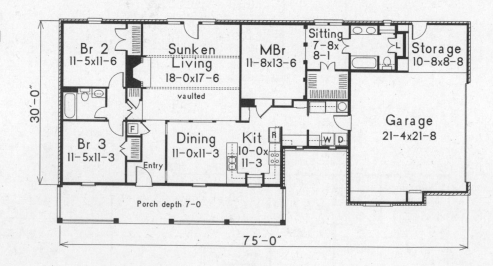

TO ORDER BLUEPRINTS USE THE FORM ON PAGE 15 OR CALL TOLL-FREE 1-877-671-6036
View thousands more home plans online at www.familyhandyman.com/homeplans

Functional Layout For Comfortable Living

1,360 total square feet of living area

Price Code A

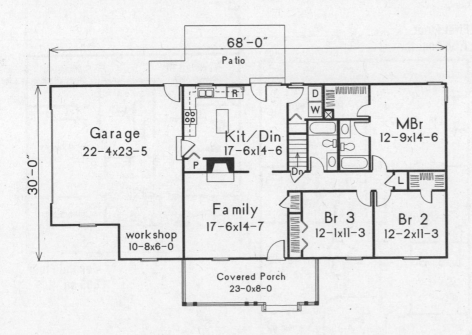

Special features

- Kitchen/dining room features island work space and plenty of dining area

- Master bedroom with large walk-in closet and private bath

- Laundry room adjacent to the kitchen for easy access

- Convenient workshop in garage

- Large closets in secondary bedrooms

- 3 bedrooms, 2 baths, 2-car side entry garage

- Basement foundation, drawings also include crawl space and slab foundations

Plan #703-MG-01240

A Cozy Ranch With Rustic Touches

© 2003, Garrell Associates, Inc.

2,272 total square feet of living area

Price Code G

Special features

- 10' ceilings throughout first floor and 9' ceilings on the second floor
- Lots of storage area on the second floor
- First floor master bedroom has a lovely sitting area with arched entry
- Second floor bedrooms share a jack and jill bath
- 3 bedrooms, 2 1/2 baths, 2-car rear entry garage
- Slab foundation

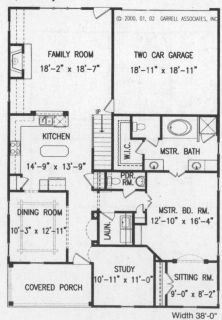

**First Floor
1,587 sq. ft.**

© 2000, 01, 02 GARRELL ASSOCIATES, INC

FAMILY ROOM
18'-2" x 18'-7"

TWO CAR GARAGE
18'-11" x 18'-11"

UP

KITCHEN
14'-9" x 13'-9"

W.I.C.

MSTR. BATH

PDR. RM.

DINING ROOM
10'-3" x 12'-11"

LAUN.

MSTR. BD. RM.
12'-10" x 16'-4"

COVERED PORCH

STUDY
10'-11" x 11'-0"

SITTING RM.
9'-0" x 8'-2"

Width 38'-0"
Depth 55'-0"

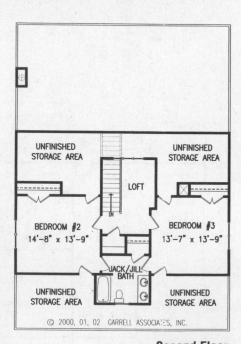

UNFINISHED STORAGE AREA

UNFINISHED STORAGE AREA

LOFT

BEDROOM #2
14'-8" x 13'-9"

BEDROOM #3
13'-7" x 13'-9"

JACK/JILL BATH

UNFINISHED STORAGE AREA

UNFINISHED STORAGE AREA

© 2000, 01, 02 GARRELL ASSOCIATES, INC.

**Second Floor
685 sq. ft.**

TO ORDER BLUEPRINTS USE THE FORM ON PAGE 15 OR CALL TOLL-FREE 1-877-671-6036
View thousands more home plans online at www.familyhandyman.com/homeplans

Country Accents Make This Home

1,568 total square feet of living area

Price Code B

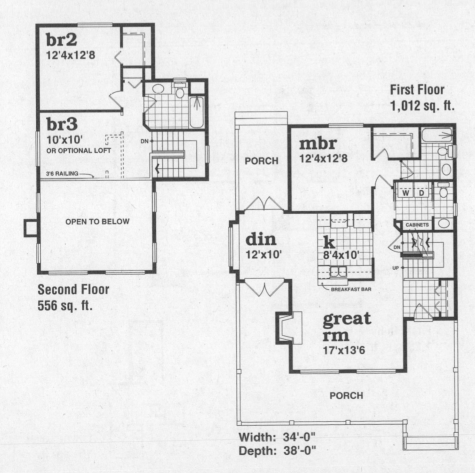

br2
12'4x12'8

br3
10'x10'
OR OPTIONAL LOFT

DN

3'6 RAILING

OPEN TO BELOW

Second Floor
556 sq. ft.

First Floor
1,012 sq. ft.

PORCH

mbr
12'4x12'8

W D

CABINETS

DN

UP

din
12'x10'

k
8'4x10'

BREAKFAST BAR

great rm
17'x13'6

PORCH

Width: 34'-0"
Depth: 38'-0"

Special features

- Master bedroom is located on first floor for convenience
- Cozy great room has fireplace
- Dining room has access to both the front and rear porches
- Two secondary bedrooms and a bath complete the second floor
- 3 bedrooms, 2 1/2 baths
- Basement or crawl space foundation, please specify when ordering

TO ORDER BLUEPRINTS USE THE FORM ON PAGE 15 OR CALL TOLL-FREE 1-877-671-6036
View thousands more home plans online at www.familyhandyman.com/homeplans

107

Summer Home Or Year-Round

1,403 total square feet of living area

Price Code A

Special features

- Impressive living areas for a modest-sized home
- Special master/hall bath has linen storage, step-up tub and lots of window light
- Spacious closets everywhere you look
- 3 bedrooms, 2 baths, 2-car drive under garage and second bath on lower level
- Basement foundation

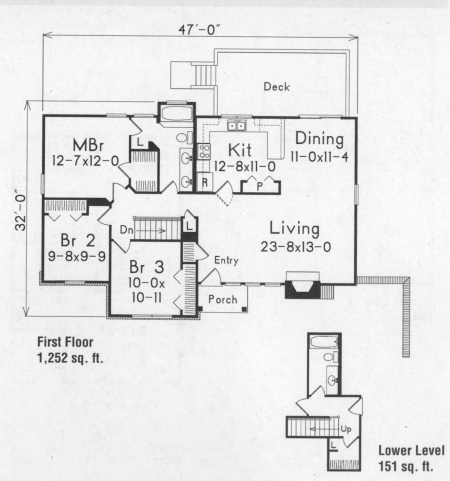

47'-0"

32'-0"

Deck

MBr
12-7x12-0

Kit
12-8x11-0

Dining
11-0x11-4

Br 2
9-8x9-9

Living
23-8x13-0

Dn

Br 3
10-0x
10-11

Entry

Porch

First Floor
1,252 sq. ft.

Up

Lower Level
151 sq. ft.

A Special Home For Views

1,684 total square feet of living area

Price Code B

Rear View

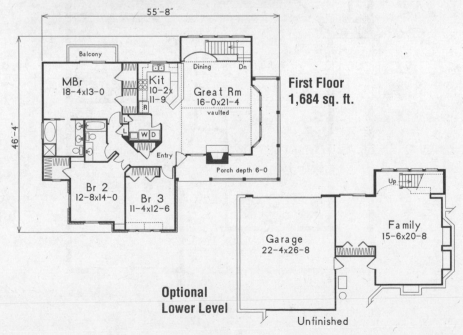

55'-8"

Balcony

MBr
18-4x13-0

Kit
10-2x
11-9

Dining   Dn

Great Rm
16-0x21-4
vaulted

**First Floor
1,684 sq. ft.**

46'-4"

W D

Entry

Porch depth 6-0

Br 2
12-8x14-0

Br 3
11-4x12-6

Up

Family
15-6x20-8

Garage
22-4x26-8

**Optional
Lower Level**

Unfinished

Special features

- Delightful wrap-around porch anchored by full masonry fireplace

- The vaulted great room includes a large bay window, fireplace, dining balcony and atrium window wall

- His and hers walk-in closets, large luxury bath and sliding doors to exterior balcony are a few fantastic features of the master bedroom

- Atrium open to 611 square feet of optional living area on the lower level

- 3 bedrooms, 2 baths, 2-car drive under garage

- Walk-out basement foundation

TO ORDER BLUEPRINTS USE THE FORM ON PAGE 15 OR CALL TOLL-FREE 1-877-671-6036
View thousands more home plans online at www.familyhandyman.com/homeplans

109

Eye-Catching Luxurious Bath

1,124 total square feet of living area

Price Code AA

Special features

- Energy efficient home with 2" x 6" exterior walls
- Wrap-around porch creates an outdoor living area
- Large dining area easily accommodates extra guests
- Sunken family room
- 2 bedrooms, 1 bath, 1-car garage
- Basement foundation

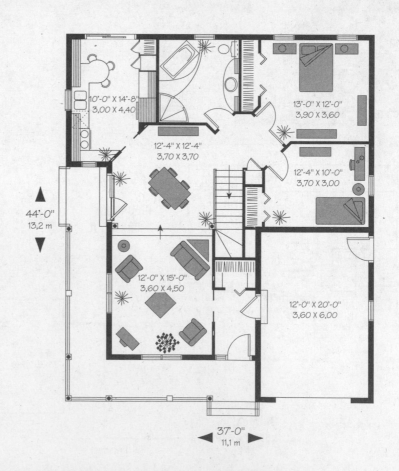

10'-0" X 14'-8"
3,00 X 4,40

13'-0" X 12'-0"
3,90 X 3,60

12'-4" X 12'-4"
3,70 X 3,70

12'-4" X 10'-0"
3,70 X 3,00

44'-0"
13,2 m

12'-0" X 15'-0"
3,60 X 4,50

12'-0" X 20'-0"
3,60 X 6,00

37'-0"
11,1 m

Four Seasons Cottage

1,484 total square feet of living area

Price Code A

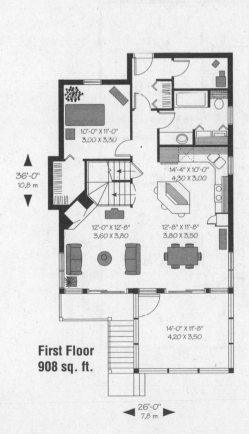

10'-0" X 11'-0"
3,00 X 3,30

14'-4" X 10'-0"
4,30 X 3,00

36'-0"
10,8 m

12'-0" X 12'-8"
3,60 X 3,80

12'-8" X 11'-8"
3,80 X 3,50

14'-0" X 11'-8"
4,20 X 3,50

First Floor
908 sq. ft.

26'-0"
7,8 m

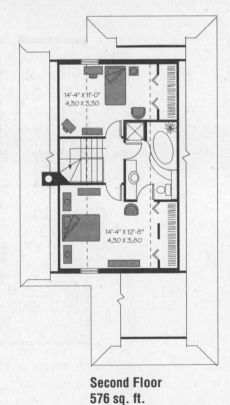

14'-4" X 11'-0"
4,30 X 3,30

14'-4" X 12'-8"
4,30 X 3,80

Second Floor
576 sq. ft.

Special features

- Energy efficient home with 2" x 6" exterior walls
- Useful screened porch is ideal for dining and relaxing
- Corner fireplace warms living room
- Snack bar adds extra counterspace in kitchen
- 3 bedrooms, 2 baths
- Basement foundation

TO ORDER BLUEPRINTS USE THE FORM ON PAGE 15 OR CALL TOLL-FREE 1-877-671-6036
View thousands more home plans online at www.familyhandyman.com/homeplans

111

Stylish Retreat For A Narrow Lot

1,084 total square feet of living area

Price Code AA

Special features

- Delightful country porch for quiet evenings
- Living room has a front feature window which invites the sun and includes a fireplace and dining area with private patio
- The U-shaped kitchen features lots of cabinets and bayed breakfast room with built-in pantry
- Both bedrooms have walk-in closets and access to their own bath
- 2 bedrooms, 2 baths
- Basement foundation

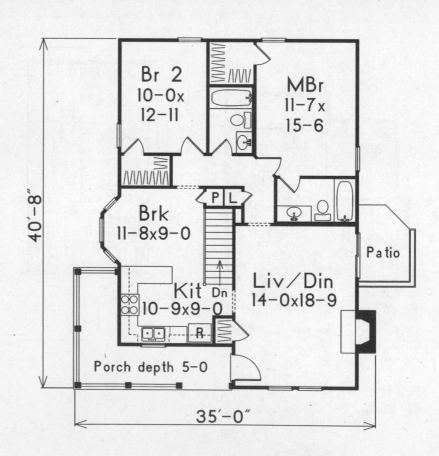

Innovative Design For That Narrow Lot

1,558 total square feet of living area

Price Code B

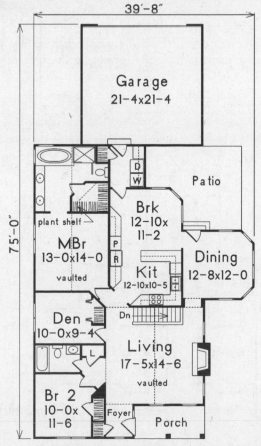

39'-8"

75'-0"

Garage
21-4x21-4

Patio

Brk
12-10x
11-2

D
W

plant shelf

MBr
13-0x14-0
vaulted

P
R

Dining
12-8x12-0

Kit
12-10x10-5

Den
10-0x9-4

Dn

Living
17-5x14-6
vaulted

Br 2
10-0x
11-6

L

Foyer

Porch

Special features

- Illuminated spaces created by visual access to outdoor living areas

- Vaulted master bedroom features private bath with whirlpool tub, separate shower and large walk-in closet

- Convenient first floor laundry has garage access

- Practical den or third bedroom

- U-shaped kitchen adjacent to sunny breakfast area

- 2 bedrooms, 2 baths, 2-car rear entry garage

- Basement foundation

Five Bedroom Home Embraces Large Family

2,828 total square feet of living area

Price Code E

Special features

- Popular wrap-around porch gives home country charm

- Secluded, oversized family room with vaulted ceiling and wet bar features many windows

- Any chef would be delighted to cook in this smartly designed kitchen with island and corner windows

- Spectacular master suite

- 5 bedrooms, 3 1/2 baths, 2-car side entry garage

- Basement foundation, drawings also include crawl space and slab foundations

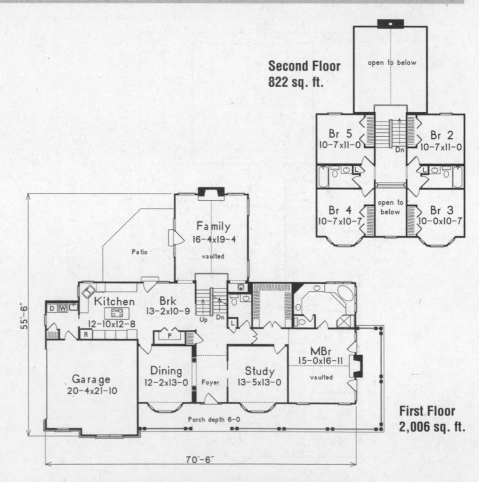

Second Floor 822 sq. ft.

open to below

Br 5 10-7x11-0

Br 2 10-7x11-0

Dn

Br 4 10-7x10-7

open to below

Br 3 10-0x10-7

Family 16-4x19-4 vaulted

Patio

Kitchen 12-10x12-8

Brk 13-2x10-9

Up Dn

Garage 20-4x21-10

Dining 12-2x13-0

Foyer

Study 13-5x13-0

MBr 15-0x16-11 vaulted

55'-6"

Porch depth 6-0

70'-6"

First Floor 2,006 sq. ft.

Massive Ranch With Classy Features

2,874 total square feet of living area

Price Code E

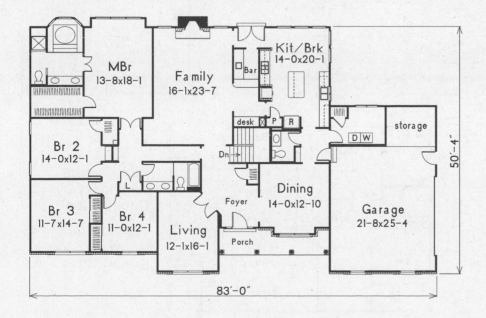

Special features

- Large family room with sloped ceiling and wood beams adjoins the kitchen and breakfast area with windows on two walls

- Large foyer opens to family room with massive stone fireplace and open stairs to the basement

- Private master bedroom with raised tub under the bay window, dramatic dressing area and a huge walk-in closet

- 4 bedrooms, 2 1/2 baths, 2-car side entry garage

- Basement foundation

Private Bedroom Area

1,550 total square feet of living area   **Price Code B**

Special features

- Wrap-around front porch is an ideal gathering place

- Handy snack bar is positioned so kitchen flows into family room

- Master bedroom has many amenities

- 3 bedrooms, 2 baths, 2-car detached garage

- Slab or crawl space foundation, please specify when ordering

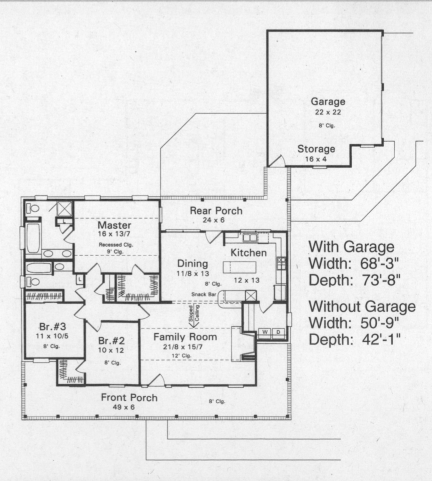

Garage
22 x 22
8' Clg.

Storage
16 x 4

Master
16 x 13/7
Recessed Clg.
9' Clg.

Rear Porch
24 x 6

Kitchen
12 x 13

Dining
11/8 x 13
8' Clg.

Snack Bar

Br. #3
11 x 10/5
8' Clg.

Br. #2
10 x 12
8' Clg.

Sloped Ceiling

Family Room
21/8 x 15/7
12' Clg.

W D

Front Porch
49 x 6   8' Clg.

With Garage
Width: 68'-3"
Depth: 73'-8"

Without Garage
Width: 50'-9"
Depth: 42'-1"

Comfortable One-Story Country Home

1,367 total square feet of living area   Price Code A

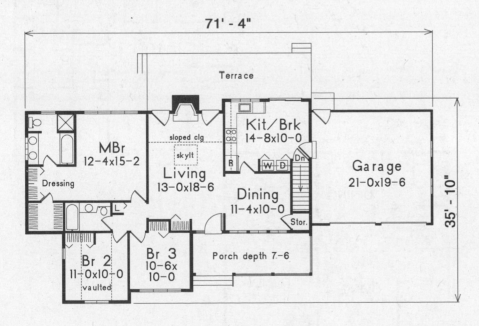

71' - 4"

35' - 10"

Terrace

Kit/Brk
14-8x10-0

sloped clg

skylt

MBr
12-4x15-2

Living
13-0x18-6

Dining
11-4x10-0

Garage
21-0x19-6

Dressing

W D

R

Dn

Stor.

L

Br 2
11-0x10-0

vaulted

Br 3
10-6x
10-0

Porch depth 7-6

Special features

- Neat front porch shelters the entrance
- Dining room has full wall of windows and convenient storage area
- Breakfast area leads to the rear terrace through sliding doors
- Large living room with high ceiling, skylight and fireplace
- 3 bedrooms, 2 baths, 2-car garage
- Basement foundation, drawings also include slab foundation

TO ORDER BLUEPRINTS USE THE FORM ON PAGE 15 OR CALL TOLL-FREE 1-877-671-6036
View thousands more home plans online at www.familyhandyman.com/homeplans

117

Three-Story Design

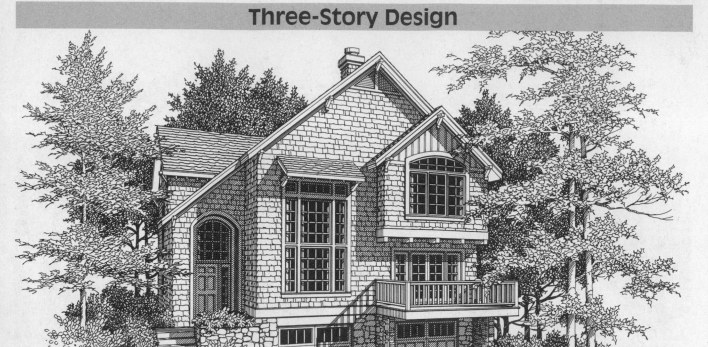

1,978 total square feet of living area

Price Code C

Special features

- Designed for a sloping lot, this multi-level home intrigues the eye
- Sunlight filters into the grand two-story foyer and living room from tall windows
- Master suite has elegant front facing windows and a private bath
- 3 bedrooms, 2 1/2 baths, 2-car drive under garage
- Walk-out basement foundation

Second Floor 872 sq. ft.

BR. 3
11/0 X 10/8

BR. 2
11/0 X 10/0

©Alan Mascord Design Associates, Inc

DN

LOFT

FOYER BELOW

©Alan Mascord Design Associates, Inc.

LIN

LIVING BELOW

SHELVES

VAULTED MASTER
15/2 X 12/0

OPT. FR. DRS.

DINING
10/6 X 12/0+

DW
15/0 X 9/0

PAN
REF

NOOK
13/10 X 8/4

DN

UP

DN

2 STORY LIVING
13/0 X 14/0

FAMILY
13/10 X 20/8

©Alan Mascord Design Associates, Inc.

35'

DECK

First Floor 1,106 sq. ft.

◄ 38' ►

Recessed Stone Entry Provides A Unique Accent

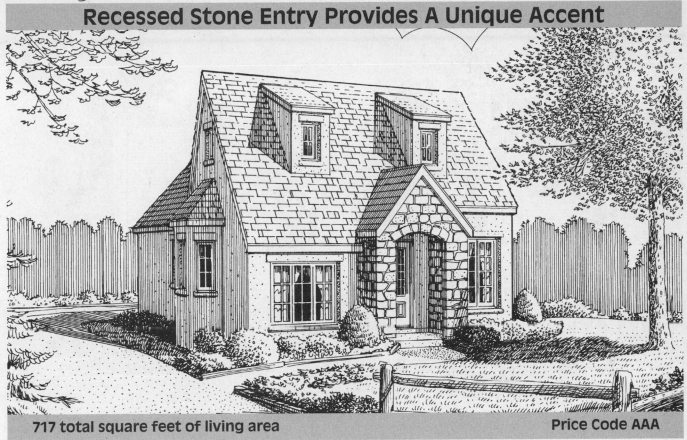

717 total square feet of living area

Price Code AAA

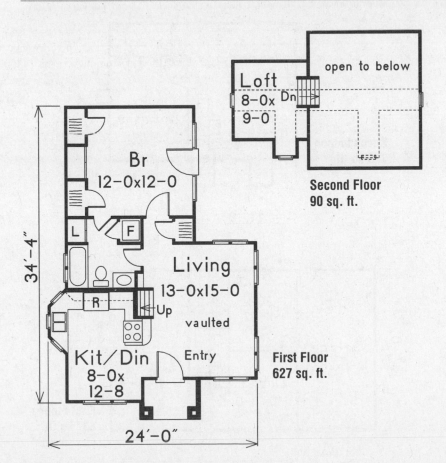

Loft
8-0x
9-0

open to below

Dn

Second Floor
90 sq. ft.

Br
12-0x12-0

L   F

Living
13-0x15-0

vaulted

Up

Entry

R

Kit/Din
8-0x
12-8

34'-4"

24'-0"

First Floor
627 sq. ft.

Special features

■ Incline ladder leads up to cozy loft area

■ Living room features plenty of windows and vaulted ceiling

■ U-shaped kitchen includes a small bay window at the sink

■ 1 bedroom, 1 bath

■ Slab foundation

Trim Colonial For Practical Living

1,582 total square feet of living area

Price Code B

Special features

- Conservative layout gives privacy to living and dining areas
- Large fireplace and windows enhance the living area
- Rear door in garage is convenient to the garden and kitchen
- Full front porch adds charm
- Dormers add light to the foyer and bedrooms
- 3 bedrooms, 2 1/2 baths, 1-car garage
- Slab foundation, drawings also include crawl space foundation

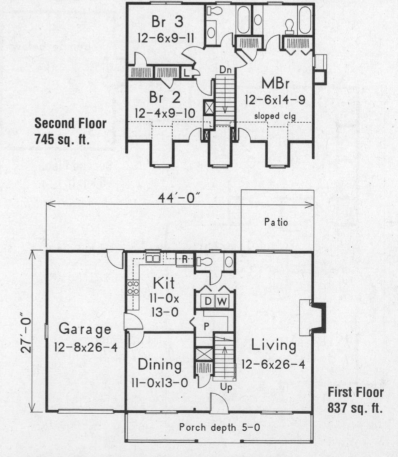

Second Floor
745 sq. ft.

Br 3
12-6x9-11

Br 2
12-4x9-10

Dn

L

MBr
12-6x14-9
sloped clg

First Floor
837 sq. ft.

44'-0"

27'-0"

Patio

Garage
12-8x26-4

Kit
11-0x
13-0

D W

P

R

Dining
11-0x13-0

Living
12-6x26-4

Up

Porch depth 5-0

Inviting Country Home

1,757 total square feet of living area

Price Code B

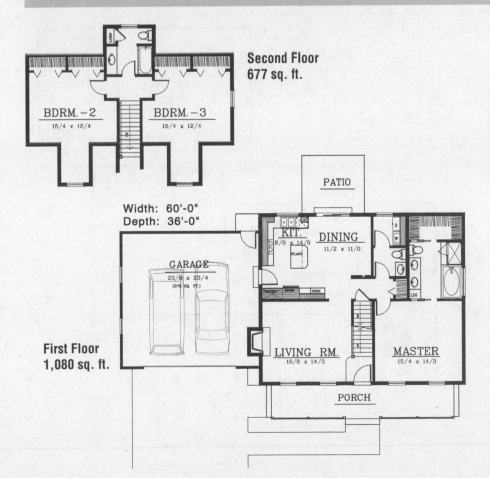

**Second Floor
677 sq. ft.**

BDRM.—2
15/4 x 12/4

BDRM.—3
15/4 x 12/4

**Width: 60'-0"
Depth: 36'-0"**

PATIO

KIT.
8/0 x 14/5

DINING
11/2 x 11/0

ISLAND

GARAGE
23/8 x 23/4
(576 SQ. FT.)

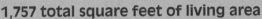

PANTRY   REFRIG.   DESK

LIN.

**First Floor
1,080 sq. ft.**

LIVING RM.
15/8 x 14/3

MASTER
15/4 x 14/3

PORCH

Special features

- Energy efficient home with 2" x 6" exterior walls
- First floor master bedroom has privacy as well as its own bath and walk-in closet
- Cozy living room includes fireplace for warmth
- 3 bedrooms, 2 1/2 baths, 2-car garage
- Crawl space or slab foundation, please specify when ordering

The Family Handyman

Angled Porch Greets Guests

2,059 total square feet of living area

Price Code C

Special features

- Large desk and pantry add to the breakfast room
- Laundry is located on second floor near bedrooms
- Vaulted ceiling in master suite
- Mud room is conveniently located near garage
- 3 bedrooms, 2 1/2 baths, 2-car garage
- Basement foundation

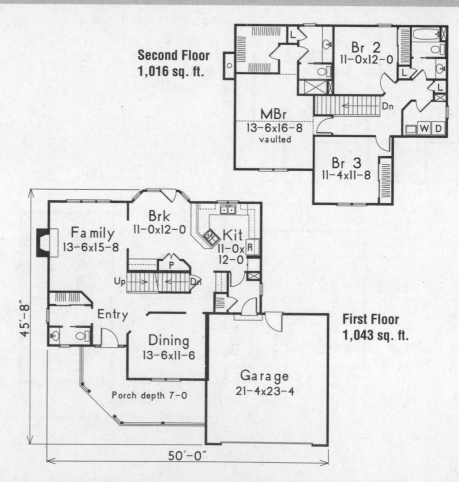

Second Floor 1,016 sq. ft.

Br 2 11-0x12-0

MBr 13-6x16-8 vaulted

Br 3 11-4x11-8

First Floor 1,043 sq. ft.

Brk 11-0x12-0

Kit 11-0x 12-0

Family 13-6x15-8

Entry

Dining 13-6x11-6

Garage 21-4x23-4

Porch depth 7-0

45'-8"

50'-0"

TO ORDER BLUEPRINTS USE THE FORM ON PAGE 15 OR CALL TOLL-FREE 1-877-671-6036
View thousands more home plans online at www.familyhandyman.com/homeplans

Scalloped Front Porch

1,374 total square feet of living area

Price Code A

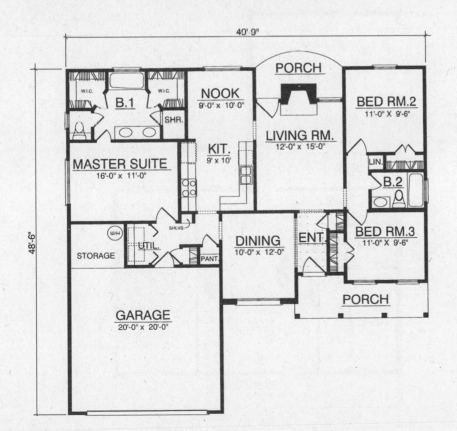

Special features

- Garage has extra storage space
- Spacious living room has fireplace
- Well-designed kitchen with adjacent breakfast nook
- Separated master suite maintains privacy
- 3 bedrooms, 2 baths, 2-car garage
- Slab or crawl space foundation, please specify when ordering

Quaint And Cozy

1,191 total square feet of living area

Price Code AA

Special features

- Energy efficient home with 2" x 6" exterior walls

- Master bedroom located near living areas for maximum convenience

- Living room has cathedral ceiling and stone fireplace

- 3 bedrooms, 2 baths, 2-car side entry garage

- Slab or crawl space foundation, please specify when ordering

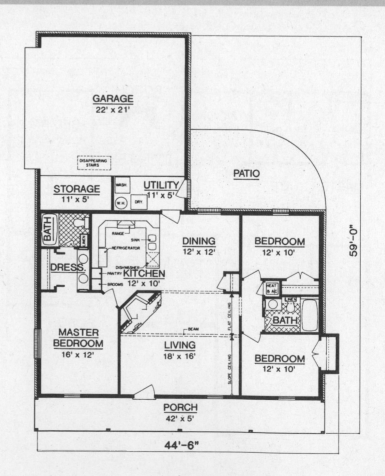

Graciously Designed Refuge

527 total square feet of living area   **Price Code AAA**

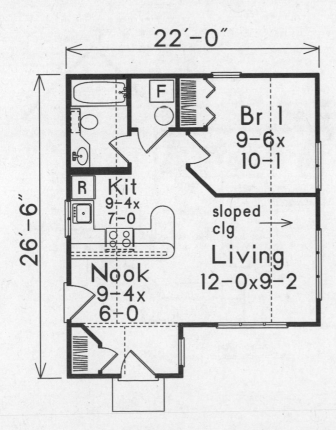

22'-0"

26'-6"

Br 1
9-6x
10-1

F

Kit
9-4x
7-0

R

sloped
clg

Living
12-0x9-2

Nook
9-4x
6-0

Special features

- Cleverly arranged home has it all
- Foyer spills into the dining nook with access to side views
- An excellent kitchen offers a long breakfast bar and borders the living room with free-standing fireplace
- A cozy bedroom has a full bath just across the hall
- 1 bedroom, 1 bath
- Crawl space foundation

Double Bays Accent Front

2,529 total square feet of living area

Price Code D

Special features

- Kitchen and breakfast area are located between the family and living rooms for easy access

- Master bedroom includes sitting area, private bath and access to covered patio

- 4 bedrooms, 3 baths, 3-car side entry garage

- Slab foundation

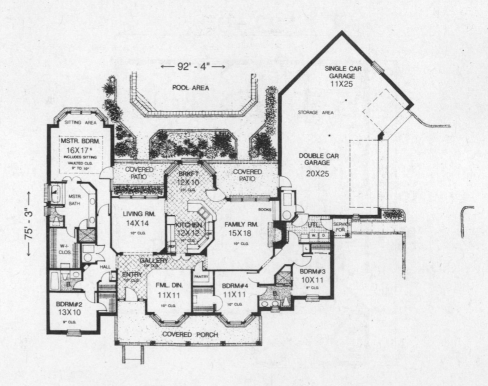

Vaulted Ceiling Adds Spaciousness

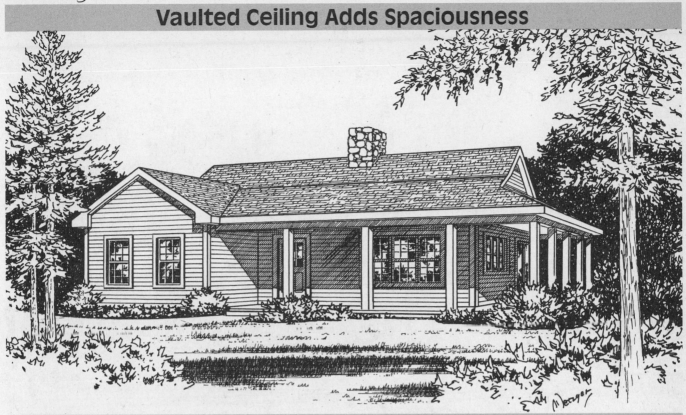

990 total square feet of living area

Price Code AA

Special features

- Wrap-around porch on two sides of this home
- Private and efficiently designed
- Space for efficiency washer and dryer unit for convenience
- 2 bedrooms, 1 bath
- Crawl space foundation

Floor plan:

43'-0"

32'-0"

Br 1
10-0x12-0

Kit
10-4x
10-10

Dining
11-4x8-10

F

vaulted clg

P R

W
D

W

Family
14-0x14-5

Br 2
12-4x11-2

L

Covered porch depth 7-0

Covered Porch Adds Charm

2,069 total square feet of living area

Price Code C

Special features

- 9' ceilings throughout this home
- Kitchen has many amenities including a snack bar
- Large front and rear porches
- 3 bedrooms, 2 1/2 baths, 2-car garage
- Slab or crawl space foundation, please specify when ordering

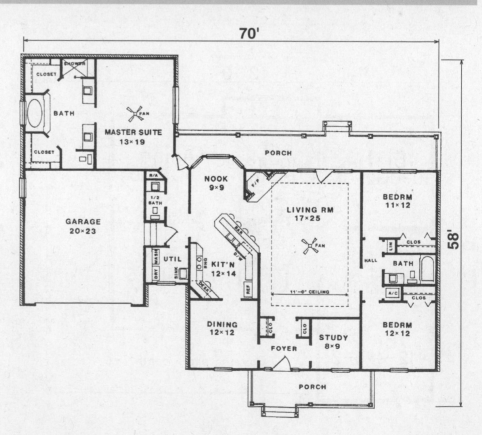

The Family Handyman

Built-In Media Center Focal Point In Living Room

1,539 total square feet of living area

Price Code B

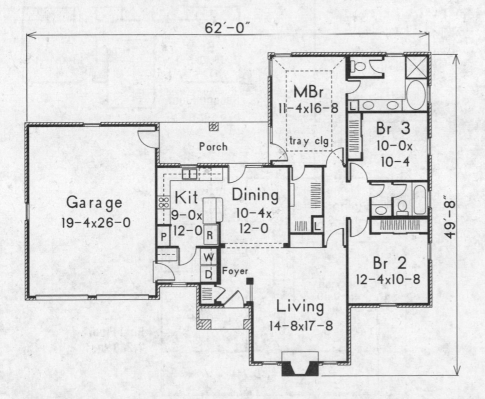

Special features

- Standard 9' ceilings
- Master bedroom features 10' tray ceiling, access to porch, ample closet space and full bath
- Serving counter separates kitchen and dining room
- Foyer with handy coat closet opens to living area with fireplace
- Handy utility room near kitchen
- 3 bedrooms, 2 baths, 2-car garage
- Slab foundation

Two-Story Foyer Adds Spacious Feeling

1,814 total square feet of living area

Price Code D

Special features

■ Large master suite includes a spacious bath with garden tub, separate shower and large walk-in closet

■ Spacious kitchen and dining area brightened by large windows and patio access

■ Detached two-car garage with walkway leading to house adds charm to this country home

■ Large front porch

■ 3 bedrooms, 2 1/2 baths, 2-car detached garage

■ Crawl space foundation, drawings also include slab foundation

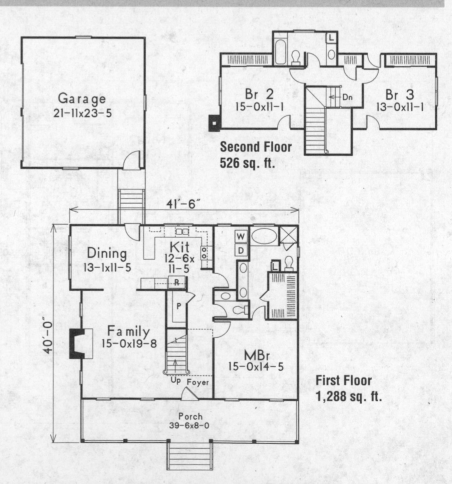

Garage
21-11x23-5

Br 2
15-0x11-1

Br 3
13-0x11-1

**Second Floor
526 sq. ft.**

41'-6"

Dining
13-1x11-5

Kit
12-6x
11-5

Family
15-0x19-8

40'-0"

MBr
15-0x14-5

Up   Foyer

**First Floor
1,288 sq. ft.**

Porch
39-6x8-0

Terrific Cottage-Style Design

1,922 total square feet of living area

Price Code C

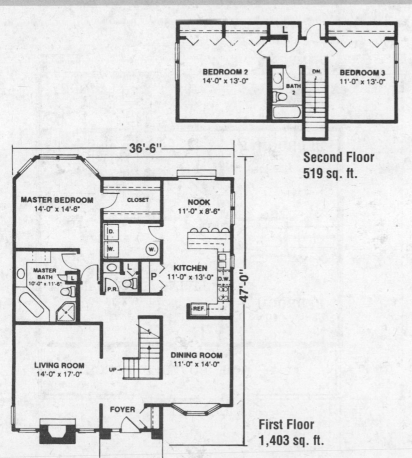

BEDROOM 2
14'-0" x 13'-0"

BATH 2

BEDROOM 3
11'-0" x 13'-0"

Second Floor 519 sq. ft.

36'-6"

MASTER BEDROOM
14'-0" x 14'-6"

CLOSET

NOOK
11'-0" x 8'-6"

MASTER BATH
10'-0" x 11'-6"

P.R.

KITCHEN
11'-0" x 13'-0"

REF.

47'-0"

DINING ROOM
11'-0" x 14'-0"

LIVING ROOM
14'-0" x 17'-0"

UP

FOYER

First Floor 1,403 sq. ft.

Special features

- Master bedroom includes many luxuries such as an oversized private bath and large walk-in closet

- Kitchen area is spacious with a functional eat-in breakfast bar and is adjacent to nook ideal as a breakfast room

- Plenty of storage is featured in both bedrooms on the second floor and in the hall

- Enormous utility room is centrally located on the first floor

- 3 bedrooms, 2 1/2 baths

- Basement foundation

Charming Country Cottage

864 total square feet of living area

Price Code AAA

Special features

- Large laundry area accesses the outdoors as well as the kitchen
- Front covered porch creates an ideal outdoor living area
- Snack bar in kitchen creates a quick and easy dining area
- 2 bedrooms, 1 bath
- Crawl space or slab foundation, please specify when ordering

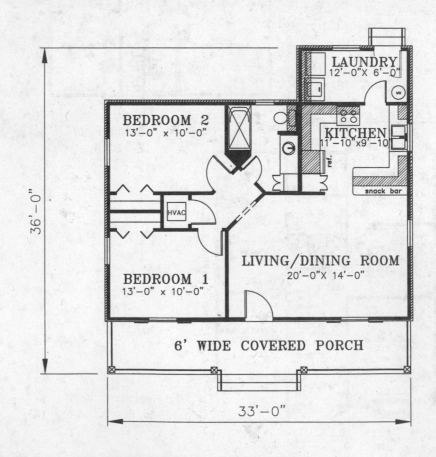

LAUNDRY
12'-0" X 6'-0"

KITCHEN
11'-10" x 9'-10"

snack bar

ref.

BEDROOM 2
13'-0" x 10'-0"

HVAC

BEDROOM 1
13'-0" x 10'-0"

LIVING/DINING ROOM
20'-0" X 14'-0"

6' WIDE COVERED PORCH

36'-0"

33'-0"

Stone Adds Charm To Exterior

1,509 total square feet of living area

Price Code B

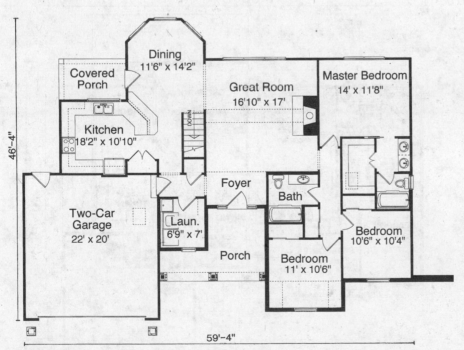

Special features

- A grand opening between the great room and dining area visually expands the living space

- The kitchen is a delightful place to prepare meals with snack bar and large pantry

- Master bedroom enjoys a private bath with double-bowl vanity and large walk-in closet

- 3 bedrooms, 2 baths, 2-car garage

- Basement foundation

Bedrooms Separated From Living Areas

1,734 total square feet of living area

Price Code B

Special features

- Large entry with coffered ceiling and display niches
- Sunken great room has 10' ceiling
- Kitchen island includes eating counter
- 9' ceiling in master bedroom
- Master bath features corner tub and double sinks
- 3 bedrooms, 2 baths, 2-car garage
- Crawl space foundation

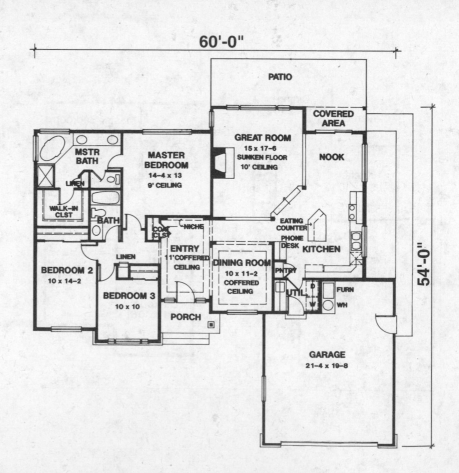

134

TO ORDER BLUEPRINTS USE THE FORM ON PAGE 15 OR CALL TOLL-FREE 1-877-671-6036
View thousands more home plans online at www.familyhandyman.com/homeplans

Central Laundry Area For Convenience

1,395 total square feet of living area

Price Code A

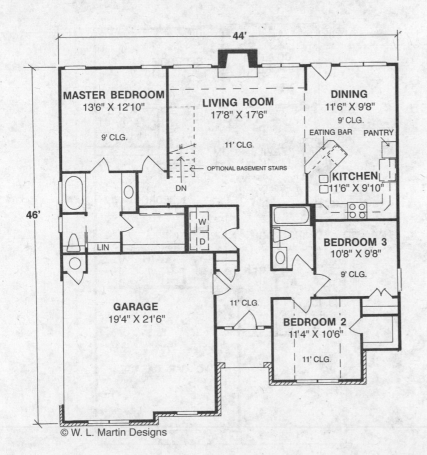

44'

MASTER BEDROOM
13'6" X 12'10"

9' CLG.

LIVING ROOM
17'8" X 17'6"

11' CLG.

OPTIONAL BASEMENT STAIRS

DN

46'

DINING
11'6" X 9'8"

9' CLG.

EATING BAR   PANTRY

KITCHEN
11'6" X 9'10"

LIN

W
D

BEDROOM 3
10'8" X 9'8"

9' CLG.

GARAGE
19'4" X 21'6"

11' CLG.

BEDROOM 2
11'4" X 10'6"

11' CLG.

© W. L. Martin Designs

Special features

- Dining and kitchen separated by angled eating area
- 11' ceilings in entrance and living room create openness
- 3 bedrooms, 2 baths, 2-car garage
- Basement foundation

TO ORDER BLUEPRINTS USE THE FORM ON PAGE 15 OR CALL TOLL-FREE 1-877-671-6036

View thousands more home plans online at www.familyhandyman.com/homeplans

Narrow Lot Design

1,093 total square feet of living area

Price Code AA

Special features

- Family room with fireplace overlooks large covered porch
- Vaulted family and dining rooms are adjacent to kitchen
- Bedroom #2 has its own entrance into bath
- Plant shelf accents vaulted foyer
- Centrally located laundry area
- 2 bedrooms, 2 baths, 2-car garage
- Slab foundation

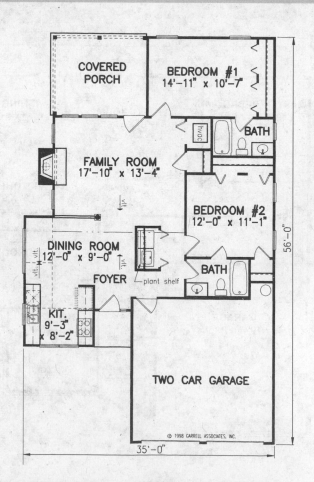

COVERED PORCH

BEDROOM #1
14'-11" x 10'-7"

BATH

FAMILY ROOM
17'-10" x 13'-4"

BEDROOM #2
12'-0" x 11'-1"

DINING ROOM
12'-0" x 9'-0"

FOYER

BATH

plant shelf

KIT.
9'-3" x 8'-2"

TWO CAR GARAGE

© 1998 CARRELL ASSOCIATES, INC.

56'-0"

35'-0"

Arched Window Is A Focal Point

© COPYRIGHT 1990 RALPH JONES & ASSOC.

1,021 total square feet of living area

Price Code AA

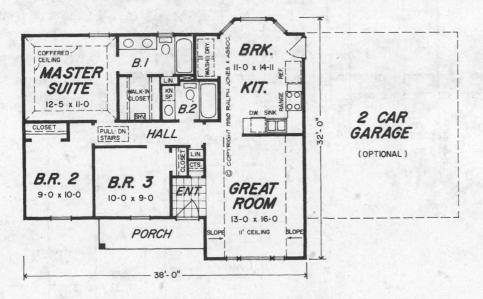

Special features

- 11' ceiling in great room expands living area

- Combination kitchen/breakfast room allows for easy preparation and cleanup

- Master suite features private bath and oversized walk-in closet

- 3 bedrooms, 2 baths, optional 2-car garage

- Slab or crawl space foundation, please specify when ordering

Quaint Alpine Style

1,563 total square feet of living area

Price Code B

Special features

- Centrally located utility room
- Double sliding glass doors add drama to living room
- Plenty of storage throughout
- Master bedroom is located on second floor for privacy and includes amenities such as a private rear balcony, dressing area and bath with front balcony
- 3 bedrooms, 2 baths
- Basement, crawl space or slab foundation, please specify when ordering

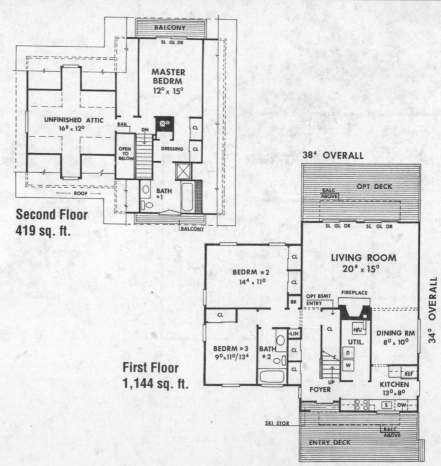

Second Floor 419 sq. ft.

First Floor 1,144 sq. ft.

Exciting Living For A Narrow Sloping Lot

1,200 total square feet of living area

Price Code A

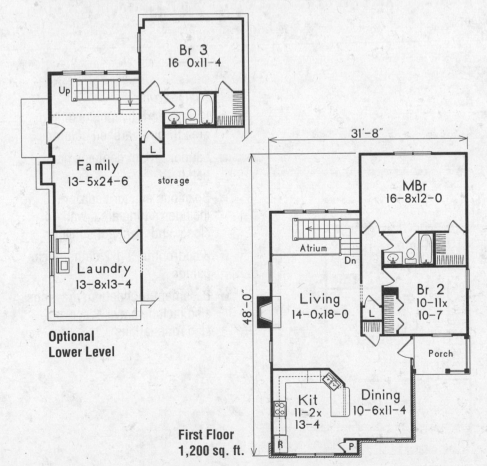

Br 3
16 0x11-4

Up

Family
13-5x24-6

storage

L

Laundry
13-8x13-4

**Optional
Lower Level**

31'-8"

MBr
16-8x12-0

Atrium

Dn

48'-0"

Living
14-0x18-0

L

Br 2
10-11x
10-7

Porch

Kit
11-2x
13-4

Dining
10-6x11-4

R

P

**First Floor
1,200 sq. ft.**

Special features

- Entry leads to a large dining area which opens to kitchen and sun drenched living room

- An expansive window wall in the two-story atrium lends space and light to living room with fireplace

- The large kitchen features a breakfast bar, built-in pantry and storage galore

- 697 square feet of optional living area on the lower level includes a family room, bedroom #3 and a bath

- 2 bedrooms, 1 bath

- Walk-out basement foundation

Covered Porch Surrounds Home

1,399 total square feet of living area

Price Code A

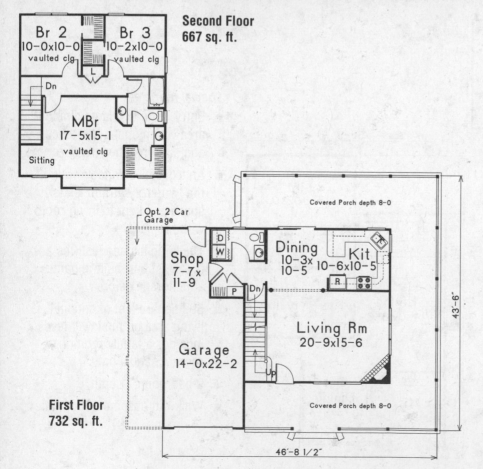

Second Floor
667 sq. ft.

Br 2
10-0x10-0
vaulted clg

Br 3
10-2x10-0
vaulted clg

Dn

MBr
17-5x15-1
vaulted clg

Sitting

Opt. 2 Car Garage

Covered Porch depth 8-0

Shop
7-7x
11-9

Dining
10-3x
10-5

Kit
10-6x10-5

Garage
14-0x22-2

Living Rm
20-9x15-6

43'-6"

Covered Porch depth 8-0

46'-8 1/2"

First Floor
732 sq. ft.

Special features

- Living room overlooks dining area through arched columns
- Laundry room contains handy half bath
- Spacious master bedroom includes sitting area, walk-in closet and plenty of sunlight
- 3 bedrooms, 1 1/2 baths, 1-car garage
- Basement foundation, drawings also include crawl space and slab foundations

Modern Rustic Design

1,118 total square feet of living area

Price Code AA

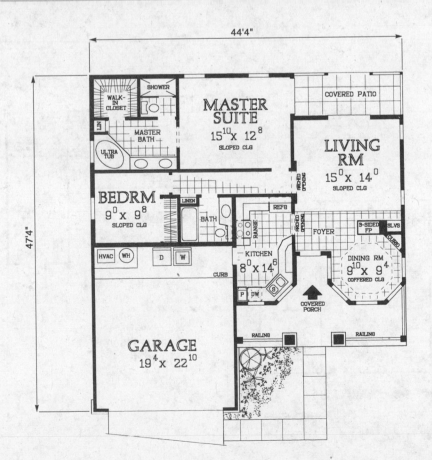

Special features

- Great room offers a sloped ceiling, fireplace with extended hearth and built-in shelves for an entertainment center
- Gourmet kitchen has a cooktop island counter and a morning room
- Master suite features a sloped ceiling, cozy sitting room, walk-in closet and a private bath with whirlpool tub
- 2 bedrooms, 2 baths, 2-car side entry garage
- Slab foundation

Cabin Cottage With French Door Entry

1,544 total square feet of living area

Price Code B

Special features

- Great room with vaulted ceiling and fireplace
- 32' x 8' grilling porch in rear
- Kitchen features a center island
- 3 bedrooms, 2 baths
- Crawl space or slab foundation, please specify when ordering

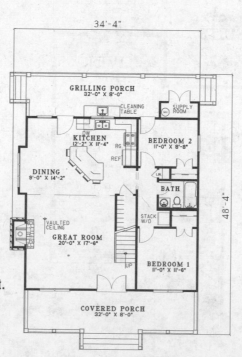

First Floor
1,031 sq. ft.

34'-4"

48'-4"

GRILLING PORCH
32'-0" X 8'-0"

CLEANING TABLE

SUPPLY ROOM

KITCHEN
12'-2" X 11'-4"

BEDROOM 2
11'-0" X 8'-8"

DINING
9'-0" X 14'-2"

BATH

STACK W/D

VAULTED CEILING

GREAT ROOM
20'-0" X 17'-6"

BEDROOM 1
11'-0" X 11'-6"

UP

COVERED PORCH
32'-0" X 8'-0"

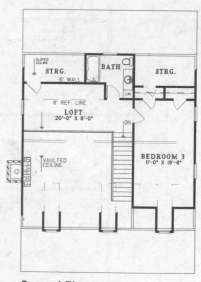

Second Floor
513 sq. ft.

SLOPED CEILING

STRG.
6' WALL

BATH

STRG.

8' REF. LINE

LOFT
20'-0" X 9'-0"

DN

VAULTED CEILING

BEDROOM 3
11'-0" X 19'-6"

Simple Roofline Makes Home Economical To Build

1,792 total square feet of living area

Price Code B

Rear View

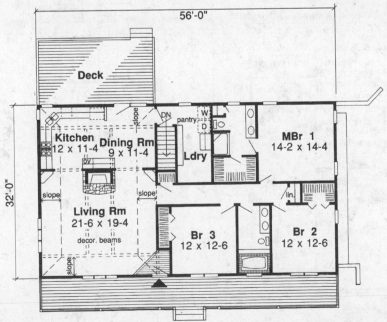

56'-0"

32'-0"

Deck

Kitchen 12 x 11-4
Dining Rm 9 x 11-4
DN
pantry
W D
Ldry
MBr 1 14-2 x 14-4
slope
ov
slope
slope
lin.
Living Rm 21-6 x 19-4
decor. beams
Br 3 12 x 12-6
Br 2 12 x 12-6

Special features

- Master bedroom has a private bath and large walk-in closet

- A central stone fireplace and windows on two walls are focal points in the living room

- Decorative beams and sloped ceiling add interest to the kitchen, living and dining rooms

- 3 bedrooms, 2 baths, 2-car drive under garage

- Basement foundation

Appealing Floor Plan For Family Living

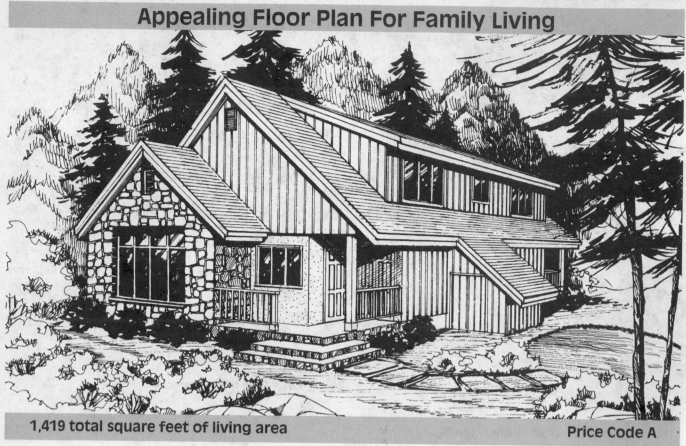

1,419 total square feet of living area

Price Code A

Special features

- Lovely sunporch at the back of the home makes a wonderful place to enjoy quiet times

- Vaulted ceiling and two sets of windows make the great room appear larger than its true size

- Exterior storage closet makes an ideal place to store lawn equipment or sporting goods

- 3 bedrooms, 2 1/2 baths

- Basement, crawl space or slab foundation, please specify when ordering

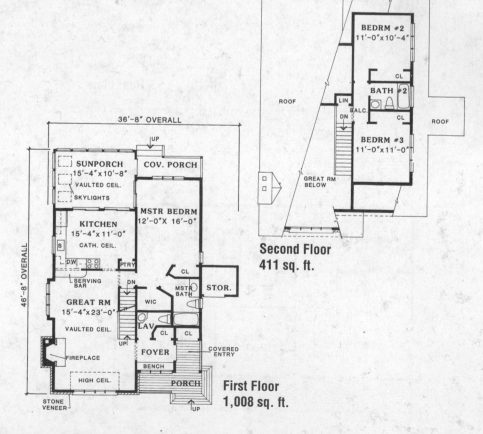

Second Floor
411 sq. ft.

First Floor
1,008 sq. ft.

Quaint Country Home

1,737 total square feet of living area

Price Code B

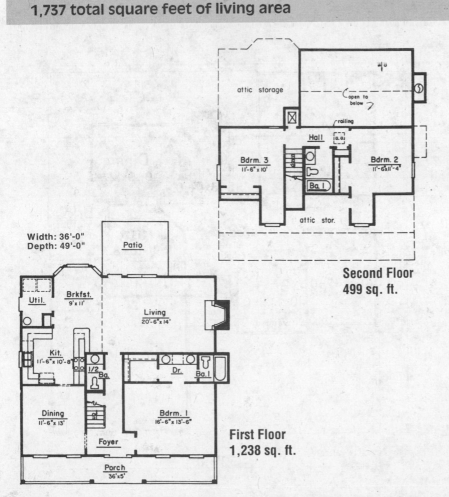

Width: 36'-0"
Depth: 49'-0"

Second Floor
499 sq. ft.

First Floor
1,238 sq. ft.

Special features

- U-shaped kitchen, sunny bayed breakfast room and living area become one large gathering area
- Living area has sloped ceilings and a balcony overlook from second floor
- Second floor includes lots of storage area
- 3 bedrooms, 2 1/2 baths
- Slab or crawl space foundation, please specify when ordering

TO ORDER BLUEPRINTS USE THE FORM ON PAGE 15 OR CALL TOLL-FREE 1-877-671-6036
View thousands more home plans online at www.familyhandyman.com/homeplans

145

Open Ranch Design Gives Expansive Look

1,630 total square feet of living area

Price Code B

Special features

- Crisp facade and full windows front and back offer open viewing

- Wrap-around rear deck is accessible from breakfast room, dining room and master bedroom

- Vaulted ceiling in living room and master bedroom

- Sitting area and large walk-in closet complement master bedroom

- Master bedroom has a private sitting area

- 3 bedrooms, 2 baths, 2-car garage

- Basement foundation

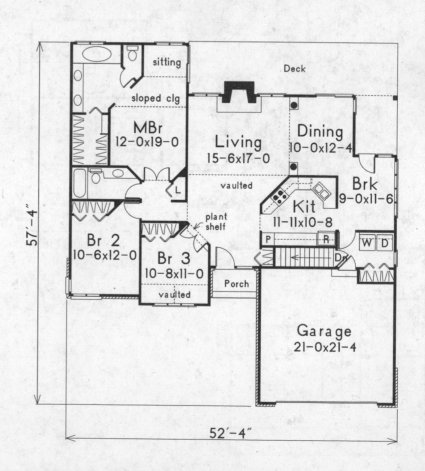

TO ORDER BLUEPRINTS USE THE FORM ON PAGE 15 OR CALL TOLL-FREE 1-877-671-6036
View thousands more home plans online at www.familyhandyman.com/homeplans

Screened Porch For Outdoor Enjoyment

1,294 total square feet of living area

Price Code A

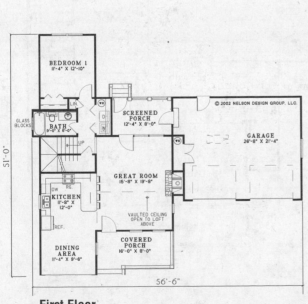

First Floor
972 sq. ft.

Second Floor
322 sq. ft.

Special features

- Second floor bedroom #2/loft has its own bath and vaulted ceilings overlooking to great room below

- Great room has cozy fireplace and accesses the front and the rear of the home

- Laundry area on the first floor is convenient to the kitchen

- 2 bedrooms, 2 baths, 2-car garage

- Crawl space or slab foundation, please specify when ordering

TO ORDER BLUEPRINTS USE THE FORM ON PAGE 15 OR CALL TOLL-FREE 1-877-671-6036
View thousands more home plans online at www.familyhandyman.com/homeplans

147

Covered Porch Adds Charm To Entrance

1,655 total square feet of living area   **Price Code B**

Special features

- Master bedroom features 9' ceiling, walk-in closet and bath with dressing area
- Oversized family room includes 10' ceiling and masonry see-through fireplace
- Island kitchen with convenient access to laundry room
- Handy covered walkway from garage to kitchen and dining area
- 3 bedrooms, 2 baths, 2-car garage
- Crawl space foundation

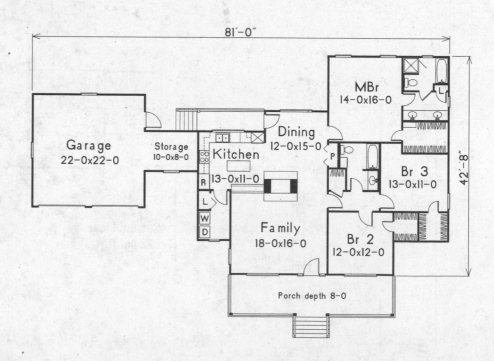

81'-0"

42'-8"

Garage
22-0x22-0

Storage
10-0x8-0

Kitchen
13-0x11-0

Dining
12-0x15-0

MBr
14-0x16-0

Br 3
13-0x11-0

Family
18-0x16-0

Br 2
12-0x12-0

Porch depth 8-0

Exciting Features Throughout

1,315 total square feet of living area

Price Code A

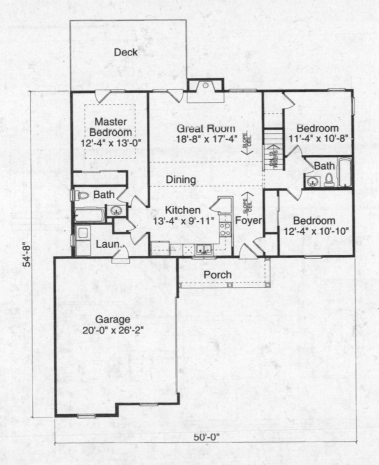

Deck

Master Bedroom
12'-4" x 13'-0"

Great Room
18'-8" x 17'-4"

SLOPE CEIL.

Bedroom
11'-4" x 10'-8"

Bath

Dining

Bath

Kitchen
13'-4" x 9'-11"

SLOPE CEIL.

Foyer

Bedroom
12'-4" x 10'-10"

Laun.

Porch

Garage
20'-0" x 26'-2"

54'-8"

50'-0"

Special features

- First floor laundry and kitchen are convenient work spaces

- Windows on both sides of the fireplace make the great room very pleasant for relaxing and enjoying views outdoors

- Open stairs to the lower level make it simple to finish the basement

- 3 bedrooms, 2 baths, 2-car garage

- Walk-out basement or basement foundation, please specify when ordering

COUNTRY FARMHOUSE APPEAL

COPYRIGHT LARRY E. BELK

1,993 total square feet of living area   **Price Code C**

Special features

- Charming front and rear porches
- 12' ceiling in living room
- Exquisite master bath with large walk-in closet
- 3 bedrooms, 2 baths, 2-car side entry garage
- Crawl space or slab foundation, please specify when ordering

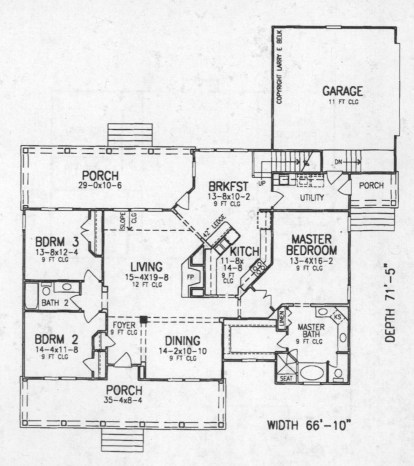

150

TO ORDER BLUEPRINTS USE THE FORM ON PAGE 15 OR CALL TOLL-FREE 1-877-671-6036
View thousands more home plans online at www.familyhandyman.com/homeplans

Foyer Is Open To Loft Above

2,008 total square feet of living area

Price Code C

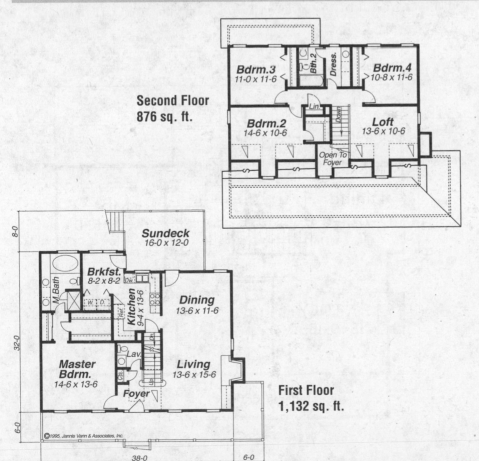

**Second Floor
876 sq. ft.**

Bdrm.3
11-0 x 11-6

Bth.2

Dress.

Bdrm.4
10-8 x 11-6

Bdrm.2
14-6 x 10-6

Lin.

Down

Loft
13-6 x 10-6

Open To
Foyer

Sundeck
16-0 x 12-0

Brkfst.
8-2 x 8-2

M.Bath

Kitchen
9-4 x 13-6

W.D.

Ref.

Dining
13-6 x 11-6

Master
Bdrm.
14-6 x 13-6

Lav.

Clo.

Living
13-6 x 15-6

Foyer

**First Floor
1,132 sq. ft.**

©1995, Jannis Vann & Associates, Inc.

38-0

8-0

32-0

6-0

6-0

Special features

- Living and dining areas join to create wonderful space for entertaining
- Master bedroom includes bath with large tub and separate shower
- Second floor includes loft space perfect for home office or playroom
- 4 bedrooms, 2 1/2 baths, 2-car drive under garage
- Basement foundation

Front Porch Adds Style To This Ranch

1,496 total square feet of living area

Price Code A

Special features

- Master bedroom features coffered ceiling, walk-in closet and spacious bath
- Vaulted ceiling and fireplace grace family room
- Dining room is adjacent to kitchen and features access to rear porch
- Convenient access to utility room from kitchen
- 3 bedrooms, 2 baths, 2-car drive under garage
- Basement foundation

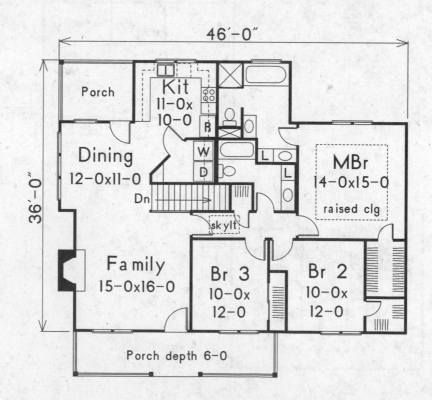

46'-0"

36'-0"

Porch

Kit 11-0x 10-0

Dining 12-0x11-0

Dn

sky lt

MBr 14-0x15-0

raised clg

Family 15-0x16-0

Br 3 10-0x 12-0

Br 2 10-0x 12-0

Porch depth 6-0

Roughing It In Luxury

| 1,200 total square feet of living area | Price Code A |

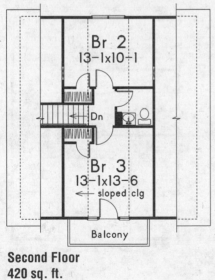

Br 2
13-1x10-1

Dn

Br 3
13-1x13-6
sloped clg

Balcony

Second Floor
420 sq. ft.

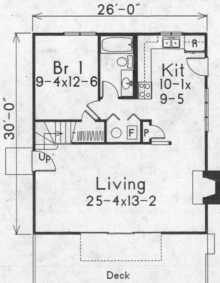

26´-0"

Br 1
9-4x12-6

Kit
10-1x
9-5

30´-0"

Up

F P

Living
25-4x13-2

First Floor
780 sq. ft.

Deck

Special features

- Ornate ranch-style railing enhances exterior while the stone fireplace provides a visual anchor

- Spectacular living room features inviting fireplace and adjoins a charming kitchen with dining area

- First floor bedroom, hall bath and two second floor bedrooms with half bath and exterior balcony complete the home

- 3 bedrooms, 1 1/2 baths

- Crawl space foundation, drawings also include slab foundation

TO ORDER BLUEPRINTS USE THE FORM ON PAGE 15 OR CALL TOLL-FREE 1-877-671-6036
View thousands more home plans online at www.familyhandyman.com/homeplans

153

A Charming Home Loaded With Extras

1,997 total square feet of living area

Price Code C

Special features

- Screened porch leads to a rear terrace with access to the breakfast room
- Living and dining rooms combine adding spaciousness to the floor plan
- Other welcome amenities include boxed windows in breakfast and dining rooms, a fireplace in living room and a pass-through snack bar in the kitchen
- 3 bedrooms, 2 1/2 baths
- Basement foundation

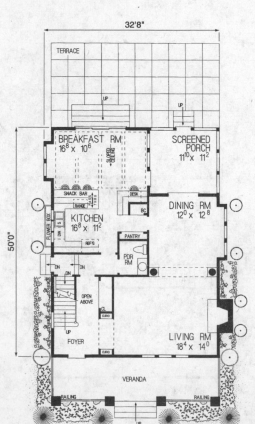

First Floor
1,111 sq. ft.

Second Floor
886 sq. ft.

154

TO ORDER BLUEPRINTS USE THE FORM ON PAGE 15 OR CALL TOLL-FREE 1-877-671-6036
View thousands more home plans online at www.familyhandyman.com/homeplans

Stylish Master Bedroom Off By Itself

1,565 total square feet of living area

Price Code B

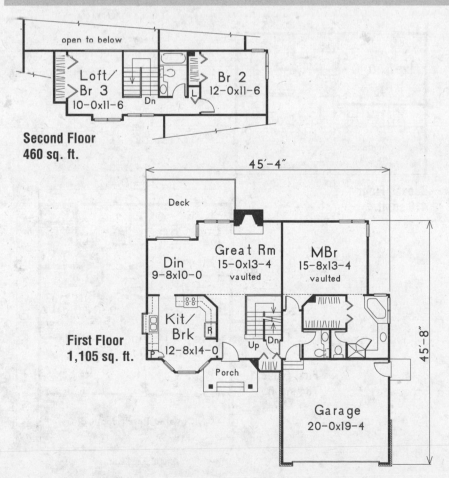

Second Floor
460 sq. ft.

First Floor
1,105 sq. ft.

Special features

- Highly-detailed exterior adds value
- Large vaulted great room with a full wall of glass opens onto the corner deck
- Loft balcony opens to rooms below and adds to the spacious feeling
- Bay-windowed kitchen with a cozy morning room
- Master bath with platform tub, separate shower and a large walk-in closet
- 3 bedrooms, 2 1/2 baths, 2-car garage
- Basement foundation

Perfect Home For Escaping To The Outdoors

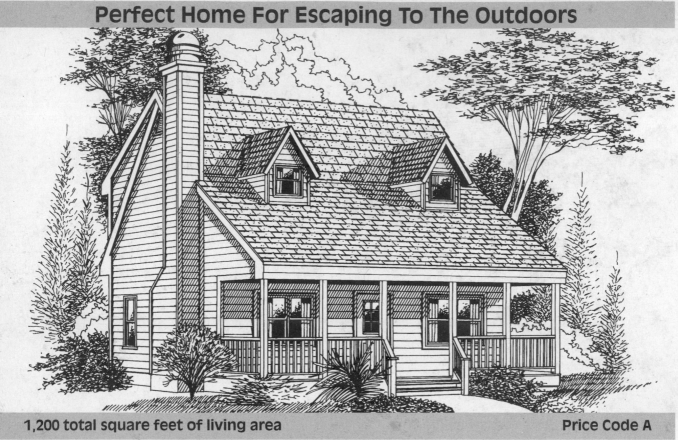

1,200 total square feet of living area

Price Code A

Special features

- Enjoy lazy summer evenings on this magnificent porch
- Activity area has fireplace and ascending stair from cozy loft
- Kitchen features built-in pantry
- Master suite enjoys large bath, walk-in closet and cozy loft overlooking room below
- 2 bedrooms, 2 baths
- Crawl space foundation

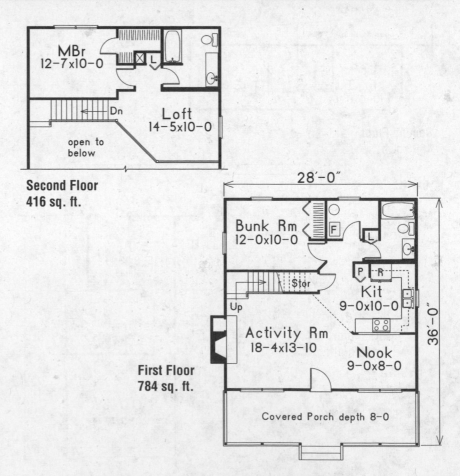

Second Floor
416 sq. ft.

MBr
12-7x10-0

Loft
14-5x10-0

open to below

Dn

First Floor
784 sq. ft.

28'-0"

36'-0"

Bunk Rm
12-0x10-0

Stor

Up

Kit
9-0x10-0

Activity Rm
18-4x13-10

Nook
9-0x8-0

Covered Porch depth 8-0

Great Relaxed Styled Plan

1,520 total square feet of living area

Price Code B

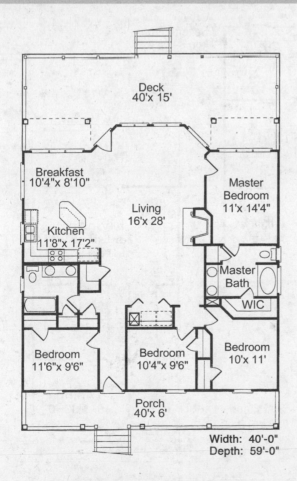

Deck
40'x 15'

Breakfast
10'4"x 8'10"

Living
16'x 28'

Kitchen
11'8"x 17'2"

Master
Bedroom
11'x 14'4"

Master
Bath

WIC

Bedroom
11'6"x 9'6"

Bedroom
10'4"x 9'6"

Bedroom
10'x 11'

Porch
40'x 6'

Width: 40'-0"
Depth: 59'-0"

Special features

- 9' ceilings throughout this home
- Living room has fireplace and large bay window that connects to oversized deck
- Master bedroom has wall of windows and terrific views to the outdoors
- 4 bedrooms, 2 baths
- Pier foundation

Large Bay Graces Dining And Master Bedroom

1,818 total square feet of living area

Price Code C

Special features

- Spacious living and dining rooms
- Master bedroom features large bay, walk-in closet, dressing area and bath
- Convenient carport and storage area
- 3 bedrooms, 2 1/2 baths, 1-car carport
- Crawl space foundation, drawings also include basement and slab foundations

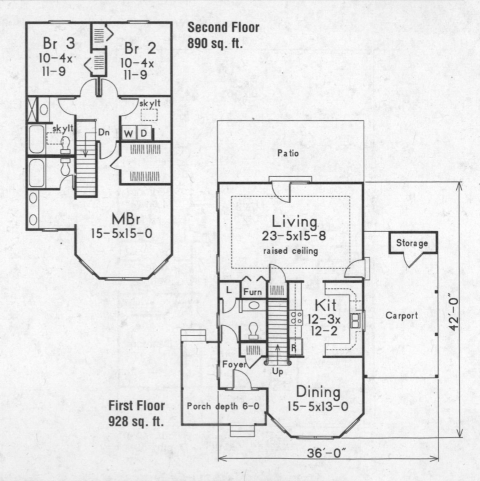

Second Floor
890 sq. ft.

Br 3
10-4x
11-9

Br 2
10-4x
11-9

skylt

skylt

Dn

W D

MBr
15-5x15-0

Patio

Living
23-5x15-8
raised ceiling

Storage

Kit
12-3x
12-2

Carport

L

Furn

Foyer

Up

R

Dining
15-5x13-0

Porch depth 6-0

First Floor
928 sq. ft.

42'-0"

36'-0"

158

TO ORDER BLUEPRINTS USE THE FORM ON PAGE 15 OR CALL TOLL-FREE 1-877-671-6036
View thousands more home plans online at www.familyhandyman.com/homeplans

Covered Breezeway To Garage

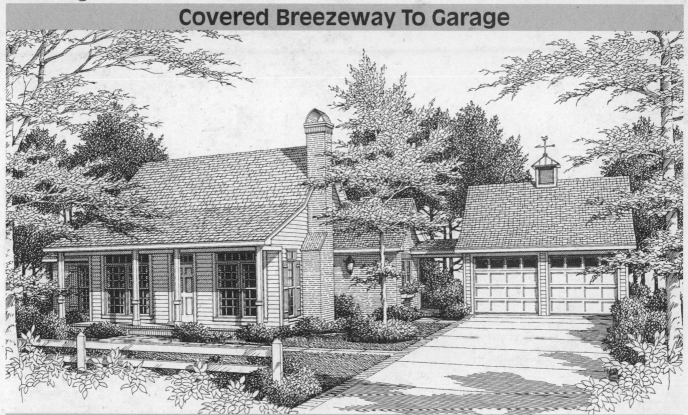

1,406 total square feet of living area

Price Code A

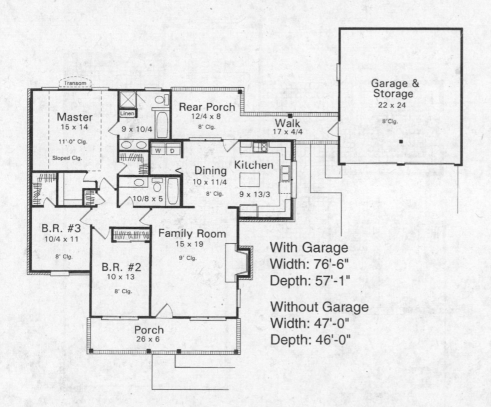

With Garage
Width: 76'-6"
Depth: 57'-1"

Without Garage
Width: 47'-0"
Depth: 46'-0"

Special features

- Master bedroom has sloped ceiling
- Kitchen and dining area merge becoming a gathering place
- Enter family room from charming covered front porch and find fireplace and lots of windows
- 3 bedrooms, 2 baths, 2-car detached garage
- Slab or crawl space foundation, please specify when ordering

TO ORDER BLUEPRINTS USE THE FORM ON PAGE 15 OR CALL TOLL-FREE 1-877-671-6036
View thousands more home plans online at www.familyhandyman.com/homeplans

159

Brick Accents Front Facade

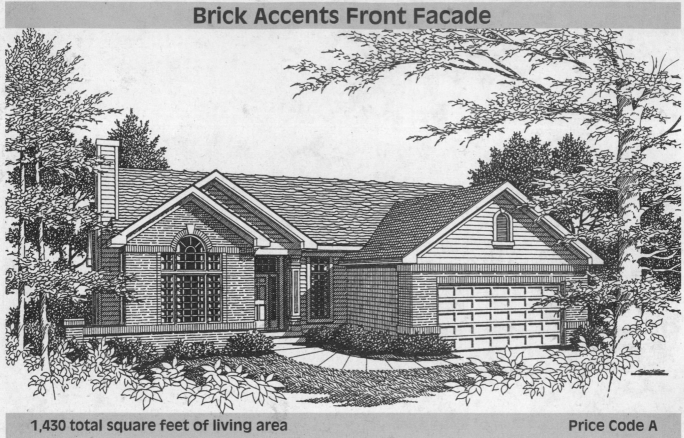

1,430 total square feet of living area

Price Code A

Special features

- Master suite features a private master bath and wall of windows
- U-shaped kitchen makes organization easy
- Great room has several windows making this a bright and cheerful place
- 2 bedrooms, 2 baths, 2-car garage
- Basement foundation

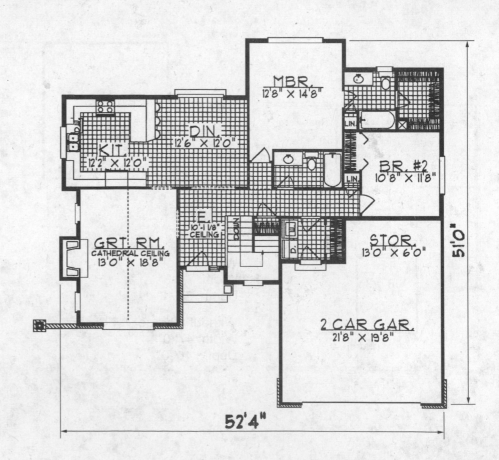

Relaxed Living In This Ranch

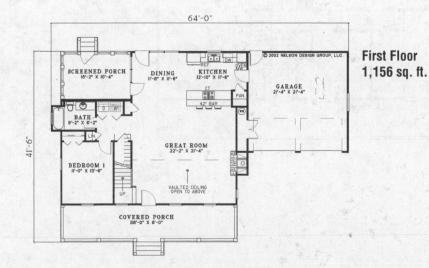

1,903 total square feet of living area

Price Code C

Second Floor
747 sq. ft.

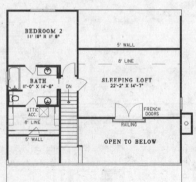

BEDROOM 2
11' 10" X 11' 8"

5' WALL

8' LINE

BATH
11'-0" X 14'-8"

DN

SLEEPING LOFT
22'-2" X 14'-7"

ATTIC ACC.

8' LINE

FRENCH DOORS

5' WALL

RAILING

OPEN TO BELOW

Special features

- Rear screened porch accesses dining area
- Sleeping loft on second floor has French doors that overlook to great room below
- Eat-in counter in kitchen overlooks great room
- 2 bedrooms, 2 baths, 2-car garage
- Crawl space or slab foundation, please specify when ordering

First Floor
1,156 sq. ft.

64'-0"

SCREENED PORCH
15'-2" X 10'-4"

DINING
11'-8" X 11'-6"

KITCHEN
12'-10" X 11'-6"

REF · DW · OVEN

© 2002 NELSON DESIGN GROUP, LLC.

GARAGE
21'-4" X 21'-4"

CT

BATH
9'-2" X 6'-2"

D · W

PAN

42" BAR

41'-6"

LIN

GREAT ROOM
22'-2" X 21'-4"

BEDROOM 1
11'-0" X 13'-6"

UP

VAULTED CEILING
OPEN TO ABOVE

COVERED PORCH
38'-0" X 8'-0"

Perfect Country Haven

1,232 total square feet of living area   **Price Code A**

Special features

- Ideal porch for quiet quality evenings

- Great room opens to dining room for those large dinner gatherings

- Functional L-shaped kitchen includes broom cabinet

- Master bedroom contains large walk-in closet and compartmented bath

- 3 bedrooms, 1 bath, optional 2-car garage

- Basement foundation, drawings also include crawl space and slab foundations

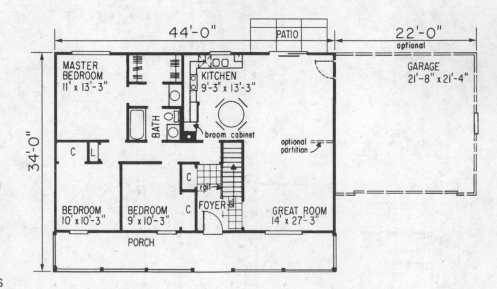

TO ORDER BLUEPRINTS USE THE FORM ON PAGE 15 OR CALL TOLL-FREE 1-877-671-6036
View thousands more home plans online at www.familyhandyman.com/homeplans

Accents Add Charm To Compact Cottage

1,359 total square feet of living area   **Price Code A**

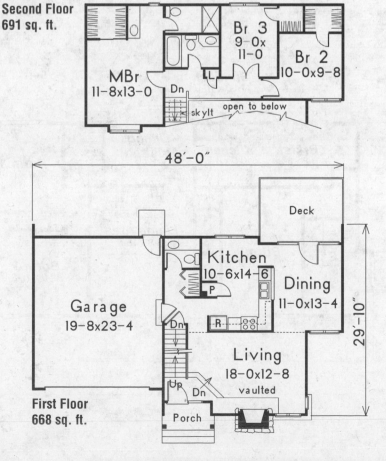

Second Floor
691 sq. ft.

MBr
11-8x13-0

Br 3
9-0x
11-0

Br 2
10-0x9-8

Dn

L

skylt   open to below

48'-0"

Deck

Kitchen
10-6x14-6

Dining
11-0x13-4

Garage
19-8x23-4

Dn

P

R

29'-10"

Living
18-0x12-8
vaulted

Up

Dn

First Floor
668 sq. ft.

Porch

Special features

- Lattice-trimmed porch, stone chimney and abundant windows lend outdoor appeal
- Spacious, bright breakfast area with pass-through to formal dining room
- Large walk-in closets in all bedrooms
- Extensive deck expands dining and entertaining areas
- 3 bedrooms, 2 1/2 baths, 2-car garage
- Basement foundation

Formal Country Charm

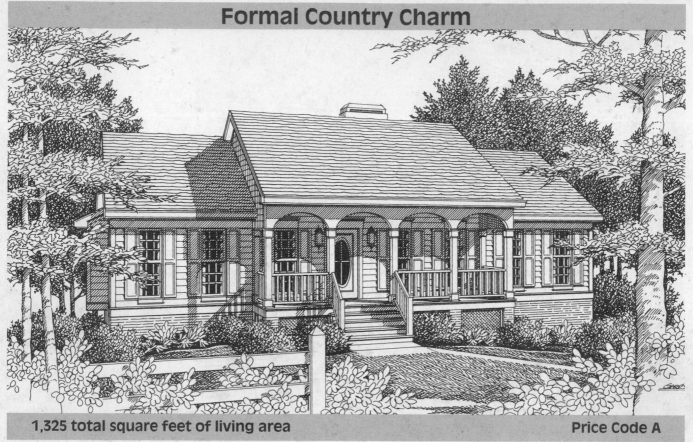

1,325 total square feet of living area

Price Code A

Special features

- Sloped ceiling and a fireplace in living area creates a cozy feeling

- Formal dining and breakfast areas have an efficiently designed kitchen between them

- Master bedroom has walk-in closet with luxurious private bath

- 3 bedrooms, 2 baths, 2-car drive under garage

- Basement foundation

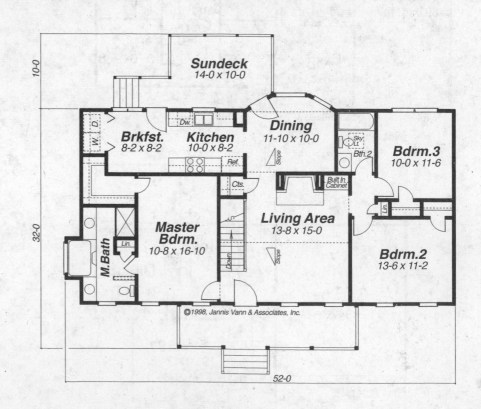

©1998, Jannis Vann & Associates, Inc.

Casual Country Home With Unique Loft

1,673 total square feet of living area

Price Code B

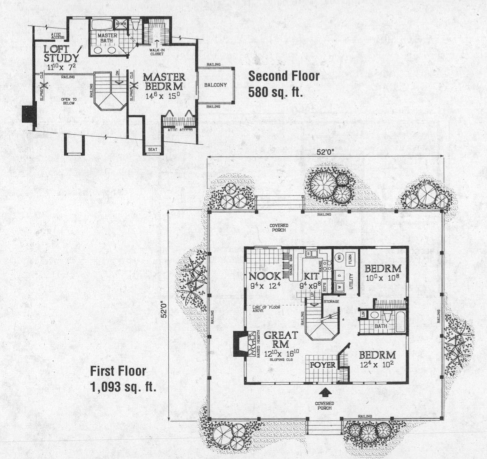

Second Floor
580 sq. ft.

First Floor
1,093 sq. ft.

Special features

- Great room flows into the breakfast nook with outdoor access and beyond to an efficient kitchen
- Master suite on second floor has access to loft/study, private balcony and bath
- Covered porch surrounds the entire home for outdoor living area
- 3 bedrooms, 2 baths
- Crawl space foundation

TO ORDER BLUEPRINTS USE THE FORM ON PAGE 15 OR CALL TOLL-FREE 1-877-671-6036
View thousands more home plans online at www.familyhandyman.com/homeplans

165

Covered Porch Highlights This Home

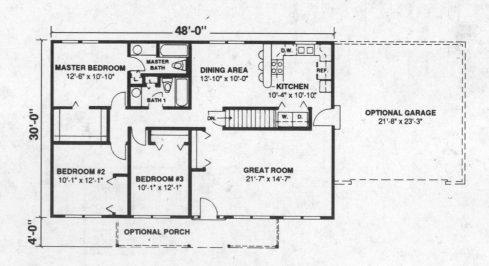

1,364 total square feet of living area

Price Code A

Special features

- Bedrooms separated from living area for privacy
- Master bedroom has private bath and large walk-in closet
- Laundry area conveniently located near kitchen
- Bright and spacious great room
- Built-in pantry in kitchen
- 3 bedrooms, 2 baths, optional 2-car garage
- Basement foundation

48'-0"

30'-0"

4'-0"

MASTER BEDROOM
12'-6" x 10'-10"

MASTER BATH

DINING AREA
13'-10" x 10'-0"

D.W.

REF.

KITCHEN
10'-4" x 10'-10"

BATH 1

DN.

W. D.

OPTIONAL GARAGE
21'-8" x 23'-3"

BEDROOM #2
10'-1" x 12'-1"

BEDROOM #3
10'-1" x 12'-1"

GREAT ROOM
21'-7" x 14'-7"

OPTIONAL PORCH

Sprawling Porch And Deck Allow Terrific Views

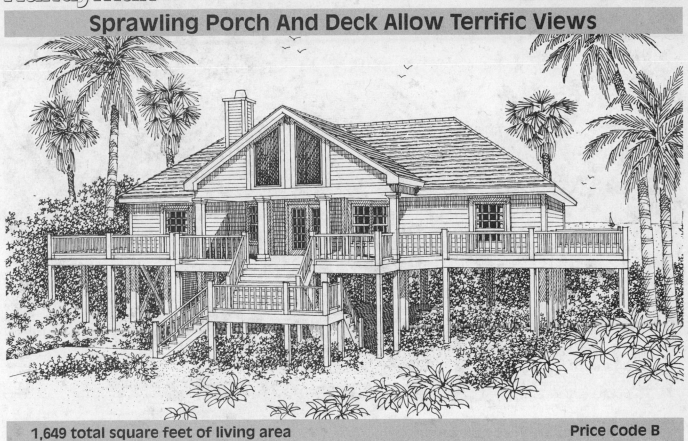

1,649 total square feet of living area

Price Code B

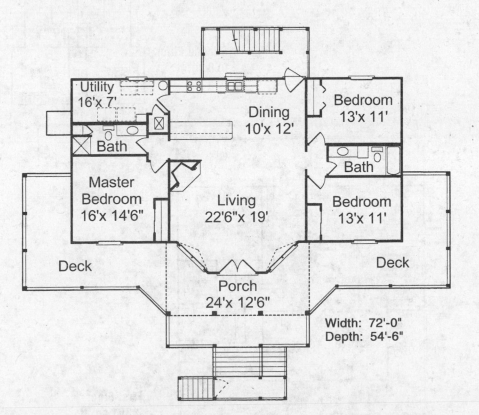

Special features

- Enormous two-story living room has lots of windows and a double-door access onto a spacious porch
- Master bedroom is separated from other bedrooms for privacy
- Well-organized kitchen has oversized counterspace for serving and dining
- 3 bedrooms, 2 baths
- Pier foundation

Floor plan labels: Utility 16' x 7', Bath, Master Bedroom 16' x 14'6", Deck, Porch 24' x 12'6", Dining 10' x 12', Living 22'6" x 19', Bedroom 13' x 11', Bath, Bedroom 13' x 11', Deck

Width: 72'-0"
Depth: 54'-6"

TO ORDER BLUEPRINTS USE THE FORM ON PAGE 15 OR CALL TOLL-FREE 1-877-671-6036
View thousands more home plans online at www.familyhandyman.com/homeplans

167

Trio Of Dormers Add Appeal

3,011 total square feet of living area

Price Code E

Special features

- 9' ceilings on the first floor
- Formal dining room has decorative columns separating it from foyer and great room
- Two secondary bedrooms share a full bath on the second floor
- Spacious master suite accesses sun room through double-doors and has a spacious master bath
- 3 bedrooms, 2 1/2 baths
- Slab or crawl space foundation, please specify when ordering

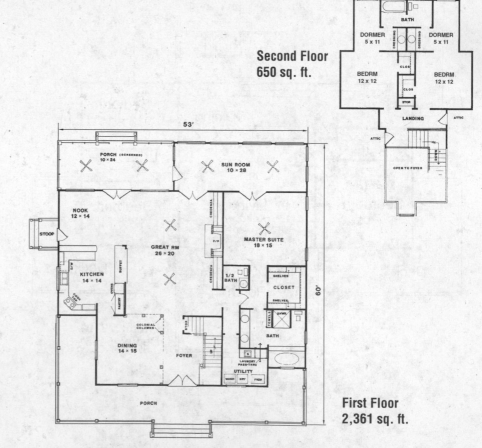

Second Floor 650 sq. ft.

BATH

DORMER 5 x 11   DORMER 5 x 11

BEDRM 12 x 12   BEDRM 12 x 12

CLOS

CLOS

STOR

LANDING   ATTIC

ATTIC

OPEN TO FOYER

First Floor 2,361 sq. ft.

53'

60'

PORCH (SCREENED) 10 x 24

SUN ROOM 10 x 28

NOOK 12 x 14

GREAT RM 26 x 20

MASTER SUITE 18 x 15

STOOP

KITCHEN 14 x 14

BUFFET

PANTRY

1/2 BATH

CLOSET

SHELVES

SHELVES

COLONIAL COLUMNS

DINING 14 x 15

FOYER

BATH

LAUNDRY PASS-THRU

UTILITY

WASH DRY FRZR

PORCH

TO ORDER BLUEPRINTS USE THE FORM ON PAGE 15 OR CALL TOLL-FREE 1-877-671-6036

View thousands more home plans online at www.familyhandyman.com/homeplans

Plan #703-FB-902

Impressive Foyer

1,856 total square feet of living area

Price Code C

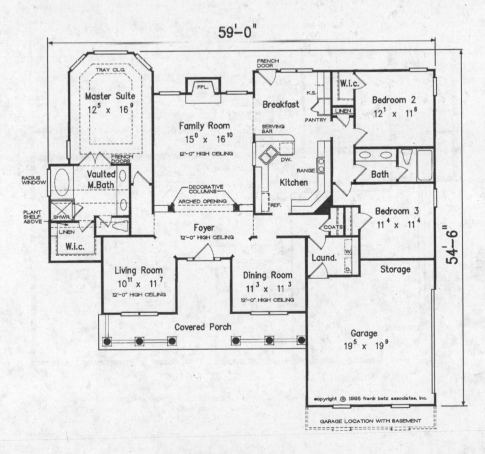

Special features

- Beautiful covered porch creates a Southern accent
- Kitchen has an organized feel with lots of cabinetry
- Large foyer has a grand entrance and leads into family room through columns and arched opening
- 3 bedrooms, 2 baths, 2-car side entry garage
- Walk-out basement, crawl space or slab foundation, please specify when ordering

Trio Of Dormers Add Appeal

2,164 total square feet of living area

Price Code C

Special features

- Country-styled front porch adds charm
- Plenty of counterspace in kitchen
- Large utility area meets big families laundry needs
- Double-doors lead to covered rear porch
- 4 bedrooms, 2 1/2 baths, 2-car side entry garage
- Slab foundation

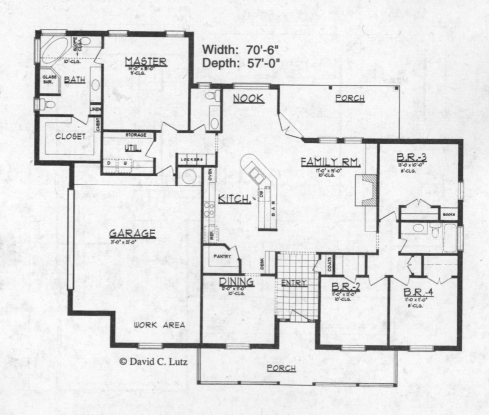

Width: 70'-6"
Depth: 57'-0"

© David C. Lutz

Wonderful Great Room

1,865 total square feet of living area

Price Code D

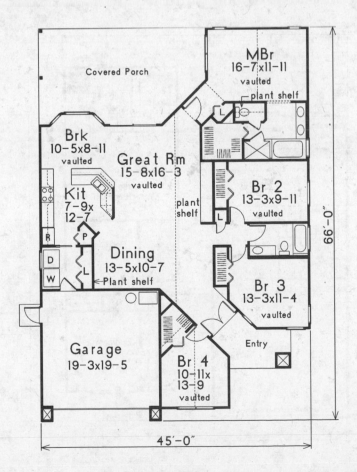

Covered Porch

MBr
16-7x11-11
vaulted

plant shelf

Brk
10-5x8-11
vaulted

Great Rm
15-8x16-3
vaulted

Kit
7-9x
12-7

plant
shelf

Br 2
13-3x9-11
vaulted

Dining
13-5x10-7
←Plant shelf

66'-0"

Garage
19-3x19-5

Br 3
13-3x11-4
vaulted

Entry

Br 4
10-11x
13-9
vaulted

45'-0"

Special features

- Large foyer opens into expansive dining area and great room

- Home features vaulted ceilings throughout

- Master suite features bath with double-bowl vanity, shower, tub and toilet in separate room for privacy

- 4 bedrooms, 2 baths, 2-car garage

- Slab foundation, drawings also include crawl space foundation

Sunny Bay In Dining Area

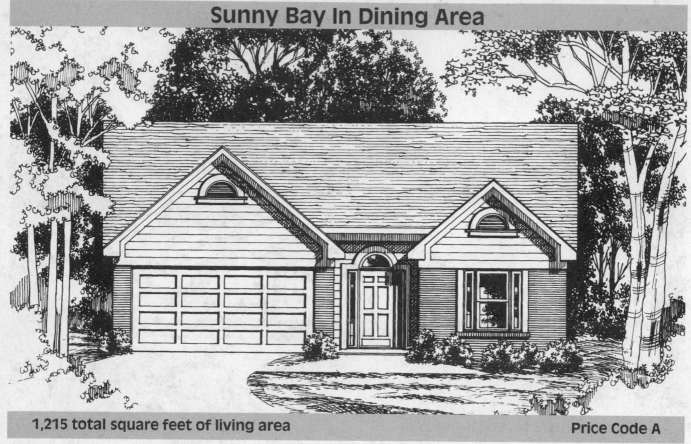

1,215 total square feet of living area

Price Code A

Special features

- Serving bar counter extends kitchen into living area
- Convenient front hall bath
- Vaulted master bedroom has spacious walk-in closet and private bath
- Efficient galley-styled kitchen has everything within reach
- 3 bedrooms, 2 baths, 2-car garage
- Crawl space, slab or walk-out basement foundation, please specify when ordering

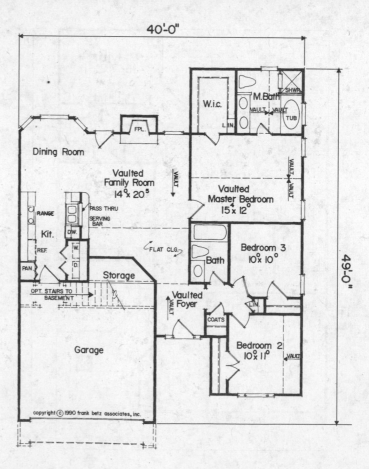

40'-0"

49'-0"

Dining Room

W.i.c. M.Bath SHWR.

VAULT VAULT TUB

LIN.

FPL.

Vaulted Family Room 14⁸ x 20⁵

PASS THRU

SERVING BAR

VAULT

Vaulted Master Bedroom 15⁴ x 12⁰

RANGE

DW.

Kit.

REF.

W. D.

FLAT CLG.

Bath

Bedroom 3 10⁰ x 10⁰

PAN.

Storage

Vaulted Foyer

LIN.

OPT. STAIRS TO BASEMENT

VAULT

COATS

Garage

Bedroom 2 10⁰ x 11⁰

VAULT

copyright © 1990 frank betz associates, inc.

Open Floor Plan Makes Home Feel Larger

1,277 total square feet of living area

Price Code A

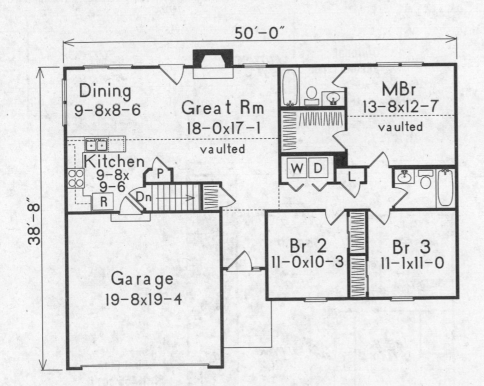

50'-0"

Dining
9-8x8-6

Great Rm
18-0x17-1
vaulted

MBr
13-8x12-7
vaulted

Kitchen
9-8x
9-6

P

W D

L

Dn R

38'-8"

Br 2
11-0x10-3

Br 3
11-1x11-0

Garage
19-8x19-4

Special features

- Vaulted ceilings in master bedroom, great room, kitchen and dining room
- Laundry closet located near bedrooms for convenience
- Compact but efficient kitchen
- 3 bedrooms, 2 baths, 2-car garage
- Basement foundation

Decorative Accents Featured On Front Porch

1,455 total square feet of living area

Price Code A

Special features

- Spacious mud room has a large pantry, space for a freezer, sink/counter area and bath with shower

- Bedroom #2 can easily be converted to a study or office area

- Optional second floor bedroom and playroom have an additional 744 square feet of living area

- 2 bedrooms, 2 baths

- Slab or crawl space foundation, please specify when ordering

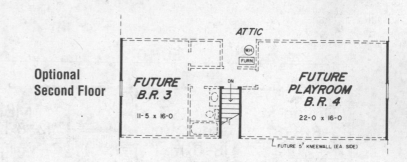

Optional Second Floor

FUTURE B.R. 3
11-5 x 16-0

ATTIC

FUTURE PLAYROOM B.R. 4
22-0 x 16-0

FUTURE 5' KNEEWALL (EA. SIDE)

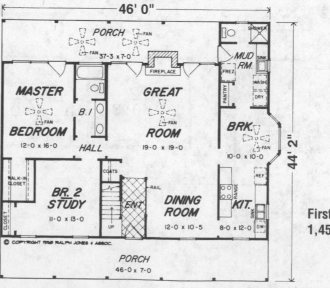

First Floor 1,455 sq. ft.

TO ORDER BLUEPRINTS USE THE FORM ON PAGE 15 OR CALL TOLL-FREE 1-877-671-6036
View thousands more home plans online at www.familyhandyman.com/homeplans

Relax On The Covered Front Porch

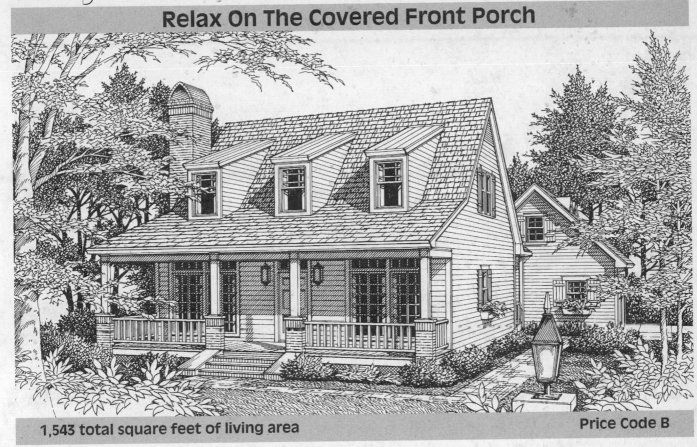

1,543 total square feet of living area

Price Code B

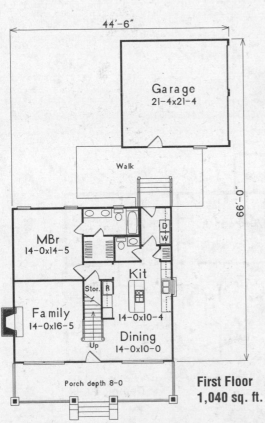

44'-6"

Garage
21-4x21-4

Walk

MBr
14-0x14-5

D
W

Stor. R

Kit
14-0x10-4

Family
14-0x16-5

Up

Dining
14-0x10-0

Porch depth 8-0

**First Floor
1,040 sq. ft.**

66'-0"

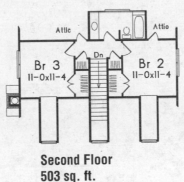

Attic

Attic

Br 3
11-0x11-4

Dn

Br 2
11-0x11-4

**Second Floor
503 sq. ft.**

Special features

- Fireplace serves as the focal point of the large family room

- Efficient floor plan keeps hallways at a minimum

- Laundry room connects the kitchen to the garage

- Private first floor master bedroom has walk-in closet and bath

- 3 bedrooms, 2 1/2 baths, 2-car detached side entry garage

- Slab foundation, drawings also include crawl space foundation

Bayed Breakfast Nook

1,442 total square feet of living area

Price Code A

Special features

- Utility room includes counterspace and closet
- Kitchen has useful center island creating extra workspace
- Vaulted master bedroom has unique double-door entry, private bath and walk-in closet
- 3 bedrooms, 2 baths, 2-car carport
- Slab foundation

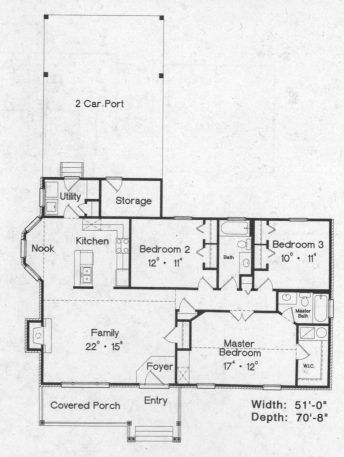

Width: 51'-0"
Depth: 70'-8"

TO ORDER BLUEPRINTS USE THE FORM ON PAGE 15 OR CALL TOLL-FREE 1-877-671-6036
View thousands more home plans online at www.familyhandyman.com/homeplans

Gabled, Covered Front Porch

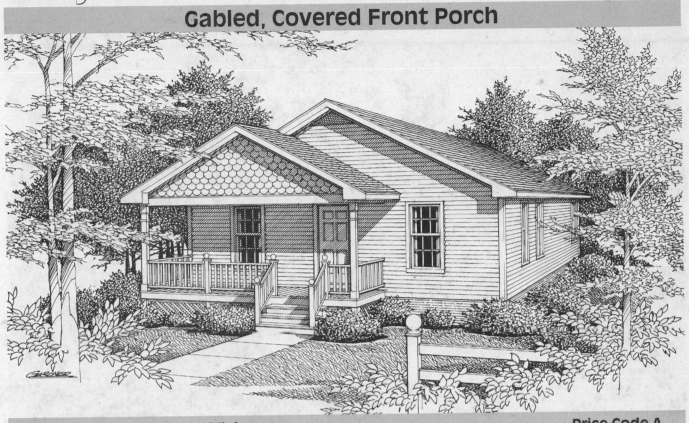

1,320 total square feet of living area

Price Code A

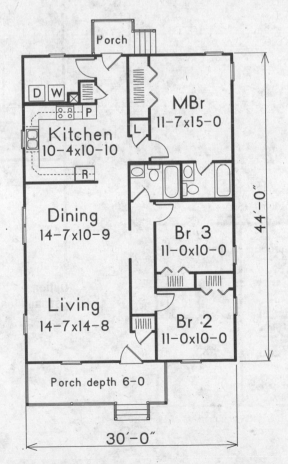

Special features

- Functional U-shaped kitchen features pantry
- Large living and dining areas join to create an open atmosphere
- Secluded master bedroom includes private full bath
- Covered front porch opens into large living area with convenient coat closet
- Utility/laundry room located near the kitchen
- 3 bedrooms, 2 baths
- Crawl space foundation

Plan #703-DH-1377

Country Colonial Feel To This Home

1,377 total square feet of living area

Price Code A

Special features

- Master bedroom has double-door access into screened porch
- Cozy dining area is adjacent to kitchen for convenience
- Great room includes fireplace
- Optional second floor has an additional 349 square feet of living area
- 3 bedrooms, 1 bath
- Crawl space or slab foundation, please specify when ordering

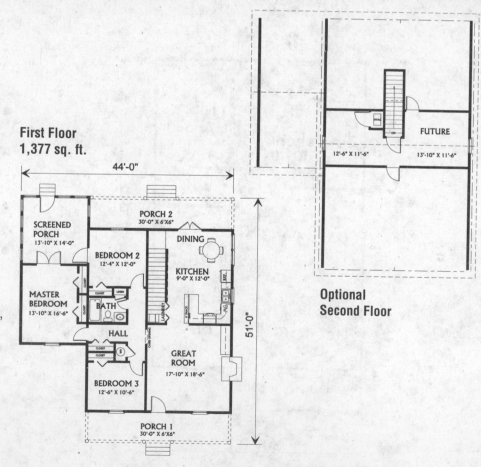

First Floor
1,377 sq. ft.

44'-0"

SCREENED PORCH
13'-10" X 14'-0"

PORCH 2
30'-0" X 6'X6"

DINING

BEDROOM 2
12'-4" X 12'-0"

KITCHEN
9'-0" X 12'-0"

MASTER BEDROOM
13'-10" X 16'-6"

BATH

LAUNDRY

HALL

GREAT ROOM
17'-10" X 18'-6"

BEDROOM 3
12'-6" X 10'-6"

PORCH 1
30'-0" X 6'X6"

51'-0"

FUTURE

12'-6" X 11'-6"   13'-10" X 11'-6"

Optional Second Floor

Ideal Starter Home

988 total square feet of living area

Price Code AA

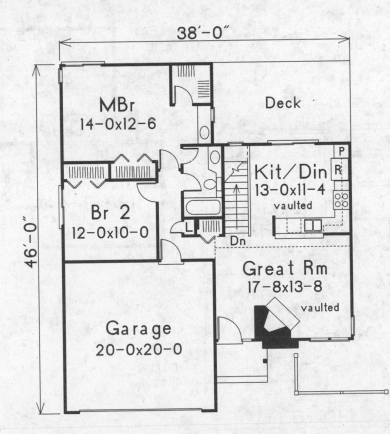

38'-0"

46'-0"

MBr
14-0x12-6

Deck

Br 2
12-0x10-0

Kit/Din
13-0x11-4
vaulted

Dn

Garage
20-0x20-0

Great Rm
17-8x13-8
vaulted

Special features

- Great room features corner fireplace
- Vaulted ceiling and corner windows add space and light in great room
- Eat-in kitchen with vaulted ceiling accesses deck for outdoor living
- Master bedroom features separate vanities and private access to the bath
- 2 bedrooms, 1 bath, 2-car garage
- Basement foundation

Double Dormers Accent This Cozy Vacation Retreat

581 total square feet of living area

Price Code AAA

Special features

- Kitchen/living room features space for dining and spiral steps leading to the loft area
- Large loft space can be easily converted to a bedroom or work area
- Entry space has a unique built-in display niche
- 1 bedroom, 1 bath
- Slab foundation

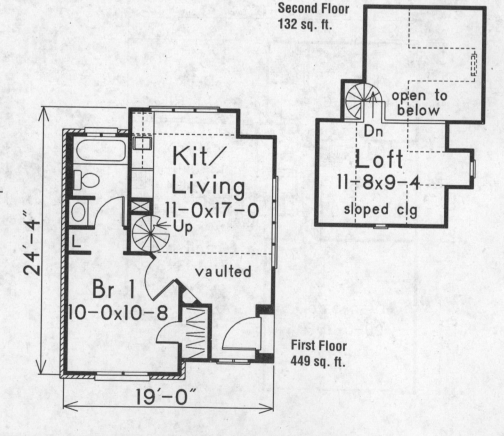

Second Floor
132 sq. ft.

open to below

Dn

Loft
11-8x9-4
sloped clg

Kit/
Living
11-0x17-0
Up

vaulted

Br 1
10-0x10-8

24'-4"

19'-0"

First Floor
449 sq. ft.

TO ORDER BLUEPRINTS USE THE FORM ON PAGE 15 OR CALL TOLL-FREE 1-877-671-6036
View thousands more home plans online at www.familyhandyman.com/homeplans

Truly Unique Design

2,104 total square feet of living area

Price Code C

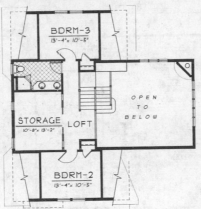

**Second Floor
669 sq. ft.**

BDRM-3
13'-4" x 10'-5"

STORAGE
10'-8" x 13'-2"

LOFT

OPEN
TO
BELOW

BDRM-2
13'-4" x 10'-5"

Special features

- 9' ceilings on the first floor
- Living room opens onto deck through double French doors
- Second floor includes large storage room
- 3 bedrooms, 2 baths, 2-car garage
- Crawl space foundation

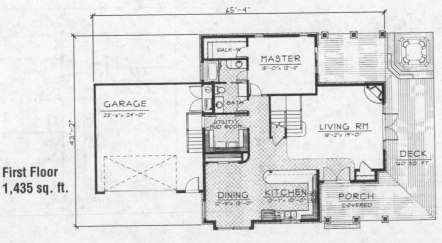

**First Floor
1,435 sq. ft.**

65'-4"

43'-2"

GARAGE
23'-6" x 24'-0"

WALK-IN

MASTER
15'-0" x 12'-11"

BATH

UTILITY
MUD ROOM

LIVING RM
18'-2" x 19'-0"

DECK
160 sq. ft.

DINING
12'-5" x 13'-0"

KITCHEN
12'-7" x 10'-0"

PORCH
COVERED

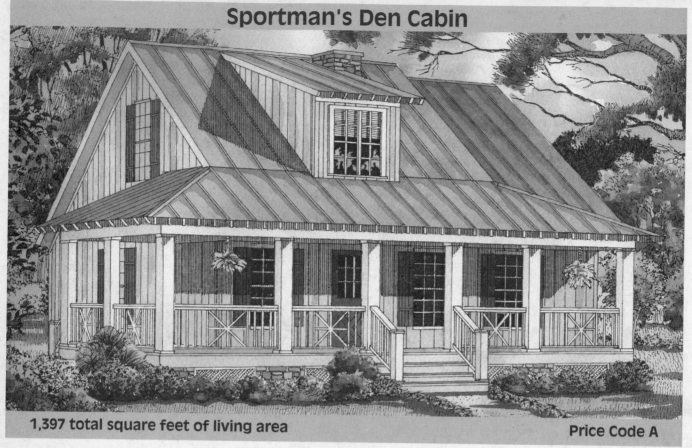

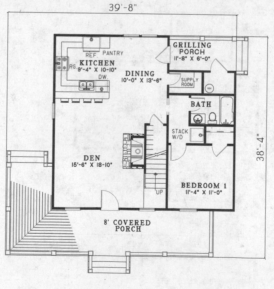

Sportman's Den Cabin

1,397 total square feet of living area

Price Code A

First Floor
890 sq. ft.

39'-8"

38'-4"

PANTRY
REF.
KITCHEN
9'-4" X 10'-10"
RG
DW
GRILLING PORCH
11'-8" X 6'-0"
DINING
10'-0" X 13'-6"
SUPPLY ROOM
BATH
DEN
15'-6" X 18'-10"
STACK W/D
UP
BEDROOM 1
11'-4" X 11'-0"
8' COVERED PORCH

Second Floor
507 sq. ft.

BATH
LIN
5' WALL
8' LINE
BEDROOM 3
11'-4" X 12'-8"
DN
BEDROOM 2
13'-4" X 14'-6"
8' LINE
5' WALL
4' WALL

Special features

- Wrap-around 8' porch adds outdoor living area to this design
- Den with fireplace has open view to kitchen with eat-in snack bar
- Supply room allows for hunting gear or tackle storage
- 3 bedrooms, 2 baths
- Crawl space or slab foundation, please specify when ordering

Graceful Southern Hospitality

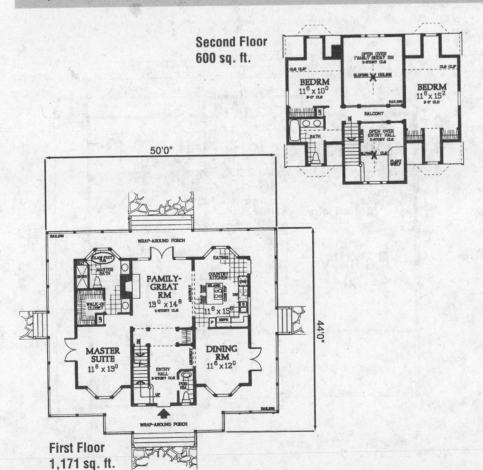

1,771 total square feet of living area

Price Code B

Second Floor
600 sq. ft.

First Floor
1,171 sq. ft.

Special features

- Efficient country kitchen shares space with a bayed eating area

- Two-story family/great room is warmed by a fireplace in winter and open to outdoor country comfort in the summer with double French doors

- First floor master suite offers a bay window and access to the porch through French doors

- 3 bedrooms, 2 1/2 baths, optional detached 2-car garage

- Basement foundation

Vacation Home Or Year-Round Living

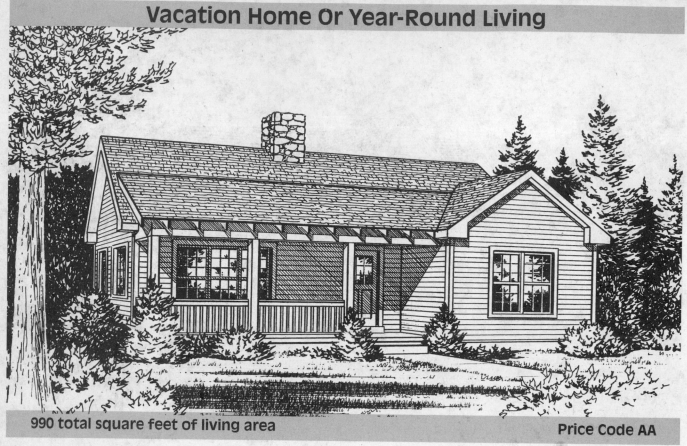

990 total square feet of living area

Price Code AA

Special features

- Covered front porch adds charming feel
- Vaulted ceilings in kitchen, family and dining rooms creates a spacious feel
- Large linen, pantry and storage closets throughout
- 2 bedrooms, 1 bath
- Crawl space foundation

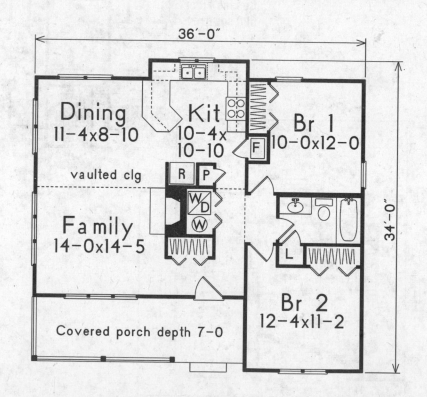

36'-0"

Dining 11-4x8-10

Kit 10-4x 10-10

Br 1 10-0x12-0

vaulted clg

Family 14-0x14-5

F

R P

W D W

L

Br 2 12-4x11-2

Covered porch depth 7-0

34'-0"

Sunny Sitting Area In Master Suite

2,545 total square feet of living area

Price Code D

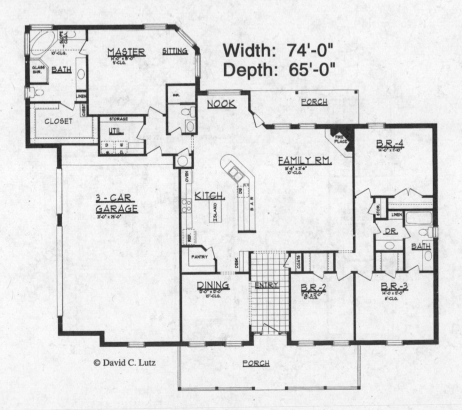

© David C. Lutz

Width: 74'-0"
Depth: 65'-0"

Special features

- Beautiful covered front porch gives country appeal
- Open family room has 10' ceiling
- Kitchen has abundant counterspace
- 4 bedrooms, 2 1/2 baths, 3-car side entry garage
- Slab foundation

Handsome Double Brick Gables

COPYRIGHT LARRY E. BELK

1,553 total square feet of living area

Price Code B

Special features

- Kitchen counter extends into great room with space for dining

- Extra storage provided in garage

- Sloped ceiling in master bedroom adds a dramatic feel

- 3 bedrooms, 2 baths, 2-car garage

- Crawl space or slab foundation, please specify when ordering

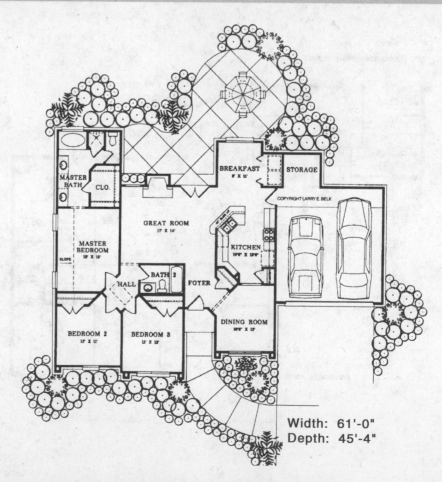

Width: 61'-0"
Depth: 45'-4"

Irresistible Cottage Adorns Any Setting

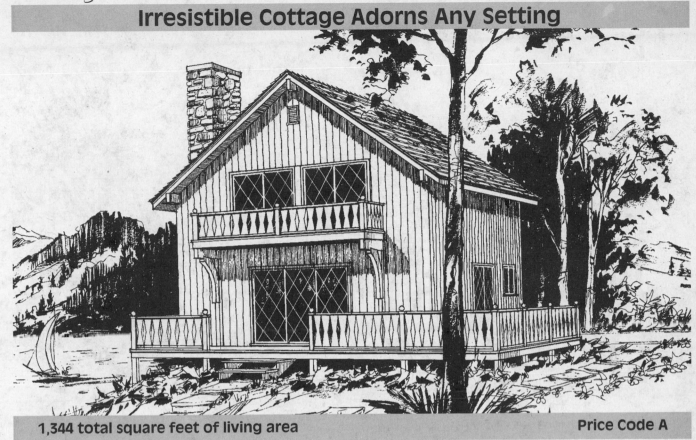

1,344 total square feet of living area

Price Code A

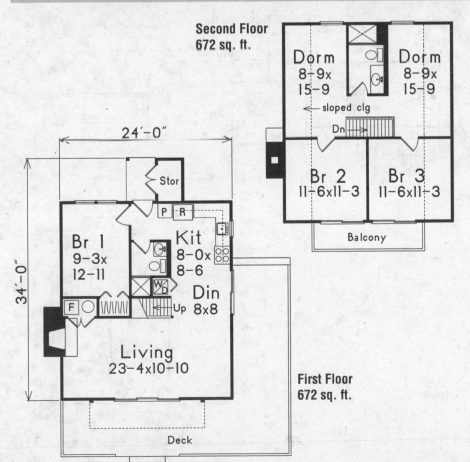

Second Floor
672 sq. ft.

Dorm
8-9x
15-9

Dorm
8-9x
15-9

← sloped clg

Dn

Br 2
11-6x11-3

Br 3
11-6x11-3

Balcony

24'-0"

Stor

P R

Br 1
9-3x
12-11

Kit
8-0x
8-6

34'-0"

F

Din
8x8

Up

W/D

Living
23-4x10-10

First Floor
672 sq. ft.

Deck

Special features

- Beautiful stone fireplace, bracketed balcony and surrounding deck create appealing atmosphere

- Enormous living room, open to dining area, enjoys views to deck through two large sliding doors

- Second floor delivers lots of sleeping area and views from exterior balcony

- 5 bedrooms, 2 baths

- Crawl space foundation, drawings also include slab foundation

Covered Front Porch

1,966 total square feet of living area

Price Code C

Special features

- Private dining room remains focal point when entering the home
- Kitchen and breakfast room join to create a functional area
- Lots of closet space in second floor bedrooms
- 3 bedrooms, 2 1/2 baths, 2-car side entry garage
- Basement foundation

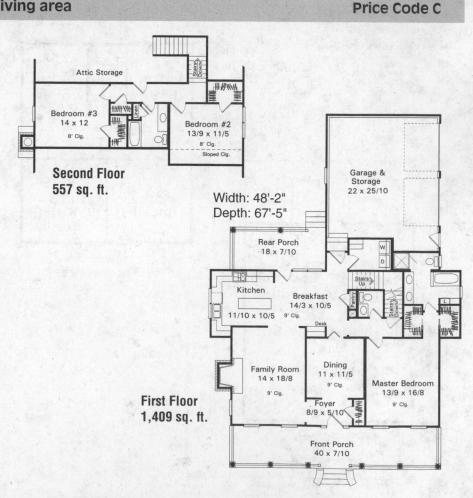

Attic Storage

Bedroom #3
14 x 12
8' Clg.

Linen

Bedroom #2
13/9 x 11/5
8' Clg.
Sloped Clg.

Stairs Down

**Second Floor
557 sq. ft.**

**Width: 48'-2"
Depth: 67'-5"**

Garage & Storage
22 x 25/10

Rear Porch
18 x 7/10

W
D

Kitchen
11/10 x 10/5

Breakfast
14/3 x 10/5
9' Clg.

Pantry

Stairs Up

Stairs Down

Desk

Family Room
14 x 18/8
9' Clg.

Dining
11 x 11/5
9' Clg.

Master Bedroom
13/9 x 16/8
9' Clg.

Foyer
8/9 x 5/10

**First Floor
1,409 sq. ft.**

Front Porch
40 x 7/10

Spacious Country Home

2,123 total square feet of living area

Price Code C

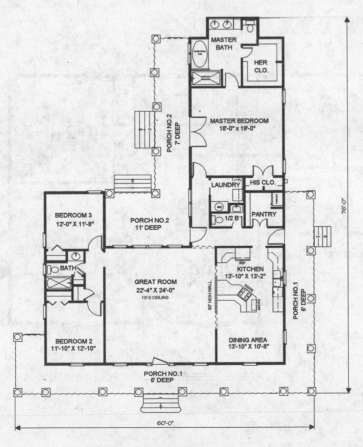

Special features

- L-shaped porch extends the entire length of this home creating lots of extra space for outdoor living

- Master bedroom is secluded for privacy and has his and hers closets, double vanity in bath and a double-door entry onto covered porch

- Efficiently designed kitchen

- 3 bedrooms, 2 1/2 baths

- Crawl space foundation

Rustic Design With Modern Features

1,000 total square feet of living area

Price Code AA

Special features

- Large mud room with separate covered porch entrance
- Full-length covered front porch
- Bedrooms on opposite sides of the home for privacy
- Vaulted ceiling creates an open and spacious feeling
- 2 bedrooms, 1 bath
- Crawl space foundation

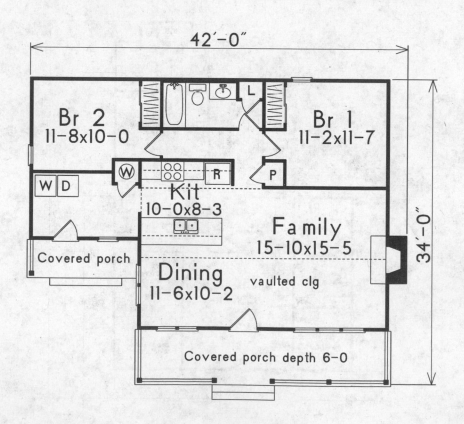

Large Built-In Desk

1,815 total square feet of living area

Price Code C

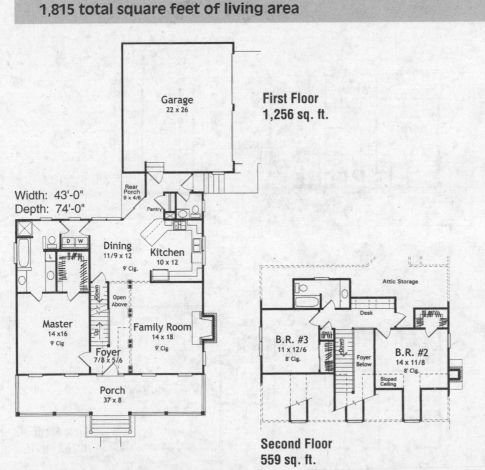

First Floor
1,256 sq. ft.

Garage
22 x 26

Rear Porch
9 x 4/6

Width: 43'-0"
Depth: 74'-0"

Pantry

Dining
11/9 x 12
9' Clg.

Kitchen
10 x 12

D W
L

Open Above

Master
14 x 16
9' Clg

Family Room
14 x 18
9' Clg.

Foyer
7/8 x 5/6

Porch
37 x 8

Attic Storage

Desk

B.R. #3
11 x 12/6
8' Clg.

Foyer Below

B.R. #2
14 x 11/8
8' Clg.

Sloped Ceiling

Second Floor
559 sq. ft.

Special features

- Second floor has built-in desk in hall; ideal as a computer work station or mini office area
- Two doors into laundry area make it handy from master bedroom and the rest of the home
- Inviting covered porch
- Lots of counterspace and cabinetry in kitchen
- 3 bedrooms, 2 1/2 baths, 2-car side entry garage
- Basement foundation

The Family **Handyman**

Plan #703-JV-2091-A

Open Floor Plan With Plenty Of Light

2,475 total square feet of living area

Price Code D

Special features

- Country feeling with wrap-around porch and dormered front

- Open floor plan with living and dining areas combined has access to a sun deck

- First floor master bedroom with many luxuries

- Bonus room on the second floor has an additional 384 square feet of living area

- 3 bedrooms, 2 1/2 baths, 2-car side entry garage

- Walk-out basement foundation

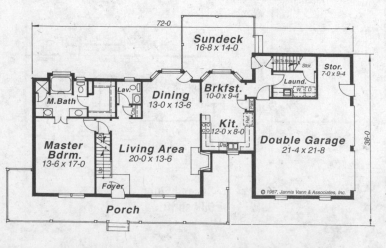

Second Floor
729 sq. ft.

Study
11-2 x 11-0

Bdrm.2
13-6 x 13-4

Bdrm.3
12-0 x 13-4

Bth.2

Bonus Rm.
11-8 x 21-10

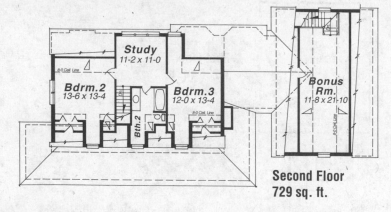

First Floor
1,362 sq. ft.

72-0

Sundeck
16-8 x 14-0

Stor.
7-0 x 9-4

Laund.

M.Bath

Lav.

Dining
13-0 x 13-6

Brkfst.
10-0 x 9-4

Master Bdrm.
13-6 x 17-0

Living Area
20-0 x 13-6

Kit.
12-0 x 8-0

Double Garage
21-4 x 21-8

Foyer

38-0

© 1987, Jannis Vann & Associates, Inc.

Porch

Rustic Haven

1,275 total square feet of living area

Price Code A

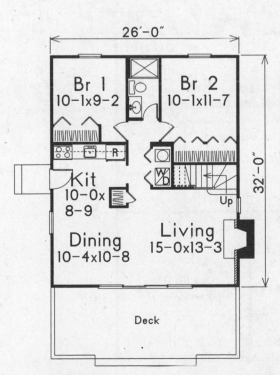

26'-0"

Br 1
10-1x9-2

Br 2
10-1x11-7

Kit
10-0x
8-9

32'-0"

Up

Dining
10-4x10-8

Living
15-0x13-3

Deck

First Floor
832 sq. ft.

Br 3
13-3x10-5

Dn

L

Br 4
13-3x10-1
← sloped clg

Balcony

Second Floor
443 sq. ft.

Special features

- Wall shingles and stone veneer fireplace all fashion an irresistible rustic appeal
- Living area features fireplace and opens to an efficient kitchen
- Two bedrooms on second floor
- 4 bedrooms, 2 baths
- Basement foundation, drawings also include crawl space and slab foundations

TO ORDER BLUEPRINTS USE THE FORM ON PAGE 15 OR CALL TOLL-FREE 1-877-671-6036
View thousands more home plans online at www.familyhandyman.com/homeplans

193

Distinguished Styling For A Small Lot

1,268 total square feet of living area

Price Code A

Special features

- Multiple gables, large porch and arched windows create classy exterior

- Innovative design provides openness in great room, kitchen and breakfast room

- Secondary bedrooms have private hall with bath

- 3 bedrooms, 2 baths, 2-car garage

- Basement foundation

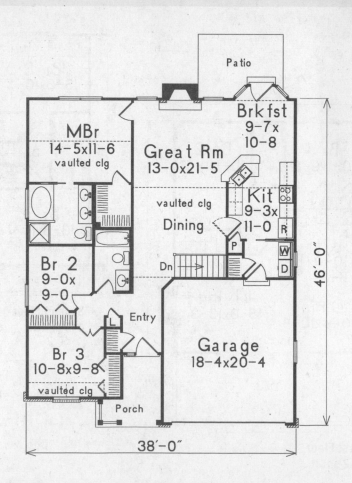

Covered Porch Adds Appeal

1,480 total square feet of living area

Price Code A

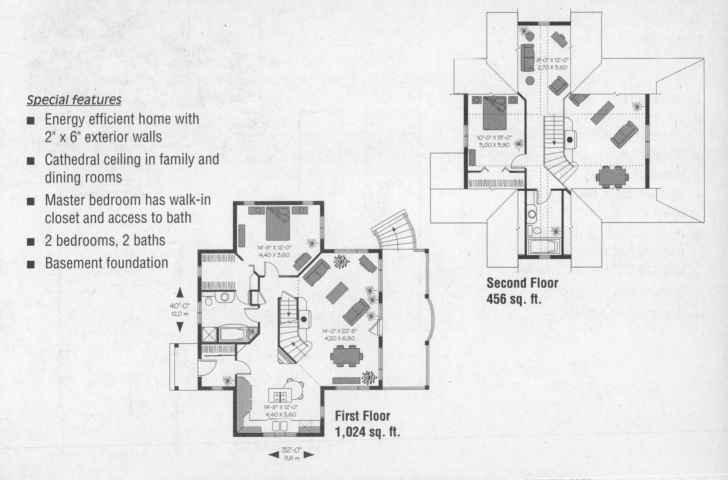

Special features

- Energy efficient home with 2" x 6" exterior walls
- Cathedral ceiling in family and dining rooms
- Master bedroom has walk-in closet and access to bath
- 2 bedrooms, 2 baths
- Basement foundation

Second Floor
456 sq. ft.

9'-0" X 12'-0"
2,70 X 3,60

10'-0" X 13'-0"
3,00 X 3,90

14'-8" X 12'-0"
4,40 X 3,60

40'-0"
12,0 m

14'-0" X 22'-8"
4,20 X 6,80

14'-8" X 12'-0"
4,40 X 3,60

First Floor
1,024 sq. ft.

32'-0"
9,6 m

TO ORDER BLUEPRINTS USE THE FORM ON PAGE 15 OR CALL TOLL-FREE 1-877-671-6036
View thousands more home plans online at www.familyhandyman.com/homeplans

195

Irresistible Paradise Retreat

1,563 total square feet of living area

Price Code B

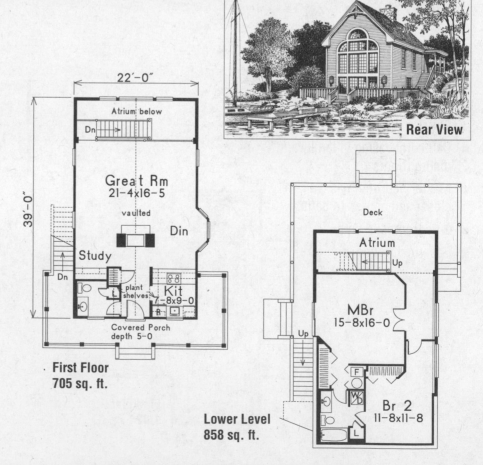

Rear View

Special features

- Enjoyable wrap-around porch and lower sundeck
- Vaulted entry is adorned with palladian window, plant shelves, stone floor and fire-place
- Huge vaulted great room has magnificient views through a two-story atrium window wall
- 2 bedrooms, 1 1/2 baths
- Basement foundation

22'-0"

Atrium below

Dn

Great Rm
21-4x16-5

vaulted

Din

Study

Dn

plant shelves

Kit
7-8x9-0

Covered Porch
depth 5-0

39'-0"

First Floor
705 sq. ft.

Deck

Atrium

Up

MBr
15-8x16-0

Up

Br 2
11-8x11-8

Lower Level
858 sq. ft.

Atrium Living For Views On A Narrow Lot

1,231 total square feet of living area

Price Code A

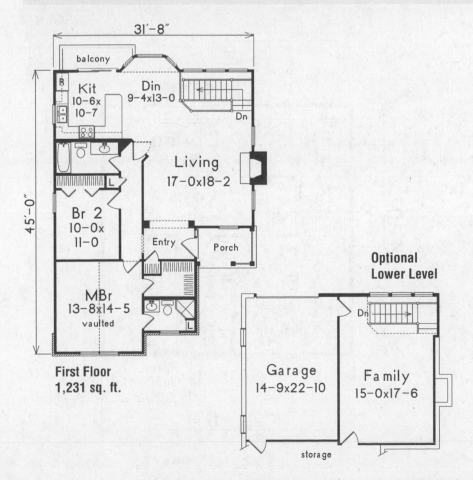

31'-8"

balcony

Kit
10-6x
10-7

Din
9-4x13-0

Dn

Living
17-0x18-2

45'-0"

Br 2
10-0x
11-0

L

Entry

Porch

MBr
13-8x14-5
vaulted

L

First Floor
1,231 sq. ft.

**Optional
Lower Level**

Dn

Garage
14-9x22-10

Family
15-0x17-6

storage

Special features

- Dutch gables and stone accents provide an enchanting appearance for a small cottage
- The spacious living room offers a masonry fireplace, atrium with window wall and is open to a dining area with bay window
- A breakfast counter, lots of cabinet space and glass sliding doors to a walk-out balcony create a sensational kitchen
- 380 square feet of optional living area on the lower level
- 2 bedrooms, 2 baths, 1-car drive under garage
- Walk-out basement foundation

TO ORDER BLUEPRINTS USE THE FORM ON PAGE 15 OR CALL TOLL-FREE 1-877-671-6036
View thousands more home plans online at www.familyhandyman.com/homeplans

197

A Cottage With Class

576 total square feet of living area

Price Code AAA

Special features

- Perfect country retreat features vaulted living room and entry with skylights and plant shelf above
- Double-doors enter a vaulted bedroom with bath access
- Kitchen offers generous storage and pass-through breakfast bar
- 1 bedroom, 1 bath
- Crawl space foundation

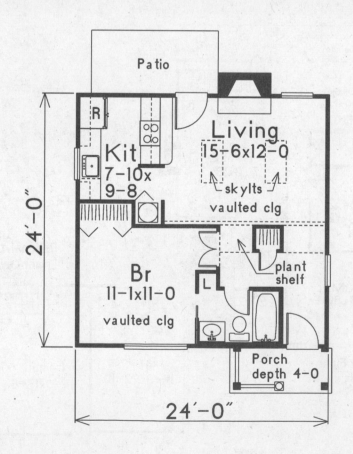

Patio

R

Kit
7-10x
9-8

Living
15-6x12-0

skylts

vaulted clg

plant
shelf

24'-0"

Br
11-1x11-0

L

vaulted clg

Porch
depth 4-0

24'-0"

Ideal Vacation Style For Views

1,650 total square feet of living area

Price Code B

First Floor
1,122 sq. ft.

Width: 37'-0"
Depth: 52'-0"

Porch
12'x 9'5"

Kitchen
8'8"x 18'

Dining
11'6"x 18'

Bedroom
13'x 10'11"

Bath

Living
16'6"x 14'5"

Bedroom
13'x 10'9"

Porch
20'6"x 5'

Deck
34'x 10'

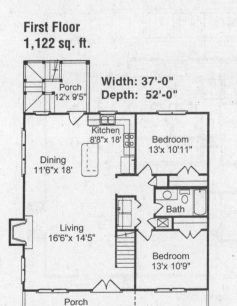

Bedroom
14'x 11'2"

Ma.
Ba.

Open to
Below

Master
Bedroom
13'x 13'6"

Second Floor
528 sq. ft.

Special features

- Master suite located on second floor for privacy
- Open living space connects to dining area
- Two-story living area features lots of windows for views to the outdoors and a large fireplace
- Efficiently designed kitchen
- 4 bedrooms, 2 baths
- Pier foundation

TO ORDER BLUEPRINTS USE THE FORM ON PAGE 15 OR CALL TOLL-FREE 1-877-671-6036
View thousands more home plans online at www.familyhandyman.com/homeplans

199

Enchanting Country Cottage

1,140 total square feet of living area   **Price Code AA**

Special features

- Open and spacious living and dining areas for family gatherings
- Well-organized kitchen with an abundance of cabinetry and a built-in pantry
- Roomy master bath features double-bowl vanity
- 3 bedrooms, 2 baths, 2-car drive under garage
- Basement foundation

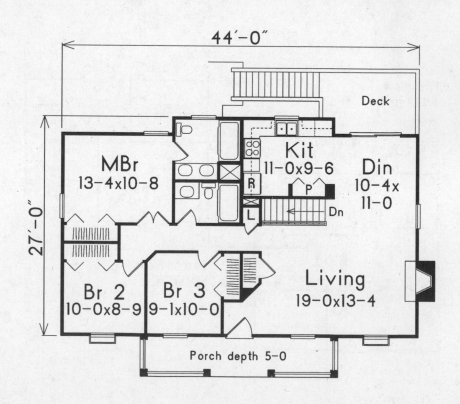

Compact Home For Functional Living

1,220 total square feet of living area

Price Code A

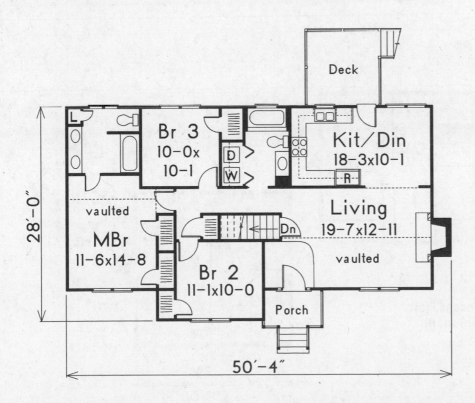

Deck

Br 3
10-0x
10-1

Kit/Din
18-3x10-1

D
W

R

Living
19-7x12-11

vaulted

MBr
11-6x14-8

vaulted

Dn

Br 2
11-1x10-0

Porch

28'-0"

50'-4"

Special features

- Vaulted ceilings add luxury to living room and master suite
- Spacious living room accented with a large fireplace and hearth
- Gracious dining area is adjacent to the convenient wrap-around kitchen
- Washer and dryer handy to the bedrooms
- Covered porch entry adds appeal
- Rear sun deck adjoins dining area
- 3 bedrooms, 2 baths, 2-car drive under garage
- Basement foundation

TO ORDER BLUEPRINTS USE THE FORM ON PAGE 15 OR CALL TOLL-FREE 1-877-671-6036
View thousands more home plans online at www.familyhandyman.com/homeplans

201

Large Patio Adds Outdoor Appeal

1,056 total square feet of living area

Price Code AA

Special features

- Energy efficient home with 2" x 6" exterior walls
- Unique fireplace becomes focal point in living and dining areas
- Three-season room off living area is cheerful and bright
- Galley-style kitchen is efficiently designed
- 2 bedrooms, 1 1/2 baths
- Basement foundation

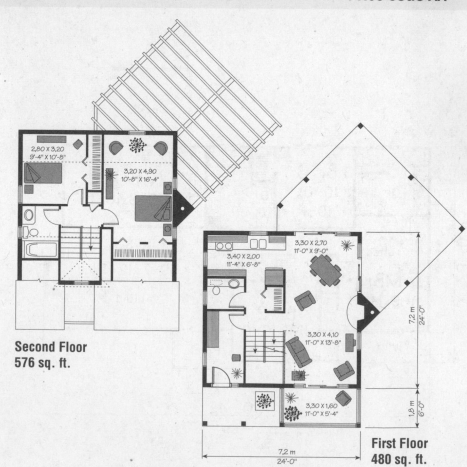

Second Floor
576 sq. ft.

2,80 X 3,20
9'-4" X 10'-8"

3,20 X 4,90
10'-8" X 16'-4"

First Floor
480 sq. ft.

3,30 X 2,70
11'-0" X 9'-0"

3,40 X 2,00
11'-4" X 6'-8"

3,30 X 4,10
11'-0" X 13'-8"

3,30 X 1,60
11'-0" X 5'-4"

7,2 m
24'-0"

1,8 m
6'-0"

7,2 m
24'-0"

TO ORDER BLUEPRINTS USE THE FORM ON PAGE 15 OR CALL TOLL-FREE 1-877-671-6036
View thousands more home plans online at www.familyhandyman.com/homeplans

Country Ranch With Open Interior

1,783 total square feet of living area

Price Code D

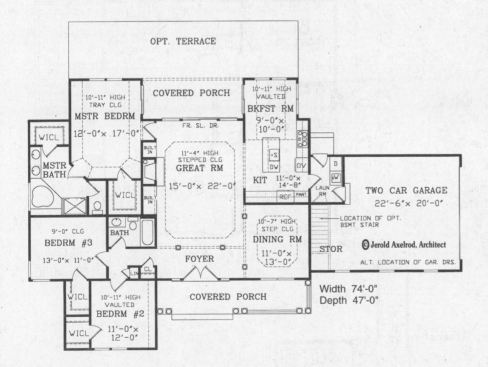

Width 74'-0"
Depth 47'-0"

Special features

- The front to rear flow of the great room, with built-ins on one side is a furnishing delight
- Bedrooms are all quietly zoned on one side
- The master bedroom is separated for privacy
- Every bedroom features walk-in closets
- 3 bedrooms, 2 baths, 2-car side entry garage
- Basement, crawl space or slab foundation, please specify when ordering

Small Home Is Remarkably Spacious

914 total square feet of living area

Price Code AA

Special features

- Large porch for leisure evenings
- Dining area with bay window, open stair and pass-through kitchen creates openness
- Basement includes generous garage space, storage area, finished laundry and mechanical room
- 2 bedrooms, 1 bath, 2-car drive under garage
- Basement foundation

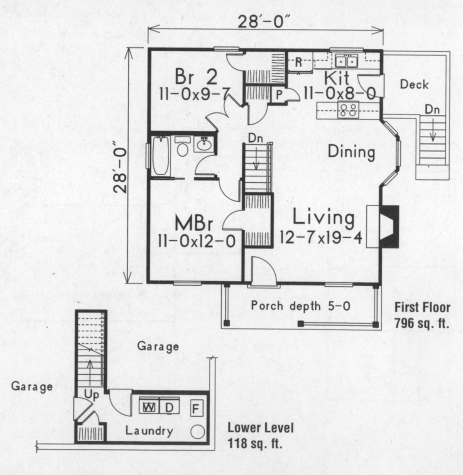

28'-0"

28'-0"

Br 2
11-0x9-7

Kit
11-0x8-0

Deck

Dn

Dn

Dining

MBr
11-0x12-0

Living
12-7x19-4

Porch depth 5-0

First Floor
796 sq. ft.

Garage

Garage

Up

W D F

Laundry

Lower Level
118 sq. ft.

TO ORDER BLUEPRINTS USE THE FORM ON PAGE 15 OR CALL TOLL-FREE 1-877-671-6036
View thousands more home plans online at www.familyhandyman.com/homeplans

Ideal Home For Lake, Mountains Or Seaside

1,711 total square feet of living area

Price Code B

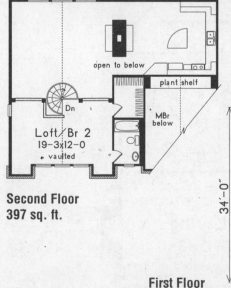

Rear View

**Second Floor
397 sq. ft.**

Loft/Br 2
19-3x12-0
vaulted

open to below

plant shelf

MBr
below

Dn

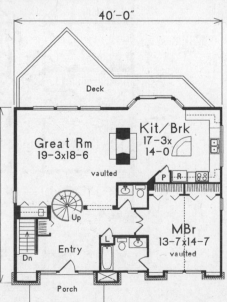

40'-0"

34'-0"

Deck

Great Rm
19-3x18-6
vaulted

Kit/Brk
17-3x
14-0

Entry

Up

Dn

MBr
13-7x14-7
vaulted

Porch

**First Floor
1,314 sq. ft.**

Special features

- Colossal entry leads to a vaulted great room with exposed beams, two-story window wall, brick fireplace, wet bar and balcony

- Bayed breakfast room shares the fireplace and joins a sun-drenched kitchen and sundeck

- Vaulted first floor master suite with double entry doors, closets and bookshelves

- Spiral stair and balcony dramatizes a loft that doubles as a spacious second bedroom

- 2 bedrooms, 2 1/2 baths

- Basement foundation

TO ORDER BLUEPRINTS USE THE FORM ON PAGE 15 OR CALL TOLL-FREE 1-877-671-6036
View thousands more home plans online at www.familyhandyman.com/homeplans

205

Three Bedroom Luxury In A Small Home

1,161 total square feet of living area

Price Code AA

Special features

- Brickwork and feature window add elegance to home for a narrow lot
- Living room enjoys a vaulted ceiling, fireplace and opens to kitchen area
- U-shaped kitchen offers a breakfast area with bay window, snack bar and built-in pantry
- 3 bedrooms, 2 baths
- Basement foundation

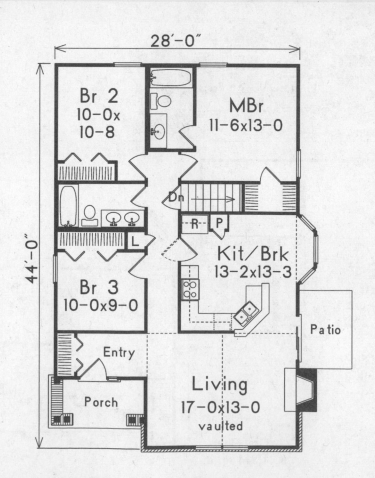

28'-0"

44'-0"

Br 2
10-0x
10-8

MBr
11-6x13-0

Dn

R P

Br 3
10-0x9-0

Kit/Brk
13-2x13-3

Patio

Entry

Living
17-0x13-0
vaulted

Porch

L

TO ORDER BLUEPRINTS USE THE FORM ON PAGE 15 OR CALL TOLL-FREE 1-877-671-6036
View thousands more home plans online at www.familyhandyman.com/homeplans

Perfect Ranch With All The Amenities

1,429 total square feet of living area

Price Code A

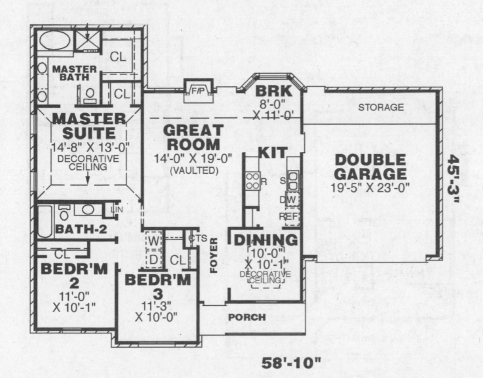

Special features

- Master bedroom features a spacious private bath and double walk-in closets
- Formal dining room has convenient access to kitchen perfect when entertaining
- Additional storage can be found in the garage
- 3 bedrooms, 2 baths, 2-car garage
- Slab foundation

Trendsetting Appeal For A Narrow Lot

1,294 total square feet of living area   Price Code A

Special features

- Great room features fireplace and large bay with windows and patio doors

- Enjoy a laundry room immersed in light with large windows, arched transom and attractive planter box

- Vaulted master bedroom with bay window and walk-in closets

- Bedroom #2 boasts a vaulted ceiling, plant shelf and half bath, perfect for a studio

- 2 bedrooms, 1 full bath, 2 half baths, 1-car rear entry garage

- Basement foundation

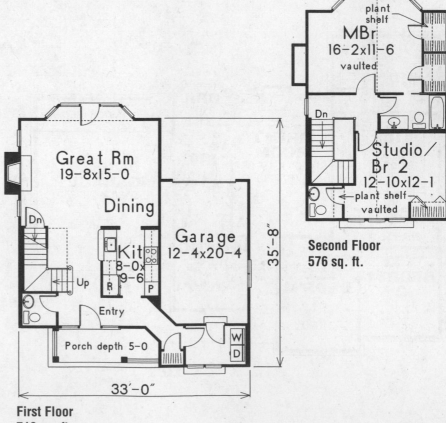

Second Floor
576 sq. ft.

MBr
16-2x11-6
vaulted

Studio/
Br 2
12-10x12-1

Great Rm
19-8x15-0

Dining

Kit
8-0x
9-6

Garage
12-4x20-4

35'-8"

Entry

Porch depth 5-0

33'-0"

First Floor
718 sq. ft.

TO ORDER BLUEPRINTS USE THE FORM ON PAGE 15 OR CALL TOLL-FREE 1-877-671-6036
View thousands more home plans online at www.familyhandyman.com/homeplans

Corner Windows Grace Library

1,824 total square feet of living area

Price Code C

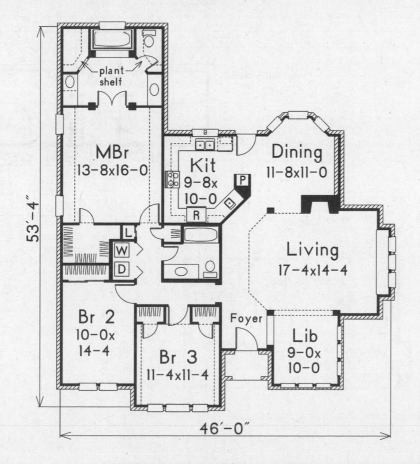

plant shelf

MBr
13-8x16-0

Kit
9-8x
10-0

Dining
11-8x11-0

Living
17-4x14-4

L
W
D

Br 2
10-0x
14-4

Br 3
11-4x11-4

Foyer

Lib
9-0x
10-0

53'-4"

46'-0"

Special features

- Living room features 10' ceiling, fireplace and media center
- Dining room includes bay window and convenient kitchen access
- Master bedroom features large walk-in closet and double-doors leading into master bath
- Modified U-shaped kitchen features pantry and bar
- 3 bedrooms, 2 baths, 2-car detached garage
- Slab foundation

TO ORDER BLUEPRINTS USE THE FORM ON PAGE 15 OR CALL TOLL-FREE 1-877-671-6036
View thousands more home plans online at www.familyhandyman.com/homeplans

209

Ideal For Entertaining

1,870 total square feet of living area　　　　**Price Code C**

Special features

- Kitchen is open to the living and dining areas
- Breakfast area has cathedral ceiling creating a sunroom effect
- Master suite is spacious with all the amenities
- Second floor bedrooms share hall bath
- 3 bedrooms, 2 1/2 baths, 2-car drive under garage
- Basement foundation

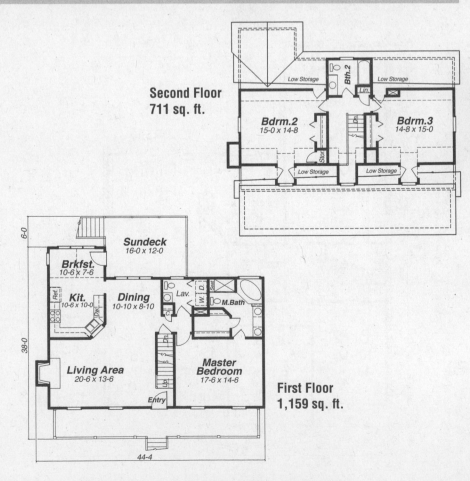

Second Floor 711 sq. ft.

First Floor 1,159 sq. ft.

Riverside Views From Covered Deck

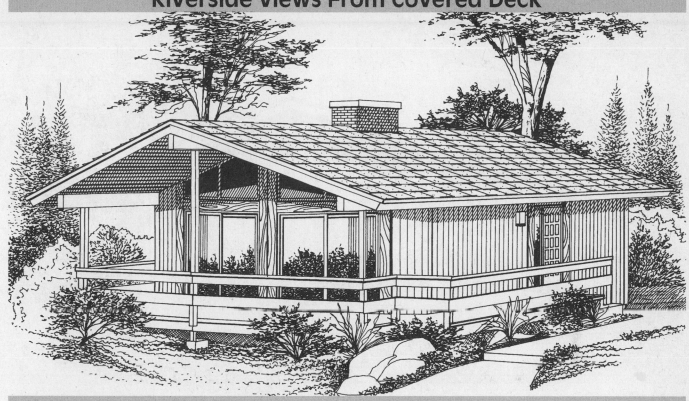

792 total square feet of living area

Price Code AAA

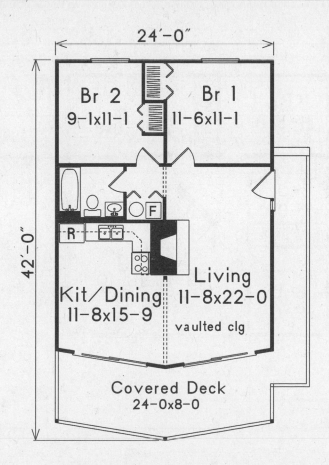

24'-0"

42'-0"

Br 2
9-1x11-1

Br 1
11-6x11-1

R

F

Kit/Dining
11-8x15-9

Living
11-8x22-0
vaulted clg

Covered Deck
24-0x8-0

Special features

- Attractive exterior features wood posts and beams, wrap-around deck with railing and glass sliding doors with transoms

- Kitchen, living and dining areas enjoy sloped ceilings, cozy fireplace and views over deck

- Two bedrooms share a bath just off the hall

- 2 bedrooms, 1 bath

- Crawl space foundation, drawings also include slab foundation

Corner Window Wall Dominates Design

784 total square feet of living area

Price Code AAA

Special features

- Outdoor relaxation will be enjoyed with this home's huge wrap-around wood deck
- Upon entering the spacious living area, a cozy free-standing fireplace, sloped ceiling and corner window wall catch the eye
- Charming kitchen features pass-through peninsula to dining area
- 3 bedrooms, 1 bath
- Pier foundation

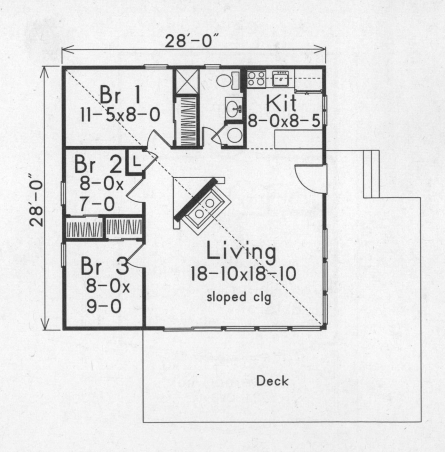

28'-0"

28'-0"

Br 1
11-5x8-0

Kit
8-0x8-5

Br 2
8-0x
7-0

Living
18-10x18-10
sloped clg

Br 3
8-0x
9-0

Deck

TO ORDER BLUEPRINTS USE THE FORM ON PAGE 15 OR CALL TOLL-FREE 1-877-671-6036
View thousands more home plans online at www.familyhandyman.com/homeplans

Multiple Decks Surround Home

1,207 total square feet of living area

Price Code A

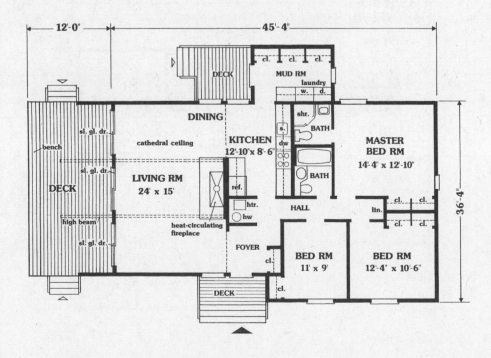

Special features

- Triple sets of sliding glass doors leading to sun deck brighten living room

- Oversized mud room has lots of extra closet space for convenience

- Centrally located heat circulating fireplace creates a focal point while warming the home

- 3 bedrooms, 2 baths

- Basement or crawl space foundation, please specify when ordering

A Vacation Oasis

1,106 total square feet of living area

Price Code AA

Special features

- Delightful A-frame provides exciting vacation style living all year long
- Sundeck accesses large living room with open soaring ceiling
- Enormous sleeping area is provided on second floor with balcony overlook to living room below
- 2 bedrooms, 1 bath
- Pier foundation

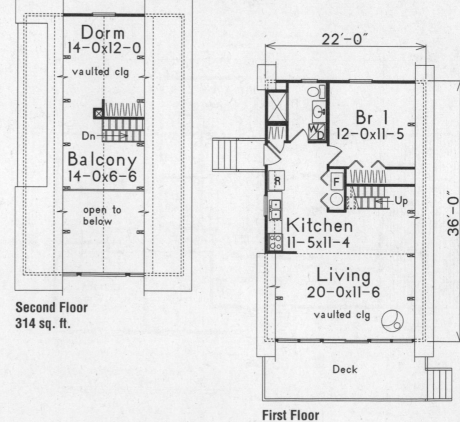

Dorm
14-0x12-0
vaulted clg

Dn

Balcony
14-0x6-6

open to below

Second Floor
314 sq. ft.

22'-0"

Br 1
12-0x11-5

Up

Kitchen
11-5x11-4

Living
20-0x11-6
vaulted clg

36'-0"

Deck

First Floor
792 sq. ft.

Fireplace Perfect For Gathering

1,631 total square feet of living area

Price Code B

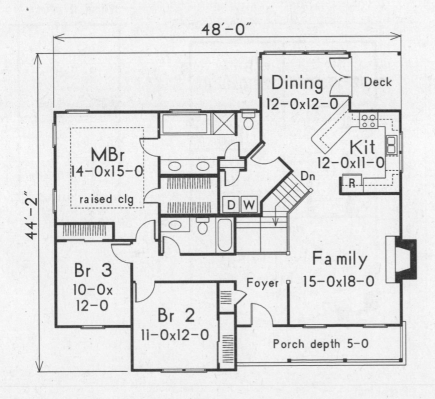

Special features

- 9' ceilings throughout this home
- Utility room conveniently located near kitchen
- Roomy kitchen and dining area boasts a breakfast bar and deck access
- Coffered ceiling accents master suite
- 3 bedrooms, 2 baths, 2-car drive under garage
- Basement foundation

Unique Yet Functional Design

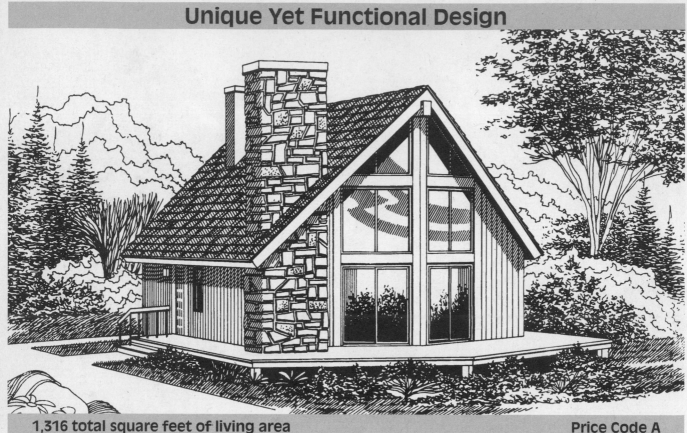

1,316 total square feet of living area

Price Code A

Special features

- Massive vaulted family/living room is accented with fireplace and views to outdoors through sliding glass doors
- Galley-style kitchen is centrally located
- Unique separate shower room near bath doubles as a convenient mud room
- 3 bedrooms, 1 bath
- Crawl space foundation

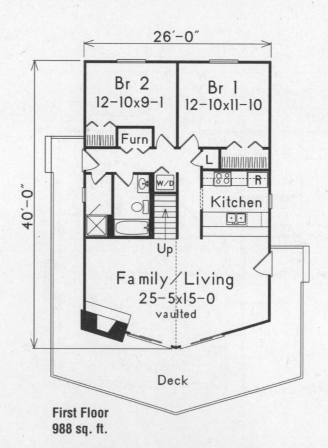

26'-0"

40'-0"

Br 2
12-10x9-1

Furn

Br 1
12-10x11-10

L

W/D

R

Kitchen

Up

Family/Living
25-5x15-0
vaulted

Deck

First Floor
988 sq. ft.

Second Floor
328 sq. ft.

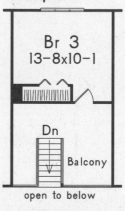

Br 3
13-8x10-1

Dn

Balcony

open to below

TO ORDER BLUEPRINTS USE THE FORM ON PAGE 15 OR CALL TOLL-FREE 1-877-671-6036
View thousands more home plans online at www.familyhandyman.com/homeplans

A Vacation Home For All Seasons

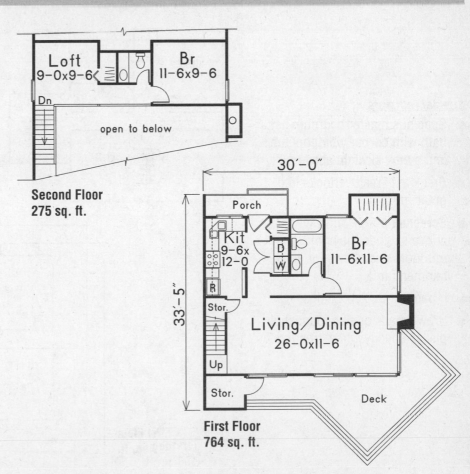

1,039 total square feet of living area

Price Code AA

Loft
9-0x9-6

Br
11-6x9-6

Dn

open to below

Second Floor
275 sq. ft.

Special features

■ Cathedral construction provides the maximum in living area openness

■ Expansive glass viewing walls

■ Two decks, front and back

■ Charming second story loft arrangement

■ Simple, low-maintenance construction

■ 2 bedrooms, 1 1/2 baths

■ Crawl space foundation

30'-0"

Porch

Kit
9-6x
12-0

Br
11-6x11-6

33'-5"

Stor.

D
W

R

Stor.

Living/Dining
26-0x11-6

Up

Stor.

Deck

First Floor
764 sq. ft.

Plan #703-GH-24724

Two-Story With Victorian Feel

1,982 total square feet of living area

Price Code C

Special features

- Spacious master bedroom has bath with corner whirlpool tub and sunny skylight above

- Breakfast area overlooks into great room

- Screened porch with skylight above extends the home outdoors and allows for entertainment area

- 4 bedrooms, 2 1/2 baths

- Crawl space or slab foundation, please specify when ordering

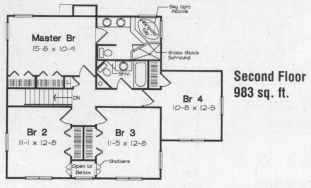

Sky light Above

Master Br
15-8 x 10-9

Glass Block Surround

Shlv.

Br 4
10-8 x 12-5

**Second Floor
983 sq. ft.**

DN

Br 2
11-1 x 12-8

Br 3
11-5 x 12-8

Open to Below

Shutters

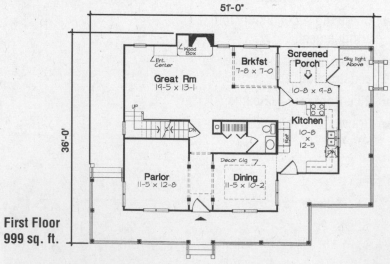

51'-0"

36'-0'

Wood Box

Ent. Center

Great Rm
19-5 x 13-1

Brkfst
7-8 x 7-0

Screened Porch
10-8 x 9-8

Sky light Above

UP

Kitchen
10-8 x 12-5

Decor Clg

Parlor
11-5 x 12-8

Dining
11-5 x 10-2

**First Floor
999 sq. ft.**

TO ORDER BLUEPRINTS USE THE FORM ON PAGE 15 OR CALL TOLL-FREE 1-877-671-6036

View thousands more home plans online at www.familyhandyman.com/homeplans

Carport With Storage

COPYRIGHTED ©1998

1,333 total square feet of living area

Price Code A

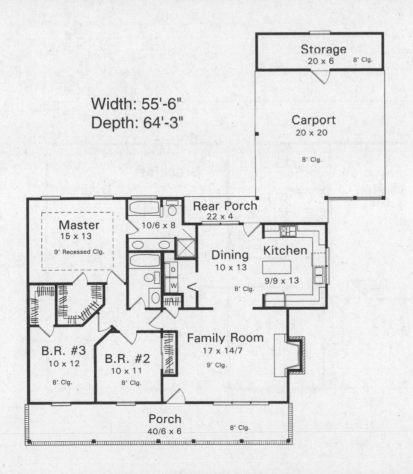

Storage
20 x 6   8' Clg.

Carport
20 x 20

8' Clg.

Width: 55'-6"
Depth: 64'-3"

Rear Porch
22 x 4

Master
15 x 13
9' Recessed Clg.

10/6 x 8

Dining
10 x 13
8' Clg.

Kitchen
9/9 x 13

D
W

B.R. #3
10 x 12
8' Clg.

B.R. #2
10 x 11
8' Clg.

Family Room
17 x 14/7
9' Clg.

Porch
40/6 x 6   8' Clg.

Special features

- Country charm with covered front porch

- Dining area looks into family room with fireplace

- Master suite has walk-in closet and private bath

- 3 bedrooms, 2 baths, 2-car attached carport

- Slab or crawl space foundation, please specify when ordering

TO ORDER BLUEPRINTS USE THE FORM ON PAGE 15 OR CALL TOLL-FREE 1-877-671-6036
View thousands more home plans online at www.familyhandyman.com/homeplans

219

Split Foyer Plan Is Always A Favorite

1,496 total square feet of living area

Price Code A

Special features

- Vaulted living and dining rooms create a spacious feel to the main living areas
- Breakfast area and kitchen combine for convenience
- Large master bath has all the amenities
- Dining area has access onto deck
- 3 bedrooms, 2 baths, 2-car drive under garage
- Slab foundation

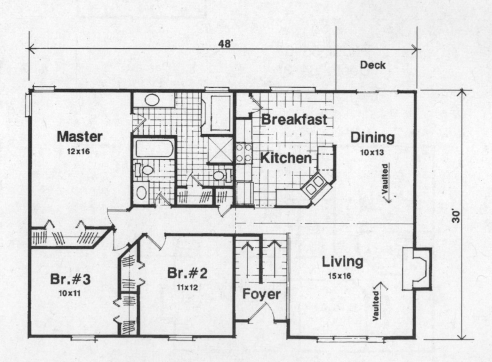

Plan #703-0216

Sheltered Entrance Opens To Stylish Features

1,661 total square feet of living area

Price Code B

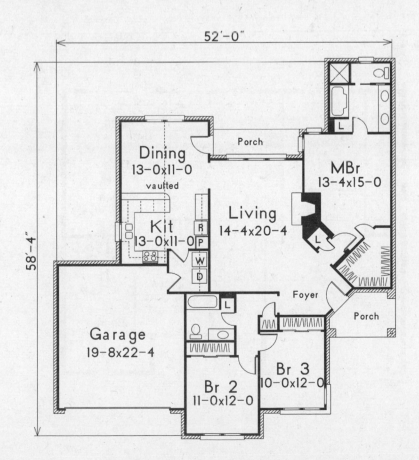

52'-0"

58'-4"

Dining
13-0x11-0
vaulted

Porch

Kit
13-0x11-0

Living
14-4x20-4

MBr
13-4x15-0

Foyer

Porch

Garage
19-8x22-4

Br 2
11-0x12-0

Br 3
10-0x12-0

Special features

- Large open foyer with angled wall arrangement and high ceiling adds to spacious living room
- Kitchen and dining area have impressive cathedral ceilings and French door allowing access to the patio
- Utility room conveniently located near kitchen
- Secluded master bedroom has large walk-in closets, unique brick wall arrangement and 10' ceiling
- 3 bedrooms, 2 baths, 2-car garage
- Slab foundation

Distinctive Interior Design Elements

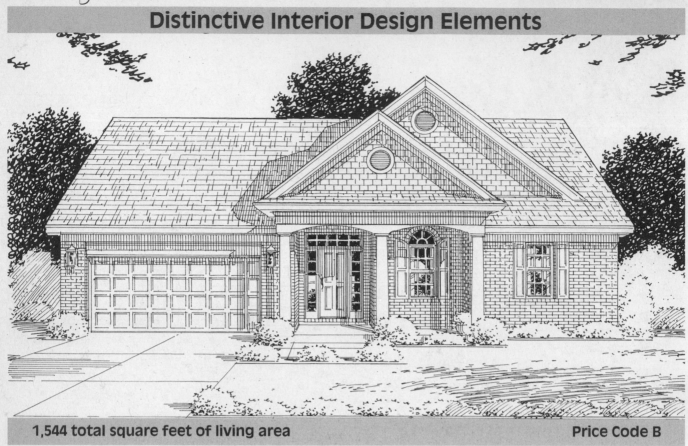

1,544 total square feet of living area

Price Code B

Special features

- A curved counter top with seating creates a delightful bar for quick meals
- Double-doors off the foyer enable one bedroom to function as a library offering flexibility
- Arched openings and sloped ceilings are nice additions to the design
- 3 bedrooms, 2 baths, 2-car garage
- Basement foundation

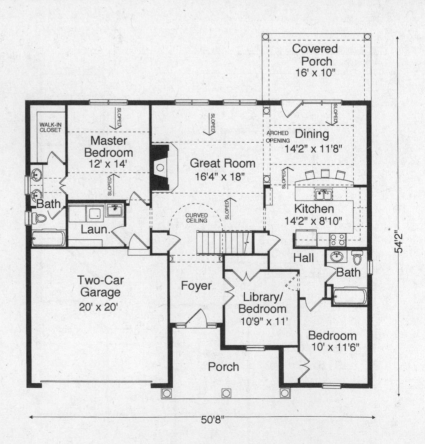

TO ORDER BLUEPRINTS USE THE FORM ON PAGE 15 OR CALL TOLL-FREE 1-877-671-6036
View thousands more home plans online at www.familyhandyman.com/homeplans

Wrap-Around Country Porch

1,875 total square feet of living area

Price Code C

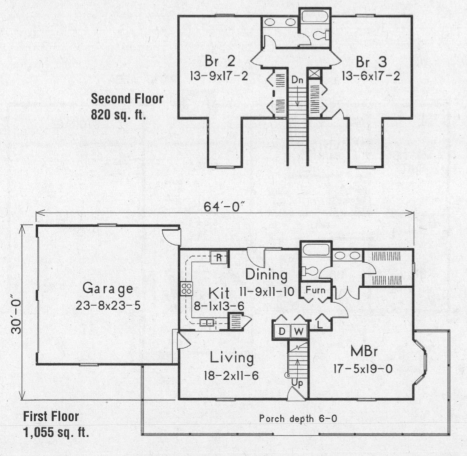

Second Floor 820 sq. ft.

Br 2
13-9x17-2

Dn

Br 3
13-6x17-2

First Floor 1,055 sq. ft.

64'-0"

30'-0"

Garage
23-8x23-5

R

Dining
11-9x11-10

Kit
8-1x13-6

Furn

D W

L

Living
18-2x11-6

Up

MBr
17-5x19-0

Porch depth 6-0

Special features

- Country-style exterior with wrap-around porch and dormers
- Large second floor bedrooms share a dressing area and bath
- Master bedroom suite includes bay window, walk-in closet, dressing area and bath
- 3 bedrooms, 2 baths, 2-car side entry garage
- Crawl space foundation, drawings also include basement and slab foundations

Rustic Styling Enhances This Ranch

1,398 total square feet of living area

Price Code A

Special features

- Country kitchen has vaulted ceiling, spacious eating bar and lots of extra space for dining

- Enormous vaulted great room has cozy fireplace flanked by windows and ceiling beams for an added rustic appeal

- Master suite bath has shower and step-up tub with stained glass ledge and plant niche accents

- 3 bedrooms, 2 baths, 2-car garage

- Slab or crawl space foundation, please specify when ordering

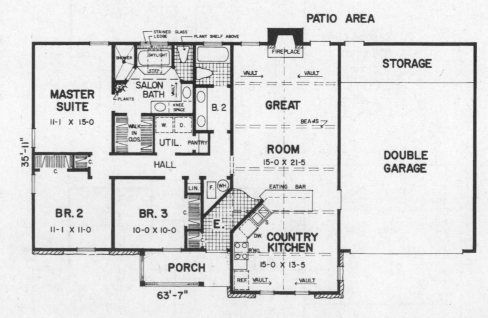

Cottage Style

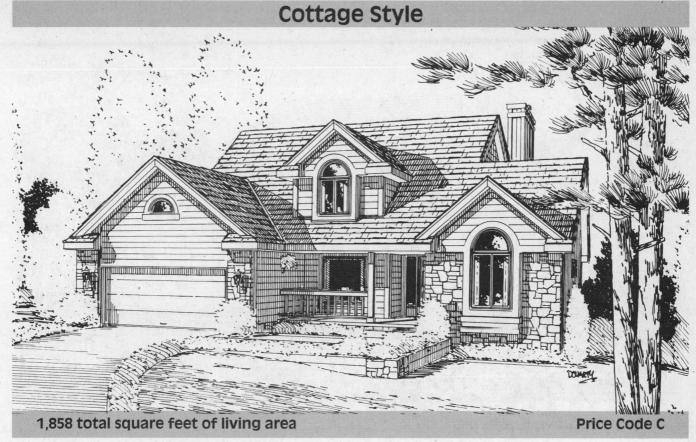

1,858 total square feet of living area

Price Code C

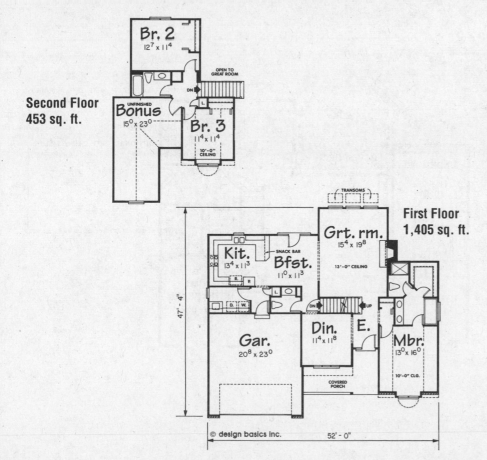

Second Floor 453 sq. ft.

Br. 2
12⁷ x 11⁴

OPEN TO GREAT ROOM

DN

UNFINISHED **Bonus**
15⁰ x 23⁰

Br. 3
11⁴ x 11⁴
10'-0" CEILING

TRANSOMS

Grt. rm.
15⁴ x 19⁸
13'-0" CEILING

First Floor 1,405 sq. ft.

Kit.
13⁴ x 11³

SNACK BAR

Bfst.
11⁰ x 11³

47'-4"

Gar.
20⁸ x 23⁰

DN · UP

Din.
11⁴ x 11⁸

E.

Mbr.
13⁰ x 16⁰
10'-0" CLG.

COVERED PORCH

© design basics inc.

52'-0"

Special features

- Transom windows in great room add a light and airy feeling
- U-shaped kitchen has lots of counter space
- Second floor includes large unfinished bonus room ideal for playroom or home office
- 3 bedrooms, 2 1/2 baths, 2-car garage
- Basement foundation

Plan #703-AX-97359

Symmetrical Design Pleasing To The Eye

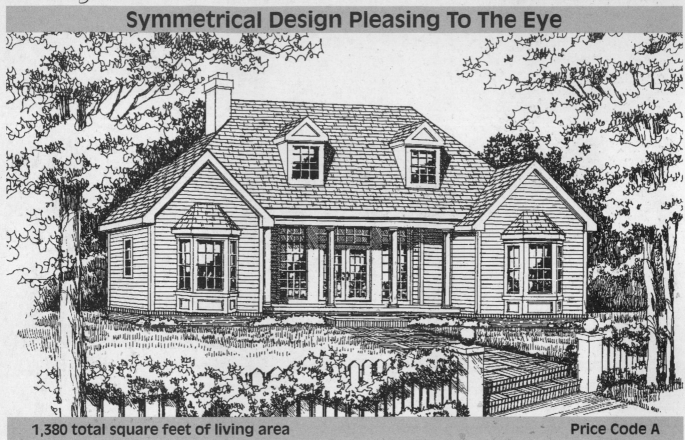

1,380 total square feet of living area

Price Code A

Special features

- Built-in bookshelves flank fireplace in great room
- Lots of storage space near laundry room and kitchen
- Covered porch has views of the backyard
- 3 bedrooms, 2 baths, optional 2-car side entry garage
- Basement, crawl space or slab foundation, please specify when ordering

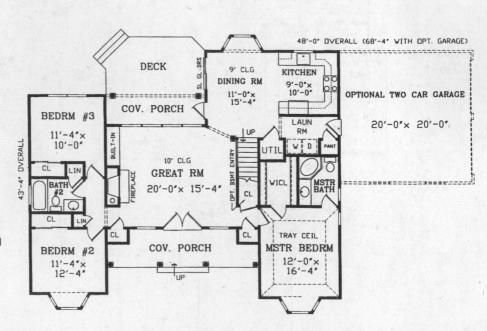

Alpine Style Creates Cozy Cabin Feel

1,577 total square feet of living area

Price Code B

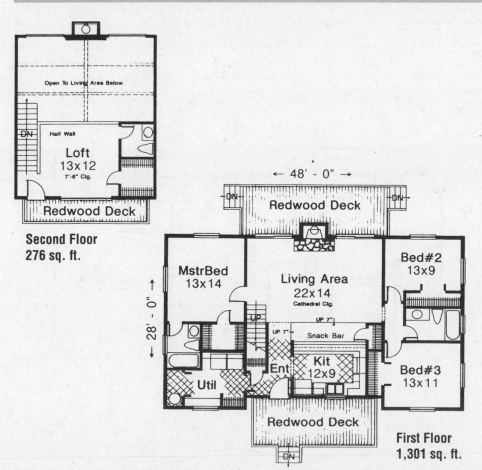

Open To Living Area Below.

DN

Half Wall

Loft
13x12
7'-6" Clg.

Redwood Deck

Second Floor
276 sq. ft.

← 48' - 0" →

DN **Redwood Deck** DN

28' - 0"

MstrBed
13x14

Living Area
22x14
Cathedral Clg.

Bed#2
13x9

UP

UP 7"

UP 7"

Snack Bar

Ent

Kit
12x9

Bed#3
13x11

Util

Redwood Deck

DN

First Floor
1,301 sq. ft.

Special features

- Large living area is a great gathering place with enormous stone fireplace, cathedral ceiling and kitchen with snack bar nearby
- Second floor loft has half-wall creating an open atmosphere
- 3 bedrooms, 2 1/2 baths
- Crawl space foundation

Distinctive Ranch

FREILING

1,962 total square feet of living area

Price Code C

Special features

- Formal dining room has a butler's pantry for entertaining
- Open living room offers a fireplace, built-in cabinetry and exceptional views to the outdoors
- Kitchen has work island and planning desk
- 3 bedrooms, 2 1/2 baths, 3-car garage
- Basement foundation

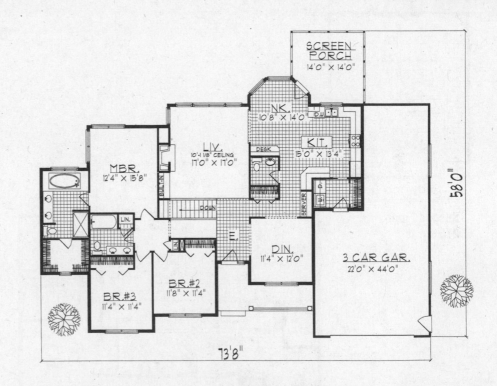

Vaulted Ceiling Frames Circle-Top Window

1,195 total square feet of living area   **Price Code AA**

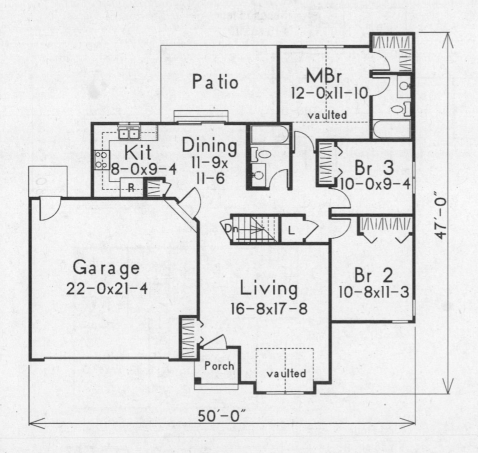

Special features

- Dining room opens onto the patio
- Master bedroom features vaulted ceiling, private bath and walk-in closet
- Coat closets located by both the entrances
- Convenient secondary entrance at the back of the garage
- 3 bedrooms, 2 baths, 2-car garage
- Basement foundation

TO ORDER BLUEPRINTS USE THE FORM ON PAGE 15 OR CALL TOLL-FREE 1-877-671-6036
View thousands more home plans online at www.familyhandyman.com/homeplans

229

Surrounding Porch For Country Views

1,428 total square feet of living area   Price Code A

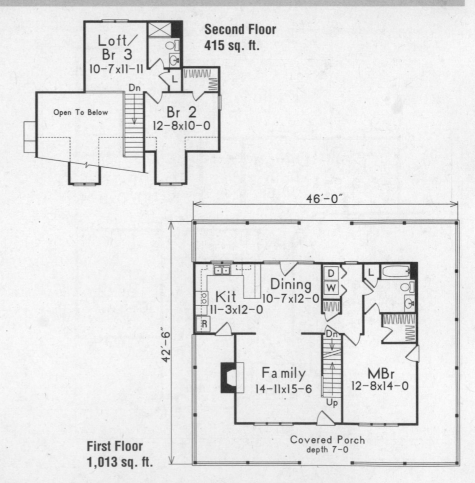

Loft/ Br 3
10-7x11-11

Second Floor
415 sq. ft.

L

Dn

Open To Below

Br 2
12-8x10-0

Special features

- Large vaulted family room opens to dining area and kitchen with breakfast bar and access to surrounding porch

- First floor master suite offers large bath, walk-in closet and nearby laundry facilities

- A spacious loft/bedroom #3 overlooking family room and an additional bedroom and bath conclude the second floor

- 3 bedrooms, 2 baths

- Basement foundation

46'-0"

Kit
11-3x12-0

Dining
10-7x12-0

D
W
L

42'-6"

Dn

Family
14-11x15-6

MBr
12-8x14-0

Up

Covered Porch
depth 7-0

First Floor
1,013 sq. ft.

Open Layout Ensures Easy Living

976 total square feet of living area

Price Code AA

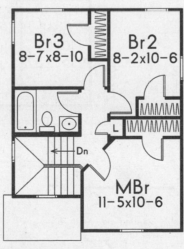

Second Floor
488 sq. ft.

Br3
8-7x8-10

Br2
8-2x10-6

MBr
11-5x10-6

Dn

L

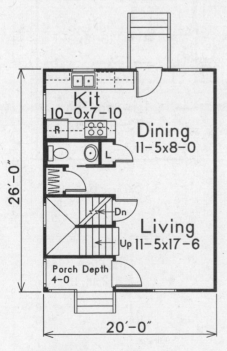

Kit
10-0x7-10

Dining
11-5x8-0

Living
Up 11-5x17-6

Dn

R

L

Porch Depth
4-0

26'-0"

20'-0"

First Floor
488 sq. ft.

Special features

- Cozy front porch opens into large living room
- Convenient half bath is located on first floor
- All bedrooms are located on second floor for privacy
- Dining room has access to the outdoors
- 3 bedrooms, 1 1/2 baths
- Basement foundation

Vacation Retreat With Attractive A-Frame Styling

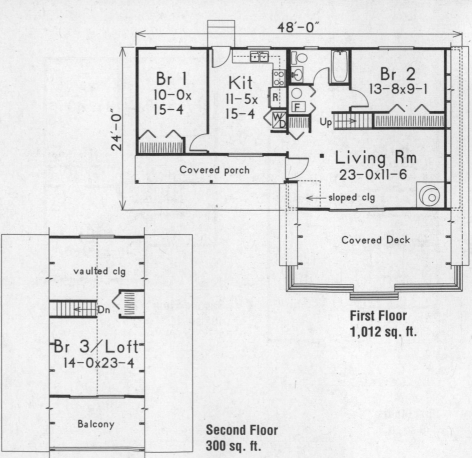

1,312 total square feet of living area

Price Code A

Special features

- Expansive deck extends directly off living area
- L-shaped kitchen is organized and efficient
- Bedroom to the left of the kitchen makes a great quiet retreat or office
- Living area flanked with windows for light
- 3 bedrooms, 1 1/2 baths
- Pier foundation

First Floor
1,012 sq. ft.

Second Floor
300 sq. ft.

232

TO ORDER BLUEPRINTS USE THE FORM ON PAGE 15 OR CALL TOLL-FREE 1-877-671-6036
View thousands more home plans online at www.familyhandyman.com/homeplans

Plan #703-HDG-99004

Covered Deck Off Breakfast Room

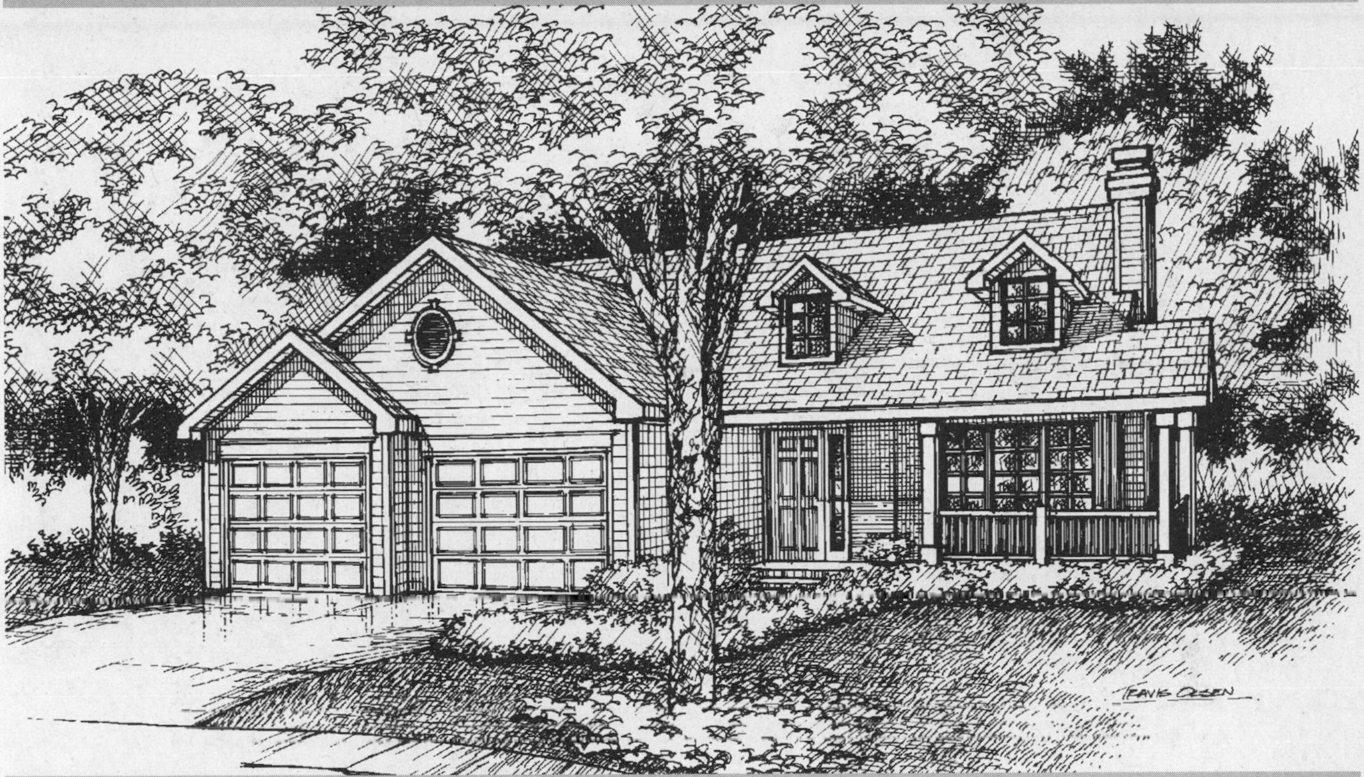

1,231 total square feet of living area **Price Code A**

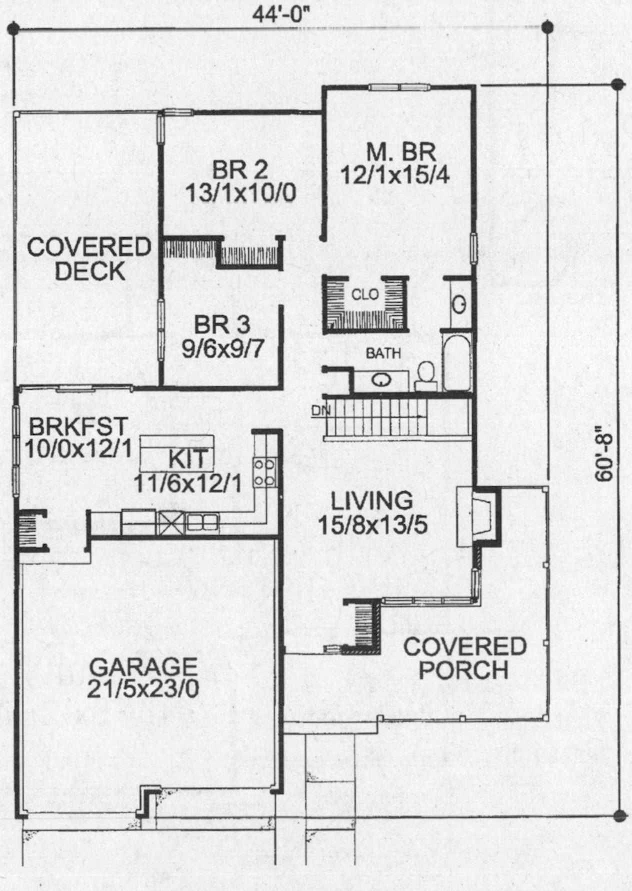
44'-0"
60'-8"
BR 2
13/1x10/0
M. BR
12/1x15/4
COVERED
DECK
CLO
BR 3
9/6x9/7
BATH
DN
BRKFST
10/0x12/1
KIT
11/6x12/1
LIVING
15/8x13/5
COVERED
PORCH
GARAGE
21/5x23/0

Special features

- Covered front porch
- Master bedroom has separate sink area
- Large island in kitchen for eat-in dining or preparation area
- 3 bedrooms, 1 bath, 2-car garage
- Basement foundation

Cottage-Style, Appealing And Cozy

828 total square feet of living area

Price Code AAA

Special features

- Vaulted ceiling in living area enhances space
- Convenient laundry room
- Sloped ceiling creates unique style in bedroom #2
- Efficient storage space under the stairs
- Covered entry porch provides cozy sitting area and plenty of shade
- 2 bedrooms, 1 bath
- Crawl space foundation

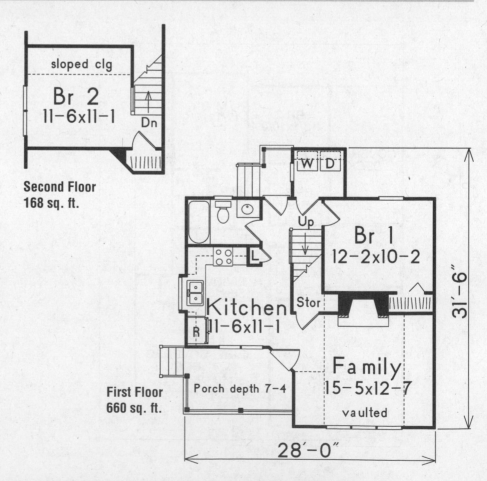

sloped clg

Br 2
11-6x11-1

Dn

Second Floor
168 sq. ft.

W D

Up

Br 1
12-2x10-2

L

Stor

Kitchen
11-6x11-1

R

Family
15-5x12-7

vaulted

31'-6"

First Floor
660 sq. ft.

Porch depth 7-4

28'-0"

TO ORDER BLUEPRINTS USE THE FORM ON PAGE 15 OR CALL TOLL-FREE 1-877-671-6036
View thousands more home plans online at www.familyhandyman.com/homeplans

Nestled Oasis Romances The Sun

1,584 total square feet of living area

Price Code B

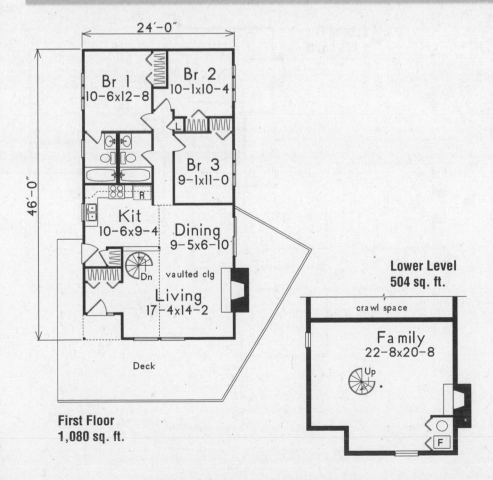

24'-0"

Br 1
10-6x12-8

Br 2
10-1x10-4

Br 3
9-1x11-0

46'-0"

Kit
10-6x9-4

Dining
9-5x6-10

vaulted clg

Dn

Living
17-4x14-2

Deck

**First Floor
1,080 sq. ft.**

**Lower Level
504 sq. ft.**

crawl space

Family
22-8x20-8

Up

F

Special features

- Vaulted living/dining room features stone fireplace, ascending spiral stair and separate vestibule with guest closet
- Space saving kitchen has an eat-in area and access to the deck
- Master bedroom adjoins a full bath
- 3 bedrooms, 2 baths
- Basement foundation, drawings also include crawl space and slab foundations

Distinctive Country Porch

2,182 total square feet of living area

Price Code C

Special features

- Meandering porch creates an inviting look

- Generous great room has four double-hung windows and gliding doors to exterior

- Highly functional kitchen features island/breakfast bar, menu desk and convenient pantry

- Each secondary bedroom includes generous closet and private bath

- 3 bedrooms, 3 1/2 baths, 2-car side entry garage

- Basement foundation

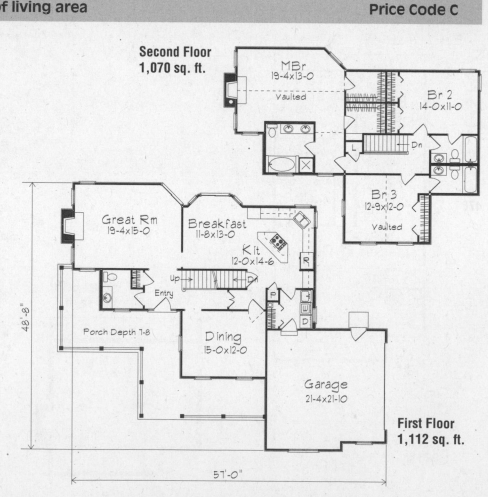

Second Floor
1,070 sq. ft.

MBr
19-4x13-0
Vaulted

Br 2
14-0x11-0

Br 3
12-9x12-0
Vaulted

Great Rm
19-4x15-0

Breakfast
11-8x13-0

Kit
12-0x14-6

Entry

Up

Dn

Porch Depth 7-8

Dining
15-0x12-0

Garage
21-4x21-10

48'-8"

57'-0"

First Floor
1,112 sq. ft.

Vaulted Living Area With Corner Fireplace

1,448 total square feet of living area

Price Code A

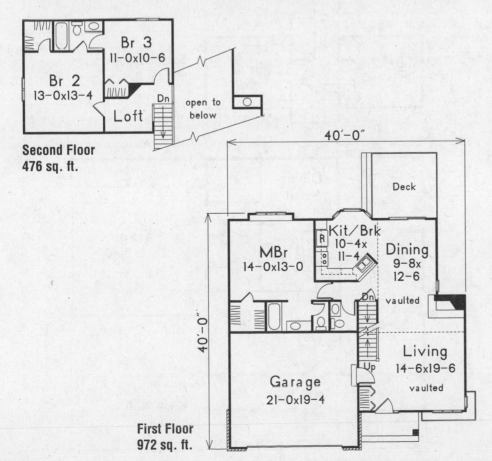

Second Floor
476 sq. ft.

Br 3
11-0x10-6

Br 2
13-0x13-4

Loft

Dn

open to below

40'-0"

Deck

MBr
14-0x13-0

Kit/Brk
10-4x
11-4

R

Dining
9-8x
12-6

40'-0"

Dn
vaulted

Living
14-6x19-6

vaulted

Up

Garage
21-0x19-4

First Floor
972 sq. ft.

Special features

- Dining room conveniently adjoins kitchen and accesses rear deck
- Private first floor master bedroom
- Secondary bedrooms share a bath and cozy loft area
- 3 bedrooms, 2 1/2 baths, 2-car garage
- Basement foundation

Roomy Two-Story Has Screened-In Rear Porch

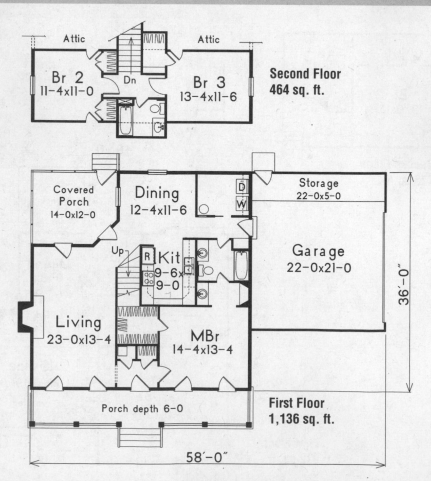

1,600 total square feet of living area

Price Code B

Special features

- Energy efficient home with 2" x 6" exterior walls

- First floor master suite accessible from two points of entry

- Master suite dressing area includes separate vanities and a mirrored make-up counter

- Second floor bedrooms with generous storage, share a full bath

- 3 bedrooms, 2 baths, 2-car side entry garage

- Crawl space foundation, drawings also include slab foundation

Attic

Br 2
11-4x11-0

Dn

Attic

Br 3
13-4x11-6

**Second Floor
464 sq. ft.**

Covered Porch
14-0x12-0

Dining
12-4x11-6

Storage
22-0x5-0

Up

Kit
9-6x
9-0

R

D
W

Garage
22-0x21-0

Living
23-0x13-4

MBr
14-4x13-4

36'-0"

Porch depth 6-0

**First Floor
1,136 sq. ft.**

58'-0"

1,550 total square feet of living area

Price Code B

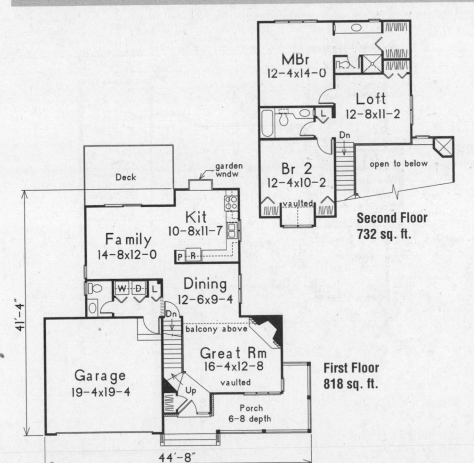

MBr
12-4x14-0

Loft
12-8x11-2

Br 2
12-4x10-2

open to below

**Second Floor
732 sq. ft.**

Deck

garden wndw

Kit
10-8x11-7

Family
14-8x12-0

Dining
12-6x9-4

balcony above

Great Rm
16-4x12-8
vaulted

Garage
19-4x19-4

Porch
6-8 depth

41'-4"

44'-8"

**First Floor
818 sq. ft.**

Special features

- Impressive front entrance with a wrap-around covered porch and raised foyer

- Corner fireplace provides a focal point in the vaulted great room

- Loft is easily converted to a third bedroom or activity center

- Large family/kitchen area includes greenhouse windows and access to the deck and utility area

- Secondary bedroom has a large dormer and window seat

- 2 bedrooms, 2 1/2 baths, 2-car garage

- Basement foundation

Country Living At Its Finest

1,993 total square feet of living area

Price Code C

Special features

- Kitchen and nook share open view onto the covered porch
- Ample-sized secondary bedrooms
- Well-designed master bath
- 3 bedrooms, 2 baths, 2-car side entry garage
- Slab foundation

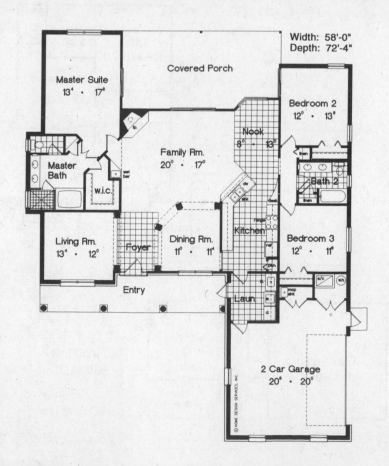

Width: 58'-0"
Depth: 72'-4"

Covered Porch

Master Suite
13⁴ • 17⁸

Master Bath

w.i.c.

wet bar

Family Rm.
20⁰ • 17⁰

Nook
8⁰ • 13⁰

Bedroom 2
12⁰ • 13⁸

Bath 2

Living Rm.
13⁴ • 12⁰

Foyer

Dining Rm.
11⁰ • 11⁴

Kitchen

Bedroom 3
12⁰ • 11⁸

Entry

Laun.

2 Car Garage
20⁰ • 20⁰

Nice-Sized Home Loaded With Charm

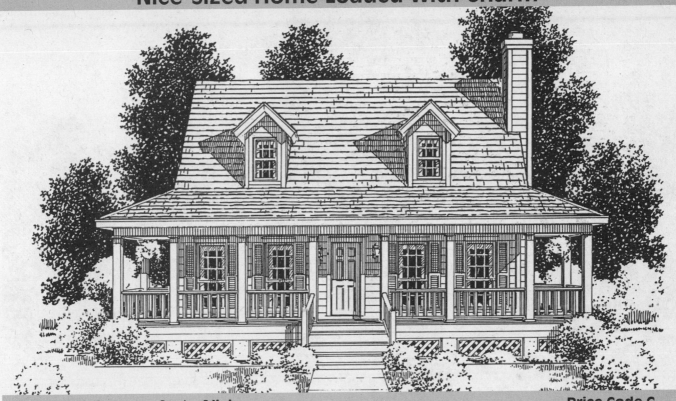

1,618 total square feet of living area

Price Code C

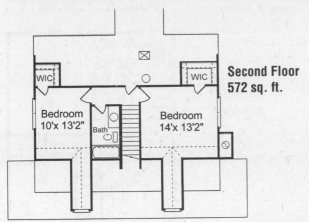

Second Floor
572 sq. ft.

WIC

WIC

Bedroom
10'x 13'2"

Bath

Bedroom
14'x 13'2"

Special features

- Secondary bedrooms with walk-in closets are located on the second floor and share a bath

- Utility room is tucked away in kitchen for convenience but out-of-sight

- Dining area is brightened by large bay window

- 3 bedrooms, 2 1/2 baths

- Slab or crawl space foundation, please specify when ordering

Width: 36'-6"
Depth: 34'-0"

Utility

Porch

Bath

Kitchen
13'6"x 12'

Dining
11'8"x 12'

WIC

Master
Bedroom
12'x 16'

WIC

Living
14'2"x 16'

First Floor
1,046 sq. ft.

Porch

Enhanced By Columned Porch

1,887 total square feet of living area

Price Code C

Special features

- Enormous great room is the heart of this home with an overlooking kitchen and dining room

- Formal dining room has lovely bay window

- Master bedroom has spacious bath with corner step-up tub, double vanity and walk-in closet

- 3 bedrooms, 2 1/2 baths, 2-car garage

- Basement foundation

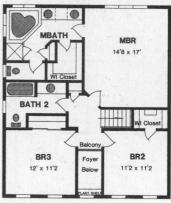

Second Floor
926 sq. ft.

MBATH

MBR
14'8 x 17'

WI Closet

BATH 2

WI Closet

Balcony

BR3
12' x 11'2

Foyer Below

BR2
11'2 x 11'2

PLANT SHELF

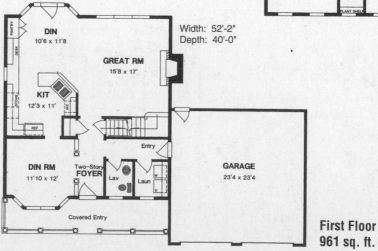

PANTRY

DESK

DIN
10'6 x 11'8

GREAT RM
15'8 x 17'

Width: 52'-2"
Depth: 40'-0"

STOVE

KIT
12'3 x 11'

REF

Entry

DIN RM
11'10 x 12'

Two-Story
FOYER

Lav

Laun

W

D

GARAGE
23'4 x 23'4

Covered Entry

First Floor
961 sq. ft.

TO ORDER BLUEPRINTS USE THE FORM ON PAGE 15 OR CALL TOLL-FREE 1-877-671-6036

View thousands more home plans online at www.familyhandyman.com/homeplans

Special Planning In This Compact Home

977 total square feet of living area

Price Code AA

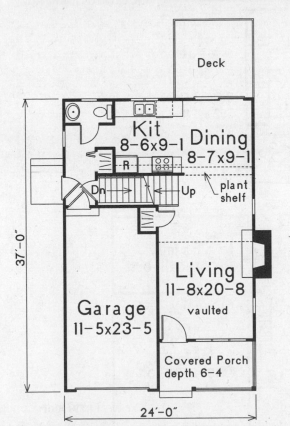

First Floor
545 sq. ft.

Deck

Kit
8-6x9-1

Dining
8-7x9-1

plant shelf

Dn

Up

Living
11-8x20-8
vaulted

Garage
11-5x23-5

Covered Porch
depth 6-4

37'-0"

24'-0"

Second Floor
432 sq. ft.

Br 2
9-1x10-1

Dn

L

Br 1
11-5x11-2

Special features

- Comfortable living room features a vaulted ceiling, fireplace, plant shelf and coat closet

- Both bedrooms are located on second floor and share a bath with double-bowl vanity and linen closet

- Sliding glass doors in dining room provide access to the deck

- 2 bedrooms, 1 1/2 baths, 1-car garage

- Basement foundation

TO ORDER BLUEPRINTS USE THE FORM ON PAGE 15 OR CALL TOLL-FREE 1-877-671-6036
View thousands more home plans online at www.familyhandyman.com/homeplans

243

Formal And Informal Gathering Rooms

1,314 total square feet of living area

Price Code A

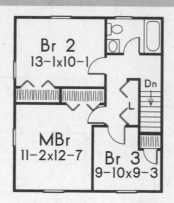

**Second Floor
552 sq. ft.**

Br 2
13-1x10-1

Dn

MBr
11-2x12-7

Br 3
9-10x9-3

Special features

- U-shaped kitchen joins cozy dining area

- Family room has direct access into garage

- Roomy closets serve the second floor bedrooms

- 3 bedrooms, 1 1/2 baths, 2-car garage

- Basement foundation, drawings also include crawl space foundation

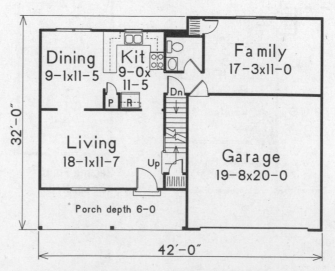

Dining
9-1x11-5

Kit
9-0x
11-5

Family
17-3x11-0

Dn

Living
18-1x11-7

Up

Garage
19-8x20-0

32'-0"

Porch depth 6-0

42'-0"

**First Floor
762 sq. ft.**

244

TO ORDER BLUEPRINTS USE THE FORM ON PAGE 15 OR CALL TOLL-FREE 1-877-671-6036
View thousands more home plans online at www.familyhandyman.com/homeplans

Unique Angled Entry

1,150 total square feet of living area

Price Code AA

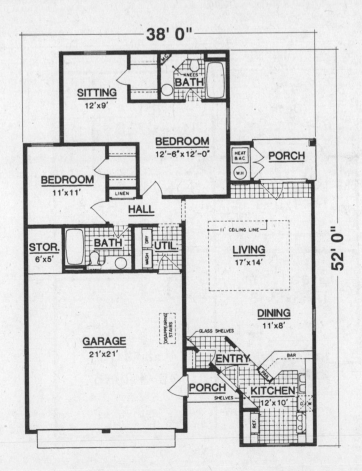

38' 0"

SITTING
12'x9'

BATH
KNEES

BEDROOM
12'-6"x12'-0"

HEAT & AC
W.H.

PORCH

BEDROOM
11'x11'

LINEN

HALL

STOR.
6'x5'

BATH

UTIL.

11' CEILING LINE

LIVING
17'x14'

52' 0"

GARAGE
21'x21'

DISAPPEARING STAIRS

GLASS SHELVES

DINING
11'x8'

BAR

ENTRY

PORCH
SHELVES

KITCHEN
12'x10'

REF

Special features

- Master suite has its own private sitting area
- Living and dining rooms have 11' high box ceilings
- Ornate trim work accents the wood sided exterior
- 2 bedrooms, 2 baths, 2-car garage
- Slab or crawl space foundation, please specify when ordering

Breakfast Bay Area Opens To Deck

1,020 total square feet of living area

Price Code AA

Special features

- Kitchen features open stairs, pass-through to great room, pantry and deck access

- Master bedroom features private entrance to bath, large walk-in closet and sliding doors to deck

- Informal entrance into home through the garage

- Great room with vaulted ceiling and fireplace

- 2 bedrooms, 1 bath, 2-car garage

- Basement foundation

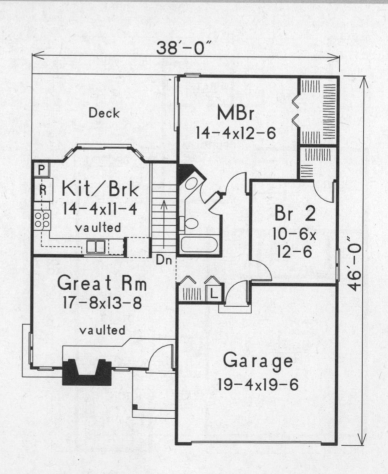

38'-0"

Deck

MBr
14-4x12-6

Kit/Brk
14-4x11-4
vaulted

Br 2
10-6x
12-6

46'-0"

Dn

Great Rm
17-8x13-8

vaulted

Garage
19-4x19-6

Shakes Accent Gables

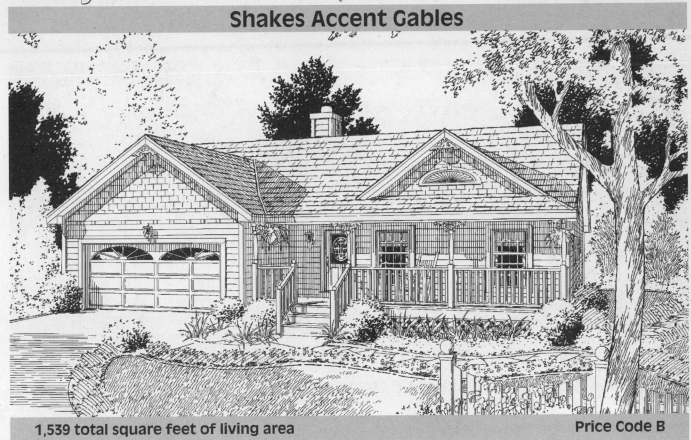

1,539 total square feet of living area

Price Code B

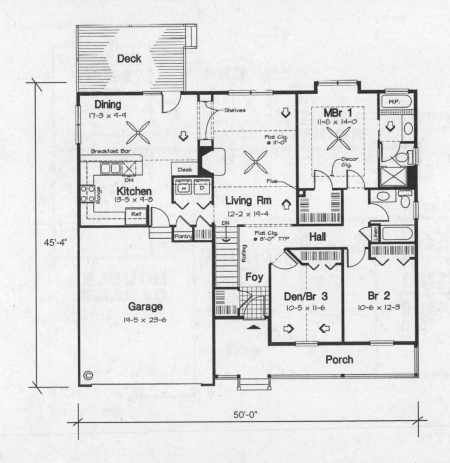

Deck

Dining
17-3 x 9-9

Shelves

MBr 1
11-8 x 14-0

Breakfast Bar

Flat Clg.
@ 11'-0"

Desk

Decor Clg.

Kitchen
13-5 x 9-8

Living Rm
12-2 x 19-4

Flue

Pantry

Flat Clg.
@ 8'-0" TYP.

Hall

Foy

Linen

45'-4"

Garage
19-5 x 23-6

Den/Br 3
10-5 x 11-6

Br 2
10-6 x 12-3

Porch

50'-0"

Special features

- A tray ceiling tops the master bedroom
- The peninsula counter in the kitchen doubles as a breakfast bar
- A walk-in closet in the foyer has space for additional storage
- 3 bedrooms, 2 baths, 2-car garage
- Basement, crawl space or slab foundation, please specify when ordering

Angled Eating Bar Great For Family Living

1,686 total square feet of living area

Price Code B

Special features

- Secondary bedrooms are separate from master suite maintaining privacy
- Island in kitchen is ideal for food preparation
- Dramatic foyer leads to great room
- Covered side porch has direct access into great room
- 3 bedrooms, 2 baths, 2-car side entry garage
- Slab foundation

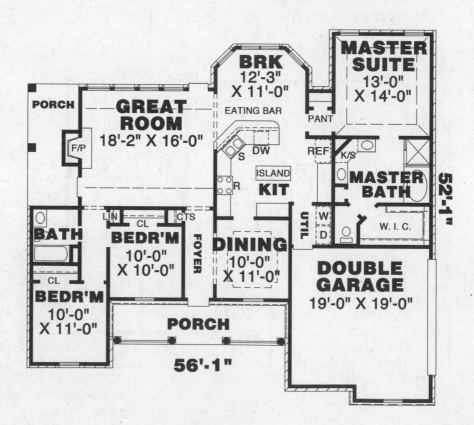

Flexible Design Is Popular

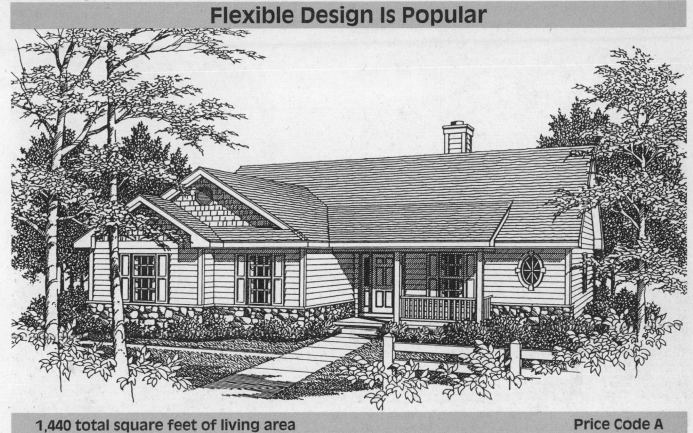

1,440 total square feet of living area

Price Code A

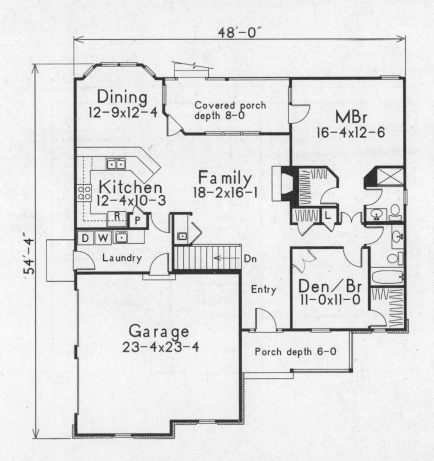

48'-0"

Dining
12-9x12-4

Covered porch
depth 8-0

MBr
16-4x12-6

Kitchen
12-4x10-3

Family
18-2x16-1

Laundry

Dn

Entry

Den/Br
11-0x11-0

Garage
23-4x23-4

Porch depth 6-0

54'-4"

Special features

- Open floor plan with access to covered porches in front and back
- Lots of linen, pantry and closet space throughout
- Laundry/mud room between kitchen and garage is a convenient feature
- 2 bedrooms, 2 baths
- Basement foundation

Handsome Stonework

1,124 total square feet of living area

Price Code AA

Special features

- Varied ceiling heights throughout this home
- Enormous bayed breakfast room overlooks great room with fireplace
- Conveniently located washer and dryer closet
- 3 bedrooms, 2 baths, 2-car drive under garage
- Walk-out basement foundation

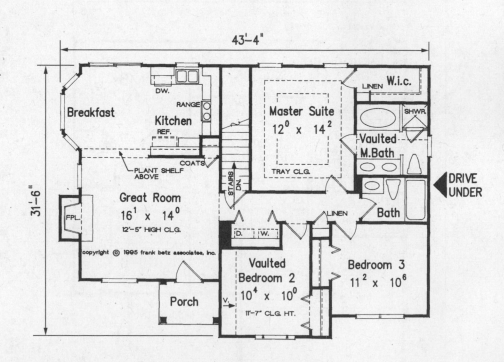

TO ORDER BLUEPRINTS USE THE FORM ON PAGE 15 OR CALL TOLL-FREE 1-877-671-6036
View thousands more home plans online at www.familyhandyman.com/homeplans

Charming Wrap-Around Porch

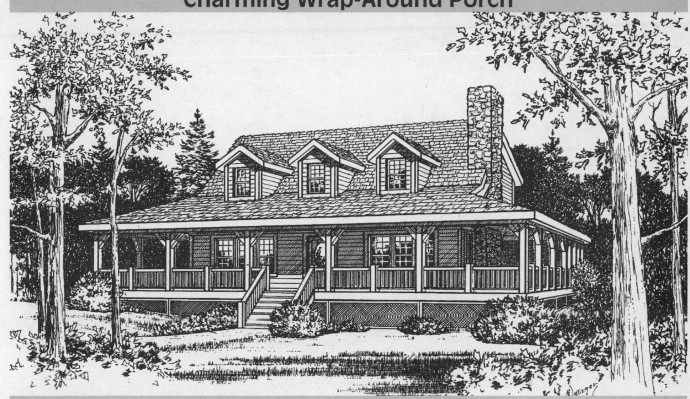

1,879 total square feet of living area   **Price Code C**

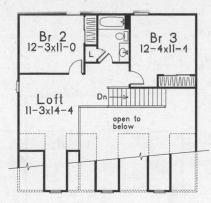

Br 2
12-3x11-0

Br 3
12-4x11-4

Loft
11-3x14-4

Dn

open to below

Second Floor
565 sq. ft.

Stor

F W

MBr
12-10x13-8

Screened Porch

P

R

Kit
11-3x9-7

W
D

Up

Dining
11-7x14-4

Great Rm
21-9x15-8

50'-0"

42'-0"

Covered porch depth 8-0

First Floor
1,314 sq. ft.

Special features

- Open floor plan on both floors makes home appear larger
- Loft area overlooks great room or can become an optional fourth bedroom
- Large walk-in pantry in kitchen and large storage in rear of home with access from exterior
- 3 bedrooms, 2 baths
- Crawl space foundation

Classic Ranch, Pleasant Covered Front Porch

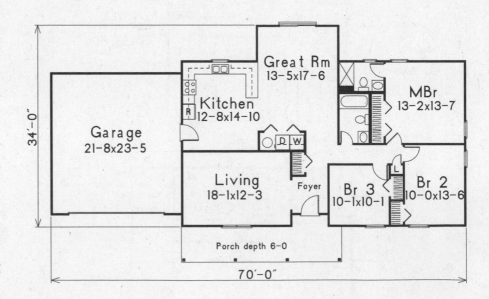

1,416 total square feet of living area

Price Code A

Special features

- Excellent floor plan eases traffic
- Master bedroom features private bath
- Foyer opens to both formal living room and informal family room
- Great room has access to the outdoors through sliding doors
- 3 bedrooms, 2 baths, 2-car garage
- Crawl space foundation, drawings also include basement foundation

Great Rm
13-5x17-6

MBr
13-2x13-7

Kitchen
12-8x14-10

Garage
21-8x23-5

34'-0"

Living
18-1x12-3

Foyer

Br 3
10-1x10-1

Br 2
10-0x13-6

Porch depth 6-0

70'-0"

High Ceilings Create A Feeling Of Luxury

1,707 total square feet of living area

Price Code C

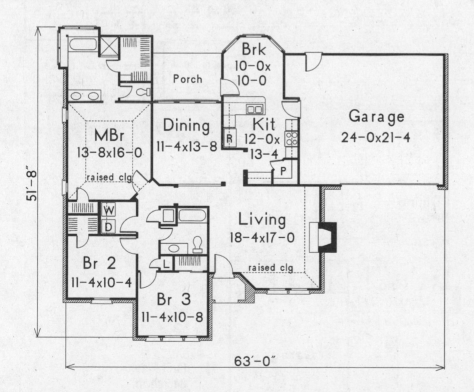

Special features

- The formal living room off the entry hall has a high sloping ceiling and prominent fireplace

- Kitchen and breakfast area allow access to garage and rear porch

- Oversized garage provides direct access to the kitchen

- Master bedroom has impressive vaulted ceiling, luxurious master bath, large walk-in closet and separate tub and shower

- Utility room conveniently located near bedrooms

- 3 bedrooms, 2 baths, 2-car garage

- Slab foundation

Floor-To-Ceiling Window

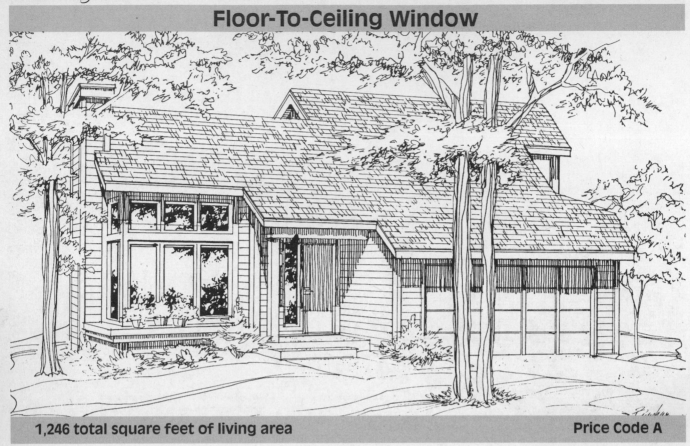

1,246 total square feet of living area

Price Code A

Special features

- Corner living room window adds openness and light
- Out-of-the-way kitchen with dining area accesses the outdoors
- Private first floor master bedroom with corner window
- Large walk-in closet is located in bedroom #3
- Easily built perimeter allows economical construction
- 3 bedrooms, 2 baths, 2-car garage
- Basement foundation

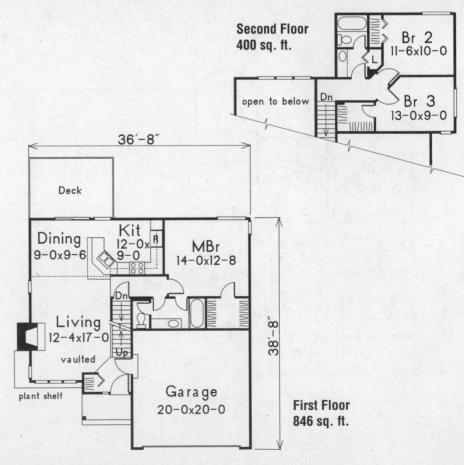

Second Floor 400 sq. ft.

Br 2 11-6x10-0

open to below

Br 3 13-0x9-0

36'-8"

Deck

Dining 9-0x9-6

Kit 12-0x 9-0

MBr 14-0x12-8

Living 12-4x17-0 vaulted

plant shelf

Garage 20-0x20-0

38'-8"

First Floor 846 sq. ft.

Expansive Wrap-Around Porch

1,668 total square feet of living area

Price Code B

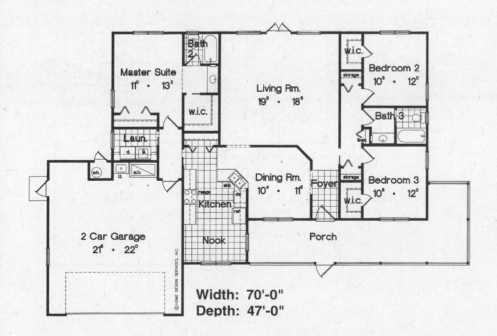

Width: 70'-0"
Depth: 47'-0"

Special features

- Master suite separated from other bedrooms for privacy
- Breakfast nook is an added bonus in kitchen
- All bedrooms include walk-in closets as well as additional storage space
- 3 bedrooms, 2 baths, 2-car garage
- Slab foundation

Handsome Octagon-Shaped Breakfast Room

Rear View

1,583 total square feet of living area

Price Code B

Special features

- Dining area is open to living room making a terrific gathering place

- Cheerful skylight in private master bath

- Living room has center fireplace creating a cozy atmosphere

- 3 bedrooms, 2 baths, 2-car garage

- Basement, crawl space or slab foundation, please specify when ordering

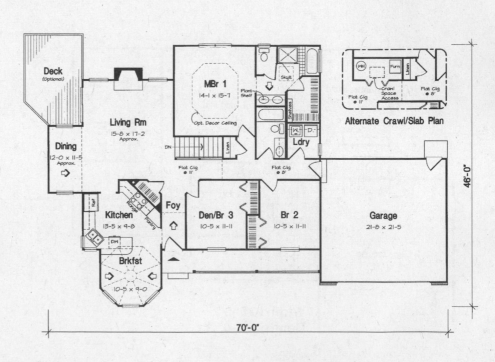

Deck (Optional)

Living Rm
15-8 x 17-2
Approx.

Dining
12-0 x 11-5
Approx.

MBr 1
14-1 x 15-7

Opt. Decor Ceiling

Skylt

Plant Shelf

DN

Flat Clg
• 11'

Ldry

Flat Clg
• 8'

Kitchen
13-5 x 9-8

Foy

Den/Br 3
10-5 x 11-11

Br 2
10-5 x 11-11

Garage
21-8 x 21-5

Ref

DW

Brkfst
10-5 x 9-0

Alternate Crawl/Slab Plan

Flat Clg
• 11'

Crawl Space Access

Flat Clg
• 8'

70'-0"

46'-0"

TO ORDER BLUEPRINTS USE THE FORM ON PAGE 15 OR CALL TOLL-FREE 1-877-671-6036

View thousands more home plans online at www.familyhandyman.com/homeplans

Cozy And Functional Design

1,285 total square feet of living area

Price Code A

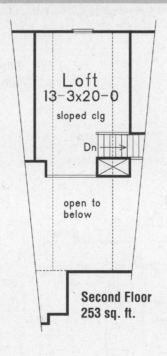

Loft
13-3x20-0
sloped clg

Dn

open to below

**Second Floor
253 sq. ft.**

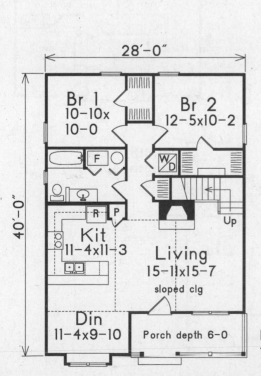

28'-0"

Br 1
10-10x
10-0

Br 2
12-5x10-2

40'-0"

W/D

F

R   P

Kit
11-4x11-3

Living
15-11x15-7
sloped clg

Up

Din
11-4x9-10

Porch depth 6-0

**First Floor
1,032 sq. ft.**

Special features

- Dining nook creates warm feeling with sunny box bay window
- Second floor loft perfect for recreation space or office hideaway
- Bedrooms include walk-in closets allowing extra storage space
- Kitchen, dining and living areas combine making perfect gathering place
- 2 bedrooms, 1 bath
- Crawl space foundation

TO ORDER BLUEPRINTS USE THE FORM ON PAGE 15 OR CALL TOLL-FREE 1-877-671-6036
View thousands more home plans online at www.familyhandyman.com/homeplans

257

All The Features

2,643 total square feet of living area

Price Code E

Special features

- Living and dining rooms combine to create a lovely area for entertaining
- Kitchen has snack bar which overlooks octagon-shaped dining area
- Family room is centrally located with entertainment center
- Private study at rear of home
- 4 bedrooms, 2 1/2 baths, 2-car side entry garage
- Basement foundation

Second Floor 768 sq. ft.

First Floor 1,875 sq. ft.

Width: 72'-8"
Depth: 50'-10"

TO ORDER BLUEPRINTS USE THE FORM ON PAGE 15 OR CALL TOLL-FREE 1-877-671-6036
View thousands more home plans online at www.familyhandyman.com/homeplans

Cozy Traditional

1,310 total square feet of living area

Price Code A

WIDTH 49–10

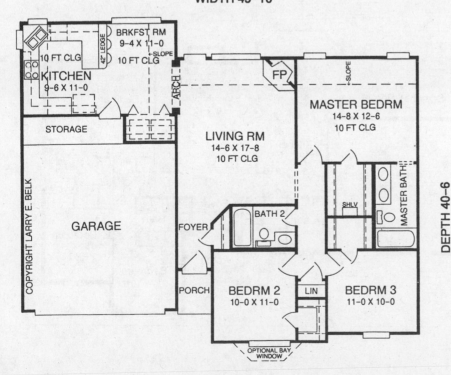

BRKFST RM
9-4 X 11-0
10 FT CLG

42" LEDGE

10 FT CLG

KITCHEN
9-6 X 11-0

STORAGE

COPYRIGHT LARRY E. BELK

GARAGE

ARCH

LIVING RM
14-6 X 17-8
10 FT CLG

FOYER

PORCH

BATH 2

FP

SLOPE

MASTER BEDRM
14-8 X 12-6
10 FT CLG

SHLV

MASTER BATH

DEPTH 40-6

BEDRM 2
10-0 X 11-0

LIN

BEDRM 3
11-0 X 10-0

OPTIONAL BAY WINDOW

Special features

- Family room features corner fireplace adding warmth
- Efficiently designed kitchen has a corner sink with windows
- Master bedroom includes large walk-in closet and private bath
- 3 bedrooms, 2 baths, 2-car garage
- Crawl space or slab foundation, please specify when ordering

Open And Spacious Feel To This Home

1,611 total square feet of living area   **Price Code B**

Special features

- Sliding doors lead to a delightful screened porch creating a wonderful summer retreat

- Master bedroom has a lavishly appointed dressing room and large walk-in closet

- The kitchen offers an abundance of cabinets and counter space with convenient access to the laundry room and garage

- 3 bedrooms, 2 baths, 2-car side entry garage

- Basement foundation

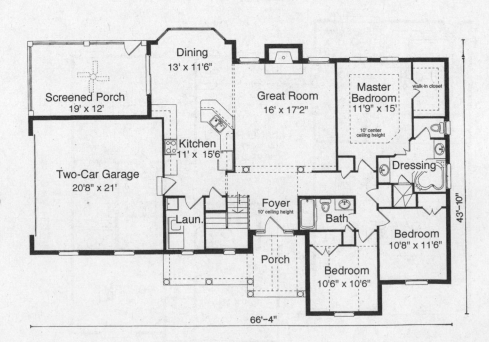

Cozy Home For Family Living

1,612 total square feet of living area   **Price Code B**

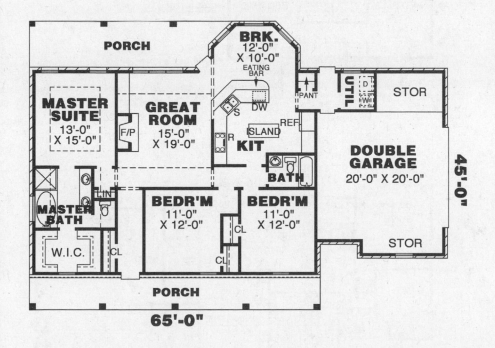

Special features

- Covered porch in rear of home creates an outdoor living area
- Master suite is separated from other bedrooms for privacy
- Eating bar in kitchen extends into breakfast area for additional seating
- 3 bedrooms, 2 baths, 2-car side entry garage
- Slab foundation

Bath With Double Dressing Areas

1,895 total square feet of living area

Price Code C

Special features

- Kitchen overlooks both the breakfast nook and living room for an open floor plan

- Living area has built-in bookshelves flanking fireplace

- Master suite has private bath and access to covered rear porch

- 3 bedrooms, 2 1/2 baths, 2-car garage

- Basement, crawl space or slab foundation, please specify when ordering

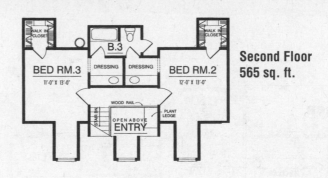

Second Floor 565 sq. ft.

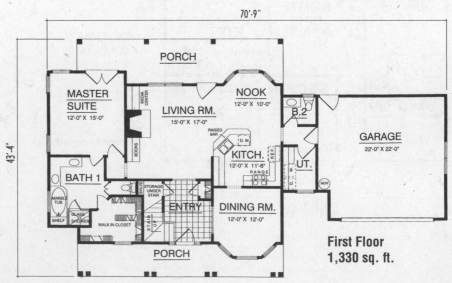

First Floor 1,330 sq. ft.

Three-Level Design Has It All

1,562 total square feet of living area

Price Code B

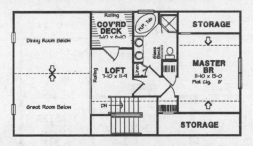

Second Floor 500 sq. ft.

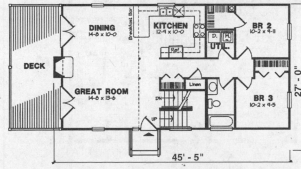

First Floor 1,062 sq. ft.

45' - 5"

27' - 0"

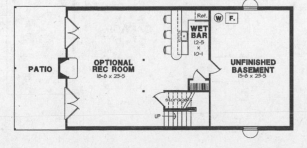

Optional Lower Level 668 sq. ft.

Special features

- Two sets of double-doors in great room and dining area fill home with sunlight

- Kitchen with breakfast bar allows for additional dining space

- Unique second floor loft is open to first floor and has a private covered deck

- Optional lower level has an additional 668 square feet of living area

- 3 bedrooms, 2 baths

- Basement foundation

Ranch-Style Home With Many Extras

1,295 total square feet of living area

Price Code A

Special features

- Wrap-around porch is a lovely place for dining

- A fireplace gives a stunning focal point to the great room that is heightened with a sloped ceiling

- The master suite is full of luxurious touches such as a walk-in closet and a lush private bath

- 2 bedrooms, 2 baths, 2-car garage

- Basement foundation

Fantastic A-Frame Get-Away

1,224 total square feet of living area

Price Code A

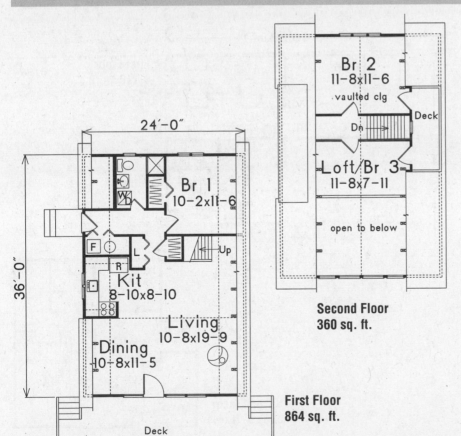

24'-0"

36'-0"

Br 1
10-2x11-6

Kit
8-10x8-10

Living
10-8x19-9

Dining
10-8x11-5

F **L** **R** **Up**

Deck

First Floor
864 sq. ft.

Br 2
11-8x11-6

vaulted clg

Dn **Deck**

Loft/Br 3
11-8x7-11

open to below

Second Floor
360 sq. ft.

Special features

- Get away to this cozy A-frame featuring three bedrooms
- Living/dining room with free-standing fireplace walks out onto a large deck
- U-shaped kitchen has a unique built-in table at end of counter for intimate gatherings
- Both second floor bedrooms enjoy their own private balcony
- 3 bedrooms, 1 bath
- Crawl space foundation

This Home Has Alpine Appeal

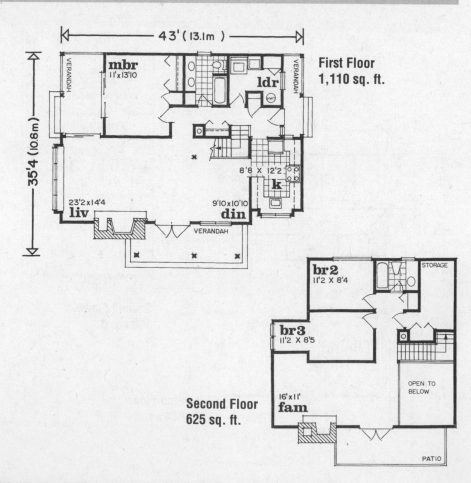

1,735 total square feet of living area

Price Code B

Special features

- Living and dining areas combine making an ideal space for entertaining

- Master bedroom accesses rear verandah through sliding glass doors

- Second floor includes cozy family room with patio deck just outside of the secondary bedrooms

- 3 bedrooms, 2 baths

- Crawl space foundation

43' (13.1m)

35'4 (10.8m)

First Floor 1,110 sq. ft.

mbr 11'x13'10

ldr

VERANDAH

liv 23'2x14'4

din 9'10x10'10

k 8'8 X 12'2

VERANDAH

Second Floor 625 sq. ft.

br2 11'2 X 8'4

STORAGE

br3 11'2 X 8'5

fam 16'x11'

OPEN TO BELOW

PATIO

Contemporary Design For Open Family Living

1,516 total square feet of living area

Price Code B

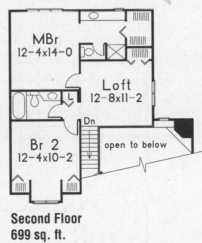

MBr
12-4x14-0

Loft
12-8x11-2

Br 2
12-4x10-2

open to below

Dn

Second Floor
699 sq. ft.

Special features

- All living and dining areas are interconnected for a spacious look and easy movement
- Covered entrance leads into sunken great room with a rugged corner fireplace
- Family kitchen combines practicality with access to other areas
- Second floor loft, opens to rooms below, converts to third bedroom
- Dormer in bedroom #2 adds interest
- 3 bedrooms, 2 1/2 baths, 2-car garage
- Basement foundation

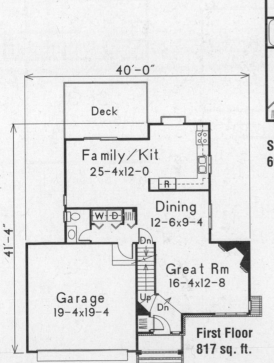

40'-0"

Deck

Family/Kit
25-4x12-0

R

W D

Dining
12-6x9-4

Dn

Great Rm
16-4x12-8

Up

Dn

Garage
19-4x19-4

41'-4"

First Floor
817 sq. ft.

TO ORDER BLUEPRINTS USE THE FORM ON PAGE 15 OR CALL TOLL-FREE 1-877-671-6036
View thousands more home plans online at www.familyhandyman.com/homeplans

267

Perfect Vacation Home

1,230 total square feet of living area

Price Code A

Special features

- Spacious living room accesses huge sun deck
- One of the second floor bedrooms features a balcony overlooking the deck
- Kitchen with dining area accesses the outdoors
- Washer and dryer tucked under stairs
- 3 bedrooms, 1 bath
- Crawl space foundation, drawings also include slab foundation

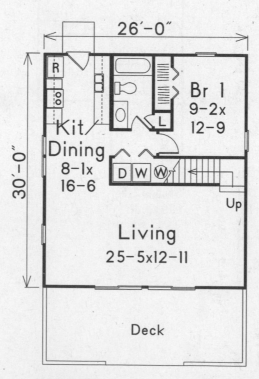

26'-0"

30'-0"

Kit/Dining
8-1x 16-6

R

D W W

Br 1
9-2x 12-9

L

Up

Living
25-5x12-11

Deck

First Floor
780 sq. ft.

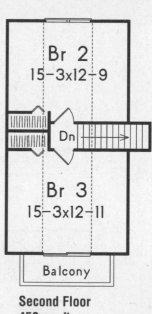

Br 2
15-3x12-9

Dn

Br 3
15-3x12-11

Balcony

Second Floor
450 sq. ft.

TO ORDER BLUEPRINTS USE THE FORM ON PAGE 15 OR CALL TOLL-FREE 1-877-671-6036
View thousands more home plans online at www.familyhandyman.com/homeplans

Chalet Cottage

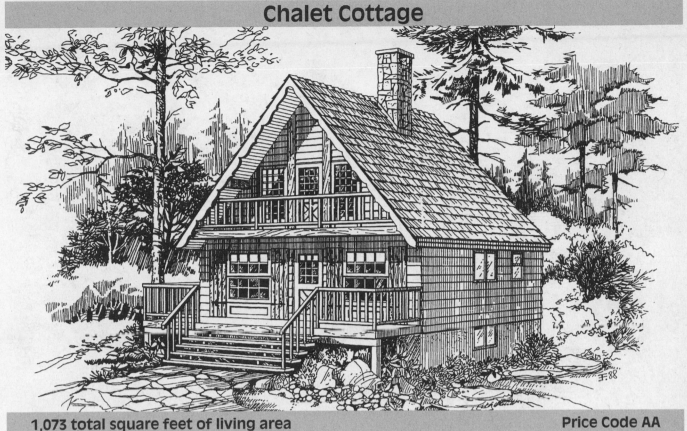

1,073 total square feet of living area

Price Code AA

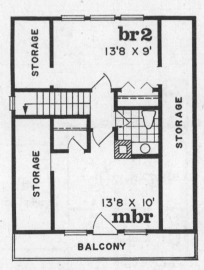

Second Floor
401 sq. ft.

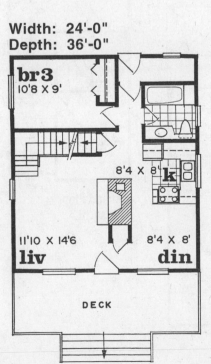

Width: 24'-0"
Depth: 36'-0"

First Floor
672 sq. ft.

Special features

- The front-facing deck and covered balcony add to outdoor living areas
- The fireplace is the main focus in the living room, separating the living room from the dining room
- Three large storage areas are found on the second floor
- 3 bedrooms, 1 1/2 baths
- Basement or crawl space foundation, please specify when ordering

TO ORDER BLUEPRINTS USE THE FORM ON PAGE 15 OR CALL TOLL-FREE 1-877-671-6036
View thousands more home plans online at www.familyhandyman.com/homeplans

269

Dining With A View

1,524 total square feet of living area

Price Code B

Special features

- Delightful balcony overlooks two-story entry illuminated by oval window
- Roomy first floor master suite offers quiet privacy
- All bedrooms feature one or more walk-in closets
- 3 bedrooms, 2 1/2 baths, 2-car garage
- Basement foundation

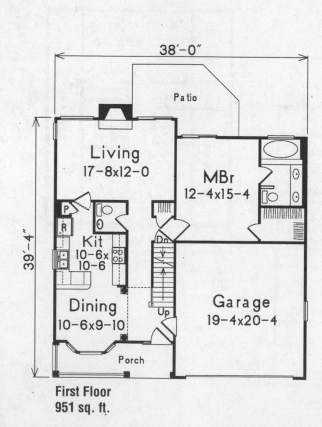

38'-0"

Patio

Living
17-8x12-0

MBr
12-4x15-4

Kit
10-6x
10-6

P
R

Dining
10-6x9-10

Dn

Up

Garage
19-4x20-4

Porch

39'-4"

First Floor
951 sq. ft.

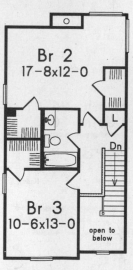

Br 2
17-8x12-0

L

Dn

Br 3
10-6x13-0

open to
below

Second Floor
573 sq. ft.

TO ORDER BLUEPRINTS USE THE FORM ON PAGE 15 OR CALL TOLL-FREE 1-877-671-6036
View thousands more home plans online at www.familyhandyman.com/homeplans

Stone Accents Create A Tudor Feel

977 total square feet of living area

Price Code AA

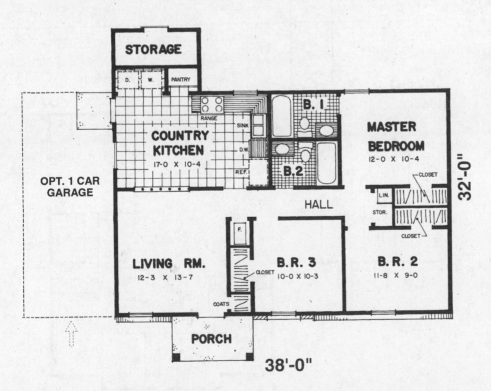

Special features

- Large storage closet ideal for patio furniture storage or lawn equipment

- Large kitchen with enough room for dining looks into oversized living room

- Front covered porch adds charm

- 3 bedrooms, 2 baths, optional 1-car garage

- Slab or crawl space foundation, please specify when ordering

Plenty Of Built-Ins

3,012 total square feet of living area

Price Code E

Special features

- Master suite has sitting area with entertainment center/library

- Utility room has a sink and includes lots of storage and counterspace

- Future space above garage has its own stairway

- Bonus area has an additional 336 square feet of living area

- 4 bedrooms, 3 1/2 baths, 2-car side entry garage

- Crawl space, slab or basement foundation, please specify when ordering

Second Floor 810 sq. ft.

First Floor 2,202 sq. ft.

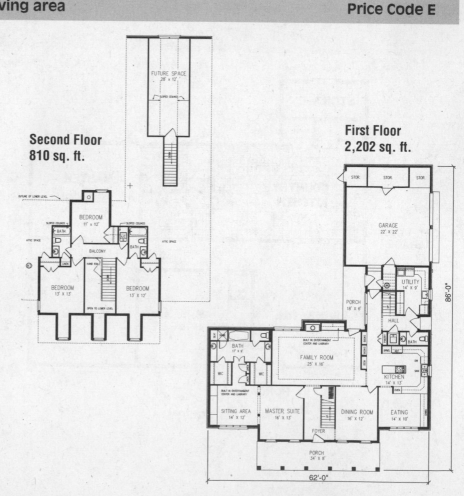

Cleverly Angled Walls Add Interest To Home

1,400 total square feet of living area

Price Code A

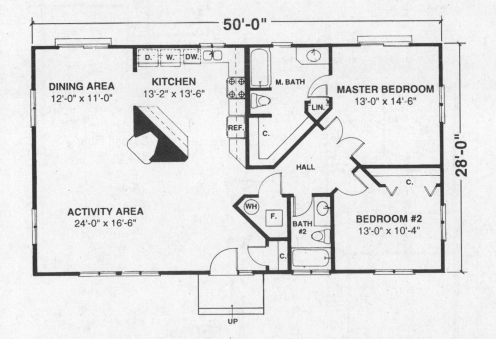

50'-0"

28'-0"

DINING AREA
12'-0" x 11'-0"

KITCHEN
13'-2" x 13'-6"

D. | W. | DW.

M. BATH

MASTER BEDROOM
13'-0" x 14'-6"

LIN.

REF.

C.

HALL

C.

ACTIVITY AREA
24'-0" x 16'-6"

WH

F.

BATH #2

BEDROOM #2
13'-0" x 10'-4"

C.

C.

UP

Special features

- Inside and out, this home is pleasingly different
- Activity area showcases large free-standing fireplace and spacious dining room with views
- Laundry area is provided in a very functional kitchen
- Master suite with double-doors is a grand bedroom with nice amenities
- 2 bedrooms, 2 baths
- Crawl space foundation

Second Floor Loft Is Ideal Office Area

1,702 total square feet of living area

Price Code B

Special features

- Second floor loft has wall of windows making this space functional and bright
- Sloped ceilings in both bedrooms
- Kitchen and dining area combine to create a terrific gathering space
- 2 bedrooms, 2 baths, 2-car garage
- Slab foundation

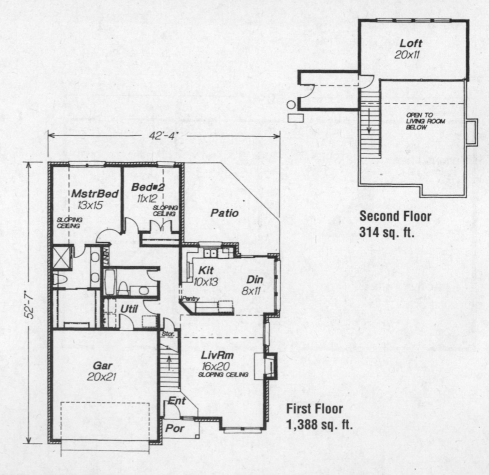

Loft
20x11

OPEN TO LIVING ROOM BELOW

Second Floor
314 sq. ft.

42'-4"

MstrBed
13x15
SLOPING CEILING

Bed#2
11x12
SLOPING CEILING

Patio

Kit
10x13

Din
8x11

Pantry

Util

Stor.

52'-7"

Gar
20x21

LivRm
16x20
SLOPING CEILING

Ent

Por

First Floor
1,388 sq. ft.

TO ORDER BLUEPRINTS USE THE FORM ON PAGE 15 OR CALL TOLL-FREE 1-877-671-6036
View thousands more home plans online at www.familyhandyman.com/homeplans

Breathtaking Balcony Overlook

1,299 total square feet of living area

Price Code A

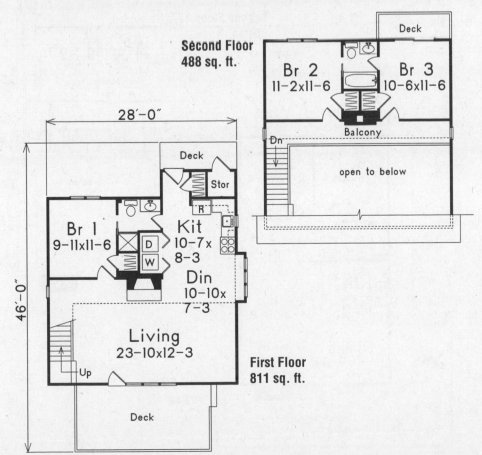

Second Floor
488 sq. ft.

Deck

Br 2
11–2x11–6

Br 3
10–6x11–6

Balcony

Dn

open to below

28'–0"

46'–0"

Deck

Stor

R

Br 1
9–11x11–6

Kit
10–7 x
8–3

D | W

Din
10–10x
7–3

Living
23–10x12–3

Up

Deck

First Floor
811 sq. ft.

Special features

- Convenient storage for skis, etc. located outside front entrance
- Kitchen and dining room receive light from box bay window
- Large vaulted living room features cozy fireplace and overlook from second floor balcony
- Two second floor bedrooms share jack and jill bath
- Second floor balcony extends over entire length of living room below
- 3 bedrooms, 2 baths
- Crawl space foundation, drawings also include slab foundation

Leisure Living With Interior Surprise

1,354 total square feet of living area

Price Code A

Special features

- Soaring ceilings highlight the kitchen, living and dining areas creating dramatic excitement

- A spectacular large deck surrounds the front and both sides of home

- An impressive U-shaped kitchen has wrap-around breakfast bar and shares fantastic views with both the first and second floors through an awesome wall of glass

- Two bedrooms with a bath, a loft for sleeping and second floor balcony overlooking living area, complete the home

- 3 bedrooms, 1 bath

- Crawl space foundation

Second Floor
394 sq. ft.

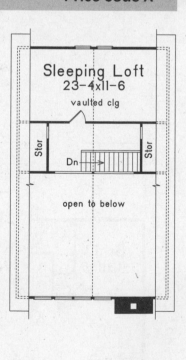

Sleeping Loft
23-4x11-6
vaulted clg

Stor

Dn

Stor

open to below

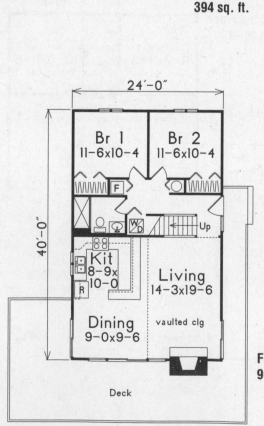

24'-0"

40'-0"

Br 1
11-6x10-4

Br 2
11-6x10-4

F

W/D

Up

Kit
8-9x
10-0

R

Living
14-3x19-6

vaulted clg

Dining
9-0x9-6

Deck

First Floor
960 sq. ft.

Contemporary Elegance With Efficiency

1,321 total square feet of living area

Price Code A

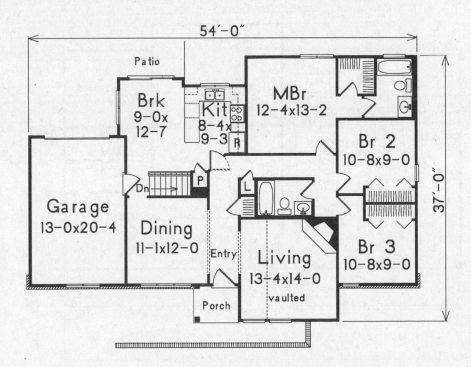

54'-0"

Patio

Brk
9-0x
12-7

Kit
8-4x
9-3

MBr
12-4x13-2

37'-0"

Garage
13-0x20-4

Dining
11-1x12-0

Dn

P

L

Entry

Living
13-4x14-0
vaulted

Br 2
10-8x9-0

Br 3
10-8x9-0

Porch

Special features

- Rear garage and elongated brick wall adds to appealing facade

- Dramatic vaulted living room includes corner fireplace and towering feature windows

- Kitchen/breakfast room is immersed in light from two large windows and glass sliding doors

- 3 bedrooms, 2 baths, 1-car rear entry garage

- Basement foundation

Cozy Country Home

2,189 total square feet of living area

Price Code C

Special features

- Study could easily be converted to a fourth bedroom

- Secluded master bedroom has all the luxuries for comfortable living

- All bedroom include spacious walk-in closets

- 3 bedrooms, 2 1/2 baths, 2-car detached garage

- Crawl space or slab foundation, please specify when ordering

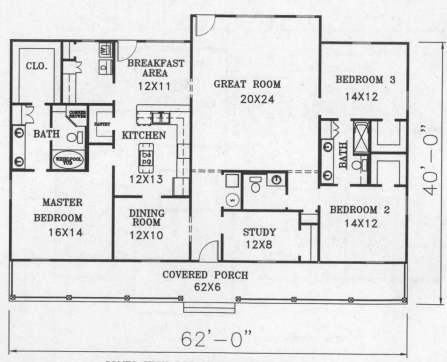

CLO.

BREAKFAST AREA
12X11

GREAT ROOM
20X24

BEDROOM 3
14X12

CORNER SHOWER

BATH

PANTRY

KITCHEN

BATH

WHIRLPOOL TUB

12X13

MASTER BEDROOM
16X14

DINING ROOM
12X10

BEDROOM 2
14X12

STUDY
12X8

COVERED PORCH
62X6

40'-0"

62'-0"

COMES WITH DETACHED GARAGE PLAN

Economical Ranch For Easy Living

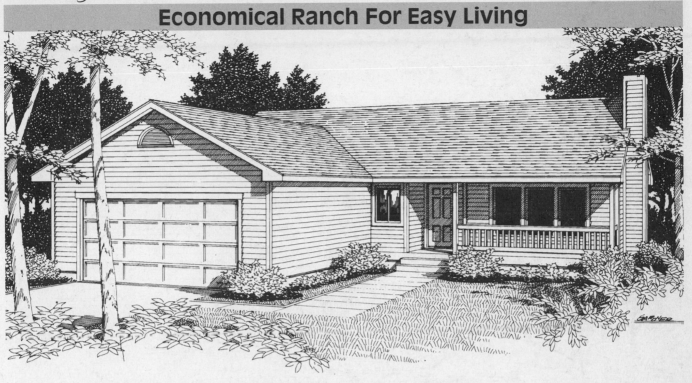

1,314 total square feet of living area

Price Code A

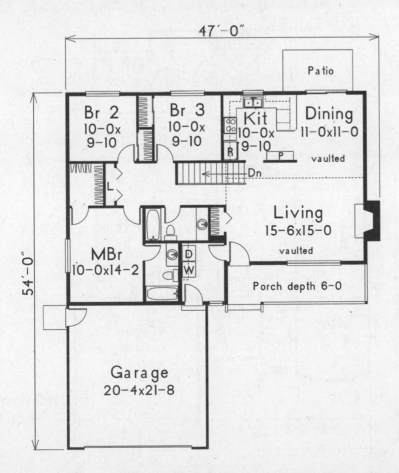

47'-0"

Patio

Br 2
10-0x
9-10

Br 3
10-0x
9-10

Kit
10-0x
9-10

Dining
11-0x11-0

vaulted

Dn

Living
15-6x15-0

vaulted

MBr
10-0x14-2

Porch depth 6-0

Garage
20-4x21-8

54'-0"

Special features

- Energy efficient home with 2" x 6" exterior walls
- Covered porch adds immediate appeal and welcoming charm
- Open floor plan combined with vaulted ceiling offers spacious living
- Functional kitchen complete with pantry and eating bar
- Cozy fireplace in the living room
- Private master bedroom features a large walk-in closet and bath
- 3 bedrooms, 2 baths, 2-car garage
- Basement foundation

TO ORDER BLUEPRINTS USE THE FORM ON PAGE 15 OR CALL TOLL-FREE 1-877-671-6036
View thousands more home plans online at www.familyhandyman.com/homeplans

279

Sweet And Simple

1,694 total square feet of living area

Price Code B

Special features

- Covered front porch is charming and inviting
- Well-designed kitchen with snack bar allows for extra seating
- Large great room with 10' ceiling adds to its spaciousness
- 3 bedrooms, 2 1/2 baths, 2-car garage
- Basement foundation

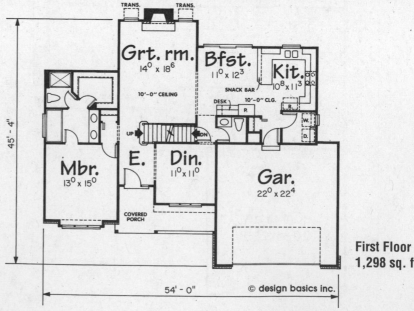

Br. 3
11⁰ x 10⁰

Br. 2
10⁴ x 11⁰

LINEN
DN

**Second Floor
396 sq. ft.**

TRANS.   TRANS.

Grt. rm.
14⁰ x 18⁶

10'-0" CEILING

Bfst.
11⁰ x 12³

SNACK BAR

Kit.
10⁸ x 11³

DESK   10'-0" CLG.

UP   DN

Mbr.
13⁰ x 15⁰

E.

Din.
11⁰ x 11⁰

Gar.
22⁰ x 22⁴

COVERED
PORCH

45' - 4"

54' - 0"

© design basics inc.

**First Floor
1,298 sq. ft.**

Plan #703-1233

Well-Designed Home Makes Great Use Of Space

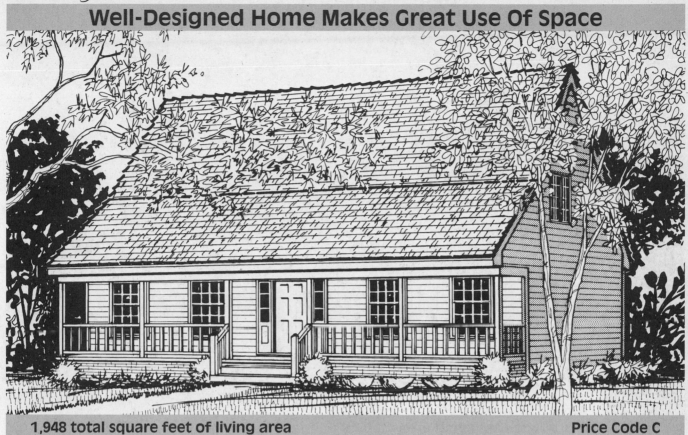

1,948 total square feet of living area

Price Code C

Second Floor
868 sq. ft.

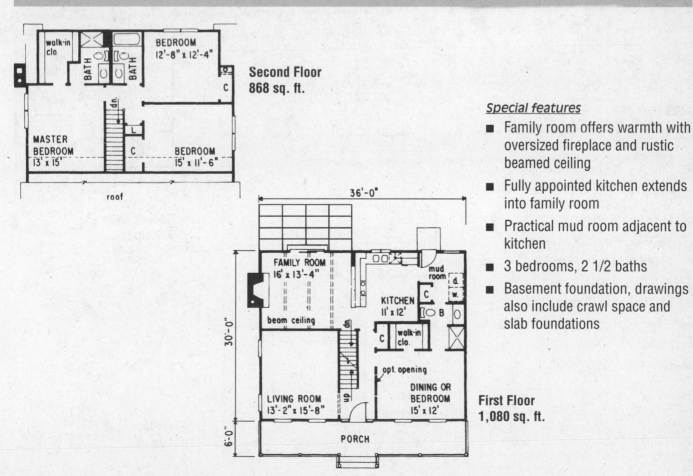

walk-in clo

BATH

BATH

BEDROOM
12'-8" x 12'-4"

C

MASTER BEDROOM
13' x 15'

dn.

C

BEDROOM
15' x 11'-6"

roof

36'-0"

FAMILY ROOM
16' x 13'-4"

beam ceiling

mud room

d. w.

KITCHEN
11' x 12'

C

B

walk-in clo.

30'-0"

dn.

LIVING ROOM
13'-2" x 15'-8"

up

opt. opening

DINING OR BEDROOM
15' x 12'

First Floor
1,080 sq. ft.

6'-0"

PORCH

Special features

- Family room offers warmth with oversized fireplace and rustic beamed ceiling
- Fully appointed kitchen extends into family room
- Practical mud room adjacent to kitchen
- 3 bedrooms, 2 1/2 baths
- Basement foundation, drawings also include crawl space and slab foundations

Country Kitchen Center Of Living Activities

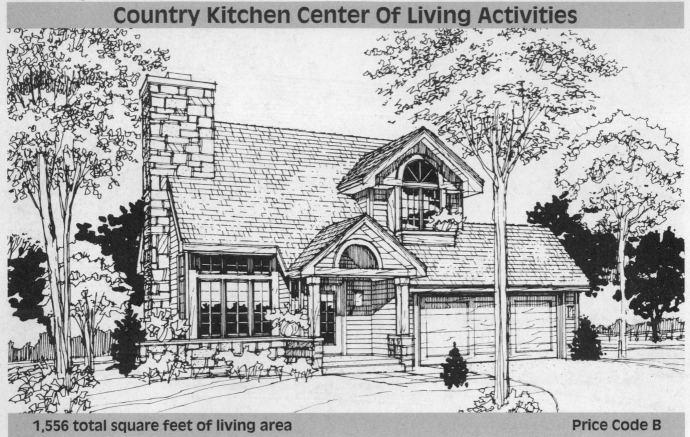

1,556 total square feet of living area

Price Code B

Special features

- A compact home with all the amenities
- Country kitchen combines practicality with access to other areas for eating and entertaining
- Two-way fireplace joins the dining and living areas
- Plant shelf and vaulted ceiling highlight the master bedroom
- 3 bedrooms, 2 1/2 baths, 2-car garage
- Basement foundation

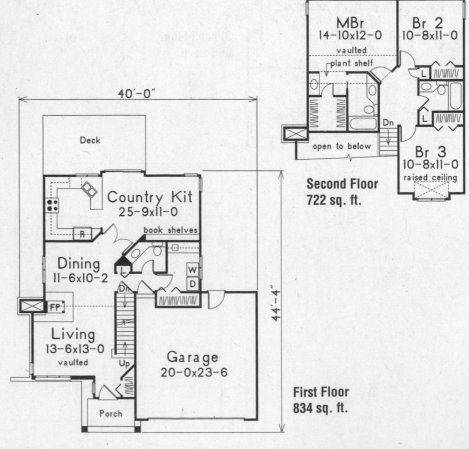

Second Floor
722 sq. ft.

MBr 14-10x12-0 vaulted
plant shelf
Br 2 10-8x11-0
open to below
Br 3 10-8x11-0 raised ceiling
Dn

40'-0"

Deck

Country Kit 25-9x11-0
book shelves
R
W D

Dining 11-6x10-2

Living 13-6x13-0 vaulted
FP
Dn
Up

Garage 20-0x23-6

Porch

44'-4"

First Floor
834 sq. ft.

Plan #703-N064

Clerestory Windows Enhance Home's Facade

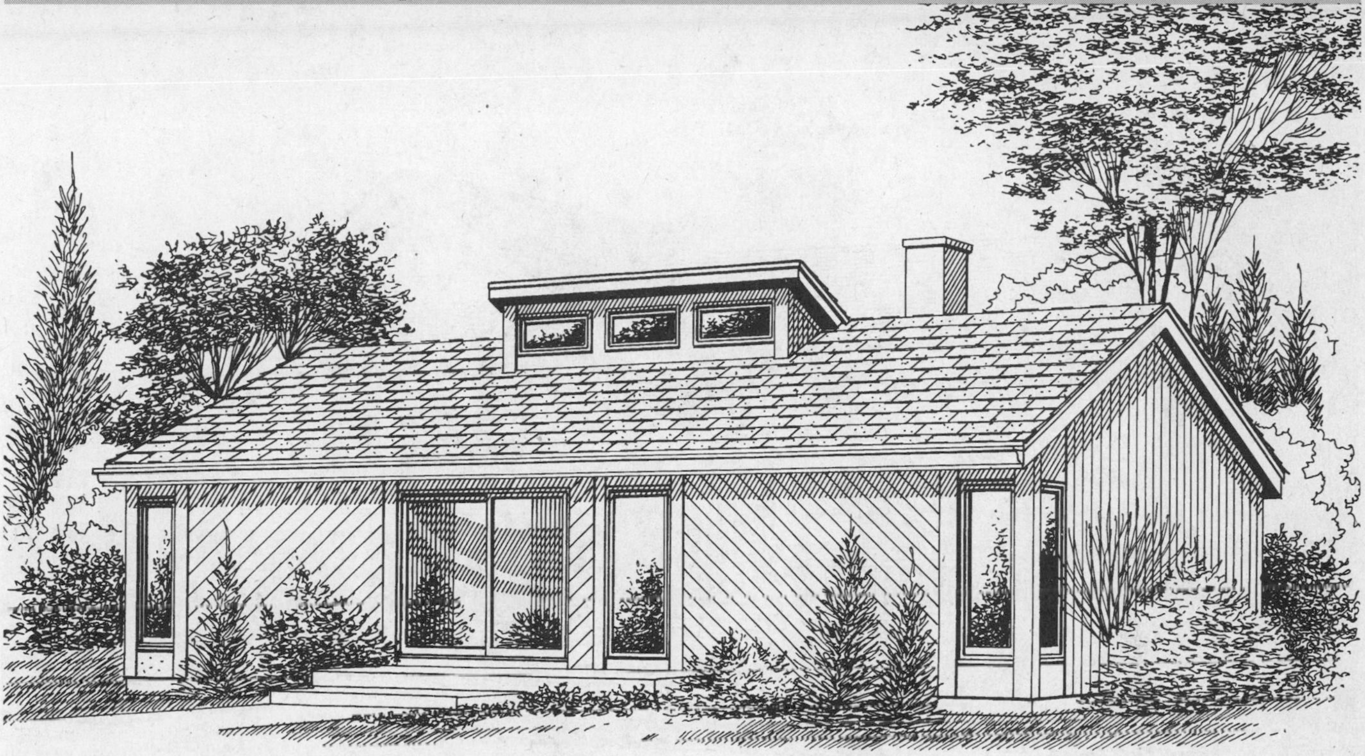

1,176 total square feet of living area **Price Code AA**

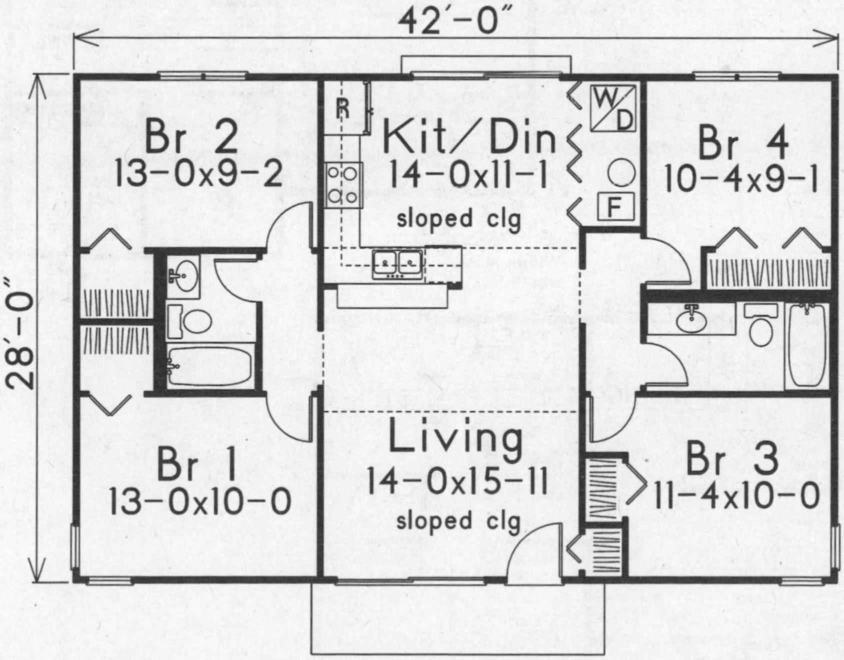
42'-0"
28'-0"
Br 2
13-0x9-2
Kit/Din
14-0x11-1
sloped clg
R
W
D
F
Br 4
10-4x9-1
Living
14-0x15-11
sloped clg
Br 1
13-0x10-0
Br 3
11-4x10-0

Special features

- Efficient kitchen offers plenty of storage, a dining area and a stylish eating bar
- A gathering space is created by the large central living room
- Closet and storage space throughout helps keep sporting equipment organized and easily accessible
- Each end of home is comprised of two bedrooms and full bath
- 4 bedrooms, 2 baths
- Crawl space foundation, drawings also include slab foundation

Split-Level Has European Style

1,224 total square feet of living area

Price Code A

Special features

- Energy efficient home with 2" x 6" exterior walls

- Charming window seats are featured in bedrooms #2 and #3

- Optional lower level has an additional 682 square feet of living area

- 3 bedrooms, 2 baths

- Basement foundation

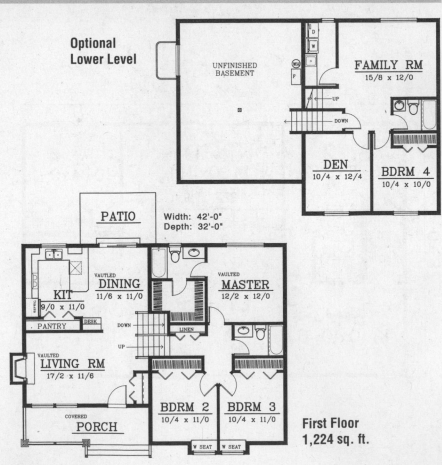

Optional Lower Level

UNFINISHED BASEMENT

FAMILY RM
15/8 x 12/0

UP

DOWN

DEN
10/4 x 12/4

BDRM 4
10/4 x 10/0

PATIO

Width: 42'-0"
Depth: 32'-0"

KIT
9/0 x 11/0

VAULTED DINING
11/6 x 11/0

VAULTED MASTER
12/2 x 12/0

PANTRY   DESK

DOWN

LINEN

UP

VAULTED LIVING RM
17/2 x 11/6

COVERED PORCH

BDRM 2
10/4 x 11/0

BDRM 3
10/4 x 11/0

W SEAT   W SEAT

First Floor
1,224 sq. ft.

Abundance Of Walk-In Closets

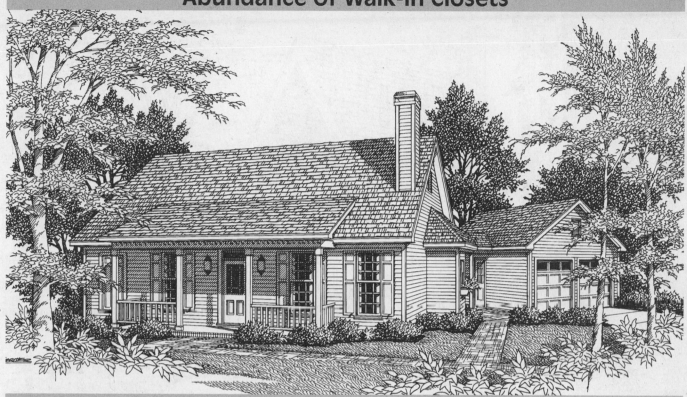

1,474 total square feet of living area

Price Code A

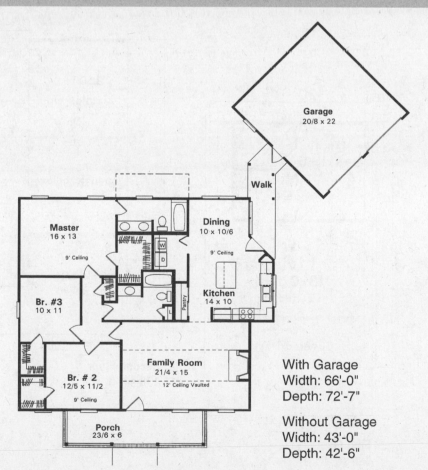

Garage
20/8 x 22

Walk

Master
16 x 13

9' Ceiling

Dining
10 x 10/6

9' Ceiling

Br. #3
10 x 11

W
D

Pantry

Kitchen
14 x 10

Family Room
21/4 x 15

12' Ceiling Vaulted

Br. # 2
12/5 x 11/2

9' Ceiling

Porch
23/6 x 6

With Garage
Width: 66'-0"
Depth: 72'-7"

Without Garage
Width: 43'-0"
Depth: 42'-6"

Special features

■ Kitchen and dining area include center eat-in island and large pantry

■ Laundry facilities and hall bath are roomy

■ Secondary bedrooms both have walk-in closets

■ 3 bedrooms, 2 baths, 2-car detached garage

■ Slab or crawl space foundation, please specify when ordering

An A-Frame For Every Environment

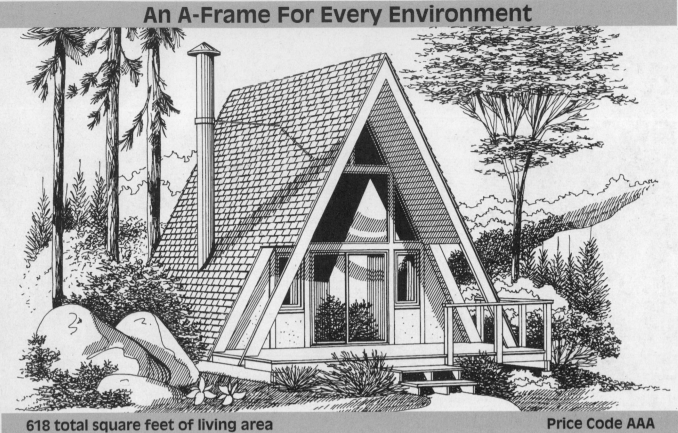

618 total square feet of living area

Price Code AAA

Special features

- Memorable family events are certain to be enjoyed on this fabulous partially covered sundeck

- Equally impressive is the living area with its cathedral ceiling and exposed rafters

- A kitchenette, bedroom and bath conclude the first floor with a delightful sleeping loft above bedroom and bath

- 1 bedroom, 1 bath

- Pier foundation

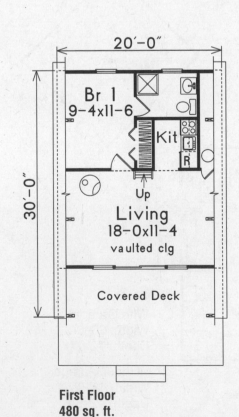

First Floor
480 sq. ft.

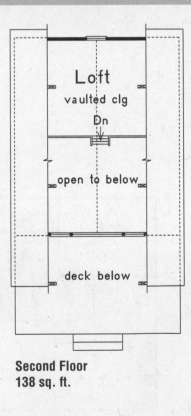

Second Floor
138 sq. ft.

TO ORDER BLUEPRINTS USE THE FORM ON PAGE 15 OR CALL TOLL-FREE 1-877-671-6036
View thousands more home plans online at www.familyhandyman.com/homeplans

1,087 total square feet of living area

Price Code AA

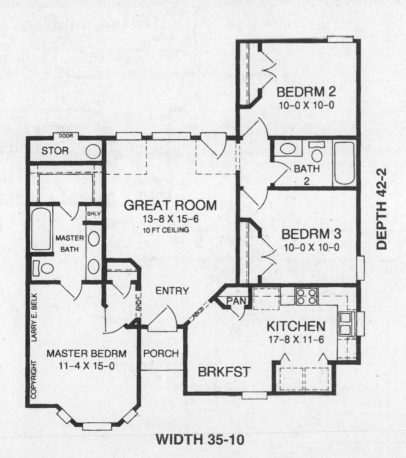

STOR
DOOR

MASTER BATH

GREAT ROOM
13-8 X 15-6
10 FT CEILING

SHLV

COPYRIGHT   LARRY E. BELK

MASTER BEDRM
11-4 X 15-0

PORCH

ENTRY

ARCH

BEDRM 2
10-0 X 10-0

BATH 2

BEDRM 3
10-0 X 10-0

DEPTH 42-2

PAN

KITCHEN
17-8 X 11-6

BRKFST

WIDTH 35-10

Special features

- Compact and efficiently designed home
- Master bedroom separate from other bedrooms for privacy
- 10' ceiling in great room
- 3 bedrooms, 2 baths
- Slab or crawl space foundation, please specify when ordering

Traditional Farmhouse Feeling With This Home

2,582 total square feet of living area   **Price Code D**

Special features

- Both the family and living rooms are warmed by hearths

- The master suite on the second floor has a bayed sitting room and a private bath with whirlpool tub

- Old-fashioned window seat in second floor landing is a charming touch

- 4 bedrooms, 3 baths, 2-car side entry garage

- Basement or crawl space foundation, please specify when ordering

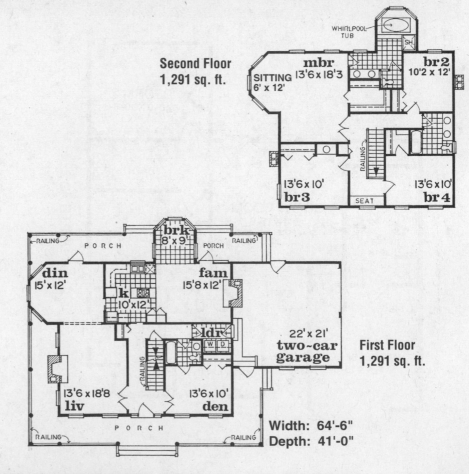

Second Floor 1,291 sq. ft.

WHIRLPOOL TUB

SH

mbr 13'6 x 18'3

br 2 10'2 x 12'

SITTING 6' x 12'

RAILING

13'6 x 10' **br 3**

SEAT

13'6 x 10' **br 4**

brk 8' x 9'

RAILING   PORCH   PORCH   RAILING

din 15' x 12'

fam 15'8 x 12'

k 10'x12'

ldr WD

22' x 21' **two-car garage**

First Floor 1,291 sq. ft.

RAILING

13'6 x 18'8 **liv**

13'6 x 10' **den**

PORCH

RAILING   RAILING

Width: 64'-6"
Depth: 41'-0"

Ski Chalet With Style

1,680 total square feet of living area

Price Code B

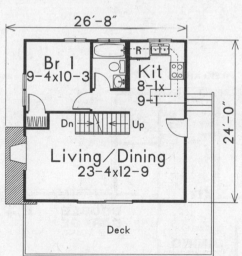

26'-8"

Br 1
9-4x10-3

KIT
8-1x
9-T

R

Dn   Up

24'-0"

Living/Dining
23-4x12-9

Deck

First Floor
576 sq. ft.

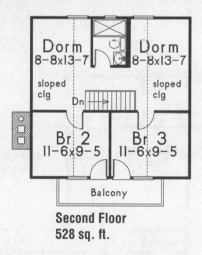

Dorm
8-8x13-7

Dorm
8-8x13-7

sloped clg

sloped clg

Dn

Br 2
11-6x9-5

Br 3
11-6x9-5

Balcony

Second Floor
528 sq. ft.

Lower Level
576 sq. ft.

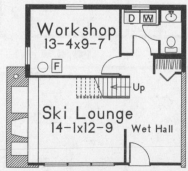

Workshop
13-4x9-7

D W

F

Up

Ski Lounge
14-1x12-9   Wet Hall

Special features

- Highly functional lower level includes wet hall with storage, laundry area, work shop and cozy ski lounge with enormous fireplace

- First floor warmed by large fireplace in living/dining area which features spacious wrap-around deck

- Lots of sleeping space for guests or a large family

- 5 bedrooms, 2 1/2 baths

- Basement foundation

TO ORDER BLUEPRINTS USE THE FORM ON PAGE 15 OR CALL TOLL-FREE 1-877-671-6036
View thousands more home plans online at www.familyhandyman.com/homeplans

289

Prominent Hall Connects Rooms

1,609 total square feet of living area   **Price Code B**

Special features

- Laundry area is adjacent to kitchen for convenience
- Two storage areas; one can be accessed from the outdoors and the other from the garage
- Eating bar overlooks from kitchen into dining area
- 3 bedrooms, 2 baths, 2-car side entry garage
- Slab foundation

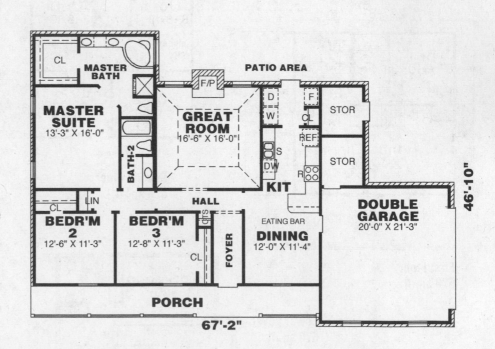

Country Charm For A Small Lot

1,169 total square feet of living area

Price Code AA

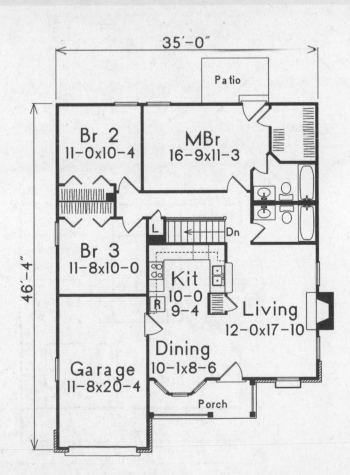

35'-0"

Patio

Br 2
11-0x10-4

MBr
16-9x11-3

Br 3
11-8x10-0

46'-4"

L

Dn

Kit
10-0
9-4

Living
12-0x17-10

Dining
10-1x8-6

Garage
11-8x20-4

Porch

Special features

- Front facade features a distinctive country appeal
- Living room enjoys a wood-burning fireplace and pass-through to kitchen
- A stylish U-shaped kitchen offers an abundance of cabinet and counterspace with view to living room
- A large walk-in closet, access to rear patio and private bath are many features of the master bedroom
- 3 bedrooms, 2 baths, 1-car garage
- Basement foundation

TO ORDER BLUEPRINTS USE THE FORM ON PAGE 15 OR CALL TOLL-FREE 1-877-671-6036
View thousands more home plans online at www.familyhandyman.com/homeplans

291

Rambling Country Bungalow

1,475 total square feet of living area

Price Code B

Special features

- Family room features a high ceiling and prominent corner fireplace

- Kitchen with island counter and garden window makes a convenient connection between the family and dining rooms

- Hallway leads to three bedrooms all with large walk-in closets

- Covered breezeway joins main house and garage

- Full-width covered porch entry lends a country touch

- 3 bedrooms, 2 baths, 2-car side entry garage

- Slab foundation, drawings also include crawl space foundation

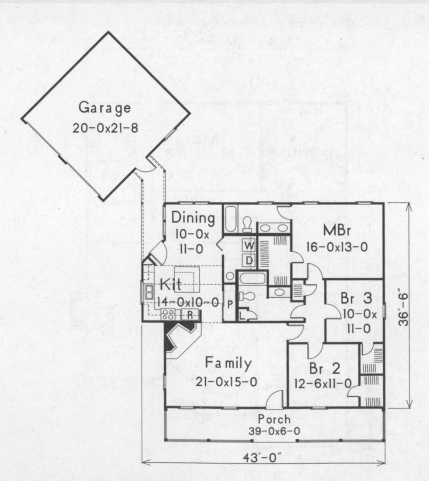

Garage
20-0x21-8

Dining
10-0x
11-0

MBr
16-0x13-0

Kit
14-0x10-0

Br 3
10-0x
11-0

Family
21-0x15-0

Br 2
12-6x11-0

Porch
39-0x6-0

36'-6"

43'-0"

Country-Style Home With Large Front Porch

1,501 total square feet of living area

Price Code B

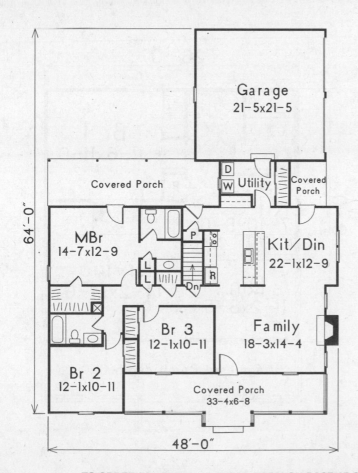

Special features

- Spacious kitchen with dining area is open to the outdoors
- Convenient utility room is adjacent to garage
- Master suite with private bath, dressing area and access to large covered porch
- Large family room creates openness
- 3 bedrooms, 2 baths, 2-car side entry garage
- Basement foundation, drawings also include crawl space and slab foundations

TO ORDER BLUEPRINTS USE THE FORM ON PAGE 15 OR CALL TOLL-FREE 1-877-671-6036
View thousands more home plans online at www.familyhandyman.com/homeplans

293

Small And Cozy Cabin

676 total square feet of living area　　　　**Price Code AAA**

Special features

- See-through fireplace between bedroom and living area adds character
- Combined dining and living areas create an open feeling
- Full-length front covered porch perfect for enjoying the outdoors
- Additional storage available in utility room
- 1 bedroom, 1 bath
- Crawl space foundation

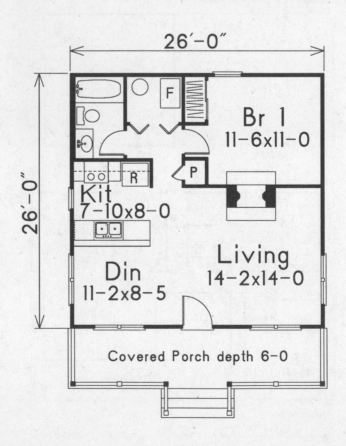

26'-0"

26'-0"

Br 1
11-6x11-0

Kit
7-10x8-0

Din
11-2x8-5

Living
14-2x14-0

Covered Porch depth 6-0

Excellent Ranch For Country Setting

2,758 total square feet of living area

Price Code E

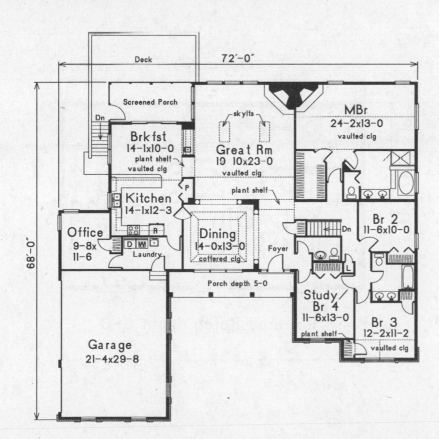

Special features

- Vaulted great room excels with fireplace, wet bar, plant shelves and skylights

- Fabulous master suite enjoys a fireplace, large bath, walk-in closet and vaulted ceiling

- Trendsetting breakfast room adjoins spacious screened porch

- Convenient office near kitchen is perfect for computer room, hobby enthusiast or fifth bedroom

- 4 bedrooms, 2 1/2 baths, 3-car side entry garage

- Basement foundation

TO ORDER BLUEPRINTS USE THE FORM ON PAGE 15 OR CALL TOLL-FREE 1-877-671-6036
View thousands more home plans online at www.familyhandyman.com/homeplans

295

Year-Round Hideaway

416 total square feet of living area   **Price Code AAA**

Special features

■ Open floor plan creates spacious feeling

■ Covered porch has rustic appeal

■ Plenty of cabinetry and workspace in kitchen

■ Large linen closet centrally located and close to bath

■ Sleeping area, 1 bath

■ Slab foundation

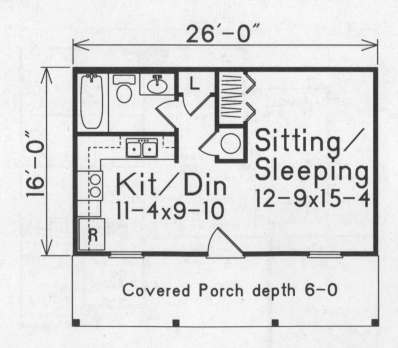

26'-0"

16'-0"

Kit/Din
11-4x9-10

Sitting/
Sleeping
12-9x15-4

Covered Porch depth 6-0

296

TO ORDER BLUEPRINTS USE THE FORM ON PAGE 15 OR CALL TOLL-FREE 1-877-671-6036
View thousands more home plans online at www.familyhandyman.com/homeplans

Lots Of Windows Creates A Cheerful Home

1,285 total square feet of living area

Price Code A

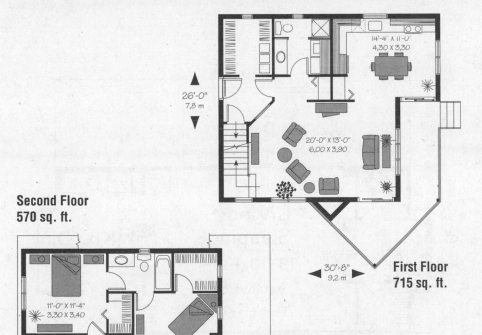

Second Floor
570 sq. ft.

26'-0"
7,8 m

14'-4" X 11'-0"
4,30 X 3,30

20'-0" X 13'-0"
6,00 X 3,90

11'-0" X 11'-4"
3,30 X 3,40

11'-8" X 19'-4"
3,50 X 5,80

30'-8"
9,2 m

First Floor
715 sq. ft.

Special features

- Energy efficient home with 2" x 6" exterior walls
- Dining and living areas both access a large wrap-around porch
- First floor bath has convenient laundry closet as well as a shower
- 2 bedrooms, 2 baths
- Basement foundation

TO ORDER BLUEPRINTS USE THE FORM ON PAGE 15 OR CALL TOLL-FREE 1-877-671-6036
View thousands more home plans online at www.familyhandyman.com/homeplans

297

Sensational Cottage Retreat

647 total square feet of living area

Price Code AAA

Special features

- Large vaulted room for living/sleeping with plant shelves on each end, stone fireplace and wide glass doors for views
- Roomy kitchen is vaulted and has a bayed dining area and fireplace
- Step down into a sunken and vaulted bath featuring a 6'-0" whirlpool tub-in-a-bay with shelves at each end for storage
- A large palladian window adorns each end of the cottage giving a cheery atmosphere throughout
- 1 living/sleeping room, 1 bath
- Crawl space foundation

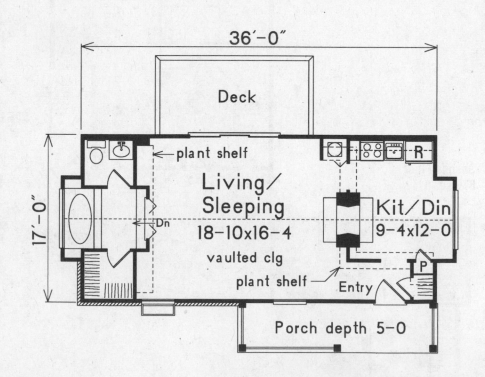

Country Farmhouse Appeal

1,907 total square feet of living area

Price Code C

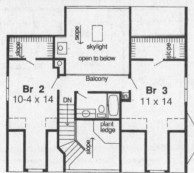

Second Floor
638 sq. ft.

Br 2
10-4 x 14

Br 3
11 x 14

Balcony

skylight
open to below

plant ledge

DN

slope

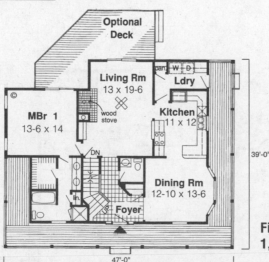

Optional Deck

Living Rm
13 x 19-6

Ldry

wood stove

Kitchen
11 x 12

MBr 1
13-6 x 14

DN

Dining Rm
12-10 x 13-6

Foyer

39'-0"

47'-0"

First Floor
1,269 sq. ft.

Special features

- Two-story living room is a surprise with skylight and balcony above

- Master bedroom positioned on first floor for convenience

- All bedrooms have walk-in closets

- 3 bedrooms, 2 1/2 baths

- Basement, crawl space or slab foundation, please specify when ordering

TO ORDER BLUEPRINTS USE THE FORM ON PAGE 15 OR CALL TOLL-FREE 1-877-671-6036
View thousands more home plans online at www.familyhandyman.com/homeplans

299

Unique Window Above Porch Adds Excitement

1,449 total square feet of living area

Price Code A

Special features

- Bayed dining room is a sunny extension off kitchen

- Master suite is secluded from other bedrooms and includes space for a stacked washer and dryer in the bath

- Two-story great room has an open feel with lots of windows and a beamed ceiling

- 2 bedrooms, 2 1/2 baths

- Crawl space foundation

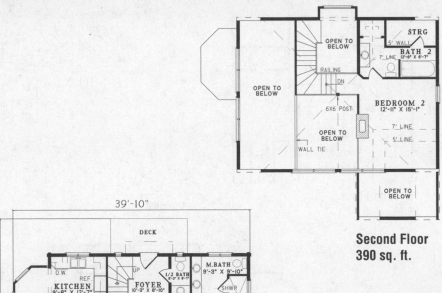

**Second Floor
390 sq. ft.**

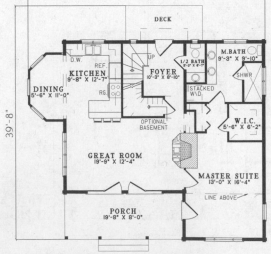

**First Floor
1,059 sq. ft.**

TO ORDER BLUEPRINTS USE THE FORM ON PAGE 15 OR CALL TOLL-FREE 1-877-671-6036

View thousands more home plans online at www.familyhandyman.com/homeplans

A Cozy Rustic Dwelling

Log Home Plans

1,769 total square feet of living area

Price Code B

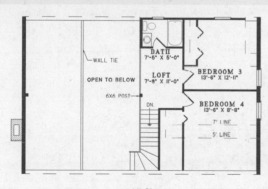

Second Floor
493 sq. ft.

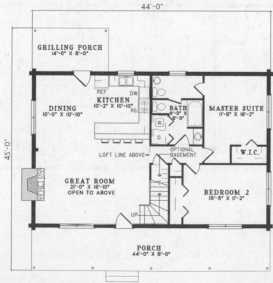

First Floor
1,276 sq. ft.

Special features

- Two-story great room has dining nearby and a cozy fireplace
- Master suite has its own half bath for convenience
- Cozy loft on second floor is a relaxing hideaway from center of activity
- 4 bedrooms, 2 1/2 baths
- Crawl space foundation

TO ORDER BLUEPRINTS USE THE FORM ON PAGE 15 OR CALL TOLL-FREE 1-877-671-6036
View thousands more home plans online at www.familyhandyman.com/homeplans

301

Sprawling Log Ranch Design

1,616 total square feet of living area

Price Code B

Special features

- Compact U-shaped kitchen designed with everything within reach
- Two sets of doors lead to an outdoor grilling porch from the cozy great room
- Large laundry room connects the garage to living areas
- 3 bedrooms, 2 baths, 2-car side entry garage
- Crawl space foundation

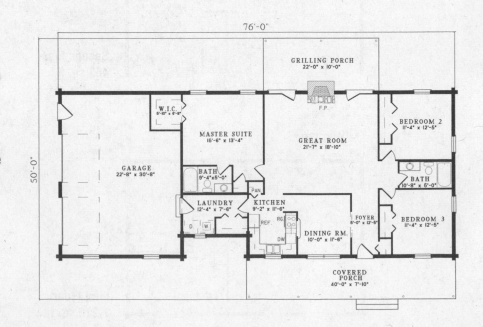

302

TO ORDER BLUEPRINTS USE THE FORM ON PAGE 15 OR CALL TOLL-FREE 1-877-671-6036
View thousands more home plans online at www.familyhandyman.com/homeplans

Plan #703-JB-1029

Wall Of Windows Adds Modern Touch

Log Home Plans

1,591 total square feet of living area   **Price Code B**

Special features

- Expansive beams span the length of the great room and dining area adding rustic appeal
- Private second floor master suite has a walk-in closet and bath
- Kitchen has dining area, breakfast bar and dining area that accesses the outdoors
- Central first floor laundry and full bath
- 3 bedrooms, 2 baths
- Crawl space foundation

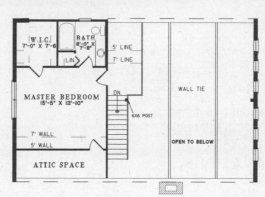

**Second Floor
199 sq. ft.**

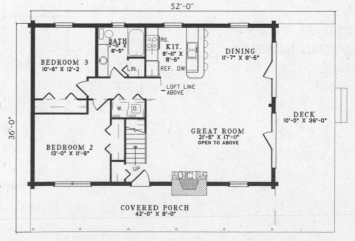

**First Floor
1,392 sq. ft.**

TO ORDER BLUEPRINTS USE THE FORM ON PAGE 15 OR CALL TOLL-FREE 1-877-671-6036
View thousands more home plans online at www.familyhandyman.com/homeplans

303

Second Floor Bridge Adds Visual Interest

2,301 total square feet of living area

Price Code D

Special features

- Centrally located dining/kitchen flows into great room offering a great place for gathering
- Relaxing screened porch adjacent to kitchen
- Private master suite has a sunny bay window and private bath
- 2 bedrooms, 2 baths
- Crawl space foundation

Second Floor 469 sq. ft.

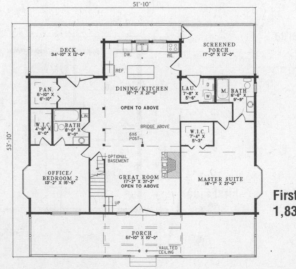

First Floor 1,832 sq. ft.

A Grand Beamed Entry With Arched Window

Log Home Plans

1,665 total square feet of living area

Price Code B

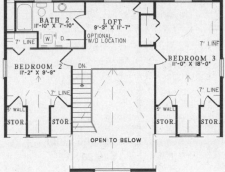

Second Floor
663 sq. ft.

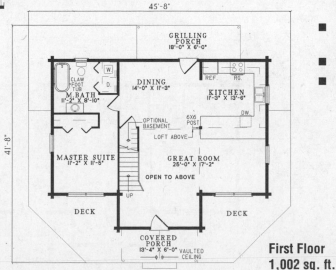

First Floor
1,002 sq. ft.

Special features

- Central loft on second floor is a nice retreat
- Oversized dining room has access to outdoor grilling porch
- A deck wraps around the home for additional outdoor living area
- First floor master suite offers privacy
- 3 bedrooms, 2 baths
- Crawl space foundation

Beams And Gables Attract Attention

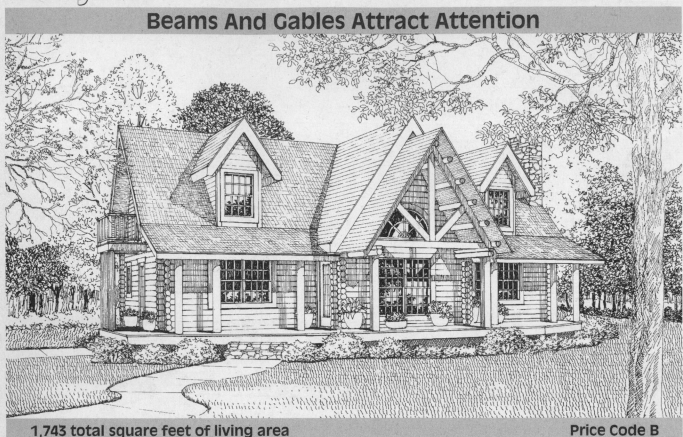

1,743 total square feet of living area

Price Code B

Special features

- Second floor loft is open to below and has access to its own private deck

- Efficiently designed kitchen has a garden window over the sink and an L-shaped counter overlooking the living and dining rooms

- Large master suite features a private entrance from the deck, luxurious bath and walk-in closet

- 2 bedrooms, 2 1/2 baths

- Crawl space foundation

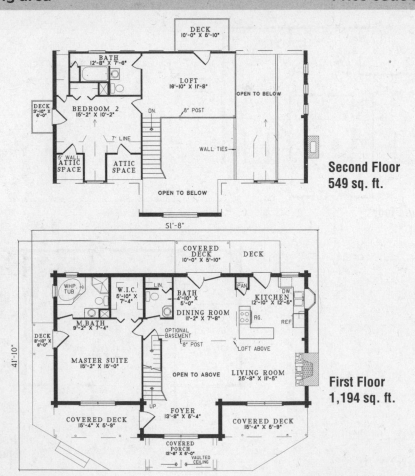

Second Floor
549 sq. ft.

First Floor
1,194 sq. ft.

TO ORDER BLUEPRINTS USE THE FORM ON PAGE 15 OR CALL TOLL-FREE 1-877-671-6036

View thousands more home plans online at www.familyhandyman.com/homeplans

Simple Log Home Style

Plan #703-JB-1060

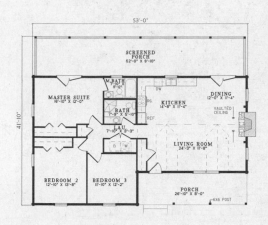

1,480 total square feet of living area   **Price Code A**

Special features

- Open living areas provide plenty of space for family gatherings
- Master suite has access directly onto covered porch
- A fireplace warms the great room
- 3 bedrooms, 2 baths,
- Crawl space foundation

Cozy Front Porch For Relaxing

Plan #703-JB-1004

Second Floor - 342 sq. ft.

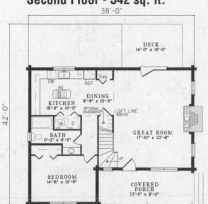

First Floor - 1,040 sq. ft.

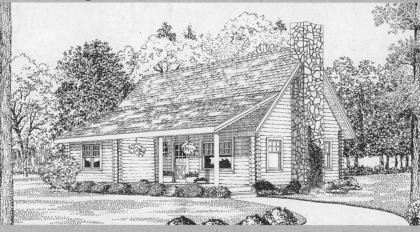

1,382 total square feet of living area   **Price Code A**

Special features

- Skylights and a two-story ceiling adds spaciousness to great room
- Second floor master suite enjoys its own private deck and bath
- Handy laundry closet is located in the kitchen for convenience
- 2 bedrooms, 2 baths
- Crawl space foundation

TO ORDER BLUEPRINTS USE THE FORM ON PAGE 15 OR CALL TOLL-FREE 1-877-671-6036
View thousands more home plans online at www.familyhandyman.com/homeplans

307

Cozy Corner Fireplace In Great Room

1,810 total square feet of living area

Price Code C

Special features

- Enormous master bath has a double vanity, corner whirlpool tub and separate shower
- Double-doors in dining room lead to a handy grilling porch
- Convenient mud room leads to laundry closet
- 3 bedrooms, 2 1/2 baths
- Crawl space foundation

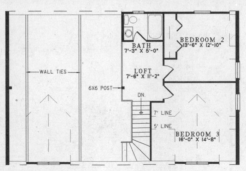

Second Floor
534 sq. ft.

BATH 7'-3" X 5'-0"
BEDROOM 2 13'-6" X 12'-10"
LOFT 7'-6" X 11'-2"
WALL TIES
6X6 POST
DN.
7' LINE
5' LINE
BEDROOM 3 16'-0" X 14'-8"

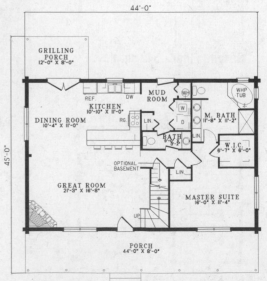

First Floor
1,276 sq. ft.

44'-0"
45'-0"
GRILLING PORCH 12'-0" X 8'-0"
REF. DW
KITCHEN 10'-10" X 11'-0"
MUD ROOM
WH
WHP TUB
DINING ROOM 10'-4" X 11'-0"
RG.
LIN
W
D
M. BATH 11'-8" X 11'-2"
LIN
BATH
LIN
W.I.C. 6'-7" X 6'-0"
OPTIONAL BASEMENT
LIN
GREAT ROOM 21'-3" X 16'-8"
UP
MASTER SUITE 16'-0" X 11'-4"
PORCH 44'-0" X 8'-0"

Large Expansive Living Spaces

Log Home Plans

2,064 total square feet of living area

Price Code C

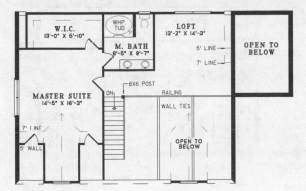

**Second Floor
774 sq. ft.**

Special features

- Second floor has a luxurious master suite, walk-in closet, private bath and a sloped loft
- Angled island extends the kitchen into dining room with bay window
- Beamed two-story great room is a cozy, rustic retreat
- 3 bedrooms, 2 baths
- Crawl space foundation

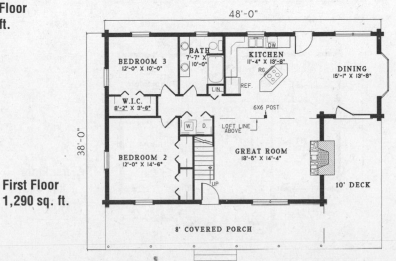

**First Floor
1,290 sq. ft.**

TO ORDER BLUEPRINTS USE THE FORM ON PAGE 15 OR CALL TOLL-FREE 1-877-671-6036
View thousands more home plans online at www.familyhandyman.com/homeplans

309

Unique Open Gable With Round Top Window

1,658 total square feet of living area   Price Code B

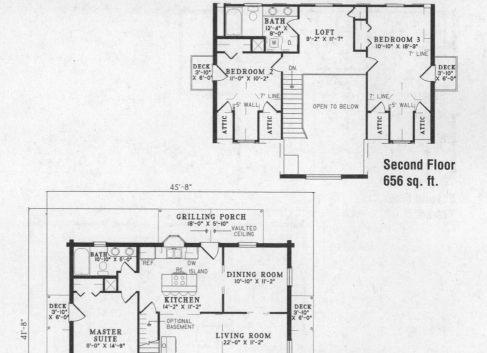

Second Floor
656 sq. ft.

First Floor
1,002 sq. ft.

Special features

- Front covered porch continues as a sun deck wrapping around the sides and allowing access to the master suite
- Kitchen with a large island and grilling porch for the chef
- Master suite is privately placed on the first floor while additional bedrooms are located on the second floor
- Spacious second floor has a loft with full bathroom and two bedrooms with dormer windows and private sun decks
- 3 bedrooms, 2 baths
- Crawl space foundation

310

TO ORDER BLUEPRINTS USE THE FORM ON PAGE 15 OR CALL TOLL-FREE 1-877-671-6036
View thousands more home plans online at www.familyhandyman.com/homeplans

Two-Story Great Room And Kitchen

Log Home Plans

1,477 total square feet of living area

Price Code A

Special features

- Spacious master suite has double closets and easy bath access

- Long counter in kitchen allows extra space for dining or food preparation

- The second floor includes a private third bedroom with bath featuring extra storage in attic

- 3 bedrooms, 2 baths

- Crawl space foundation

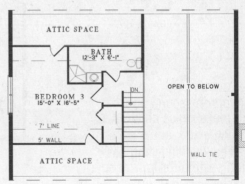

**Second Floor
346 sq. ft.**

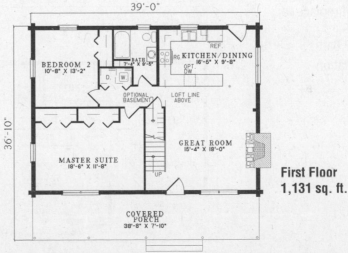

**First Floor
1,131 sq. ft.**

Stunning Dormers Attract Attention

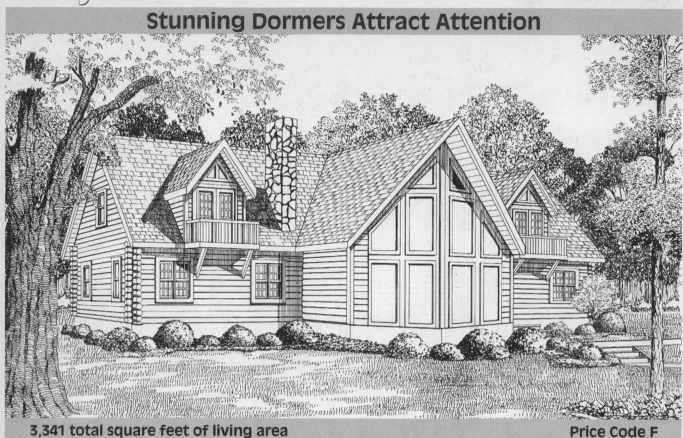

3,341 total square feet of living area

Price Code F

Special features

- Large loft on second floor would make a nice children's play area

- Oversized kitchen island has enough seating for four people

- Breath-taking great room has a two-story beamed ceiling, wall of windows and a fireplace for warmth

- 3 bedrooms, 2 1/2 baths

- Crawl space foundation

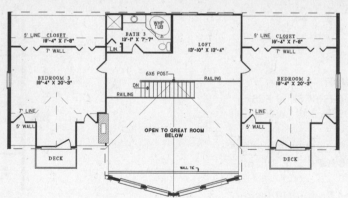

**Second Floor
1,215 sq. ft.**

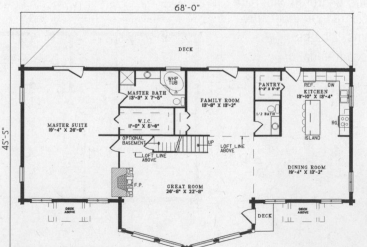

**First Floor
2,126 sq. ft.**

Wrap-Around Deck Enhances Home

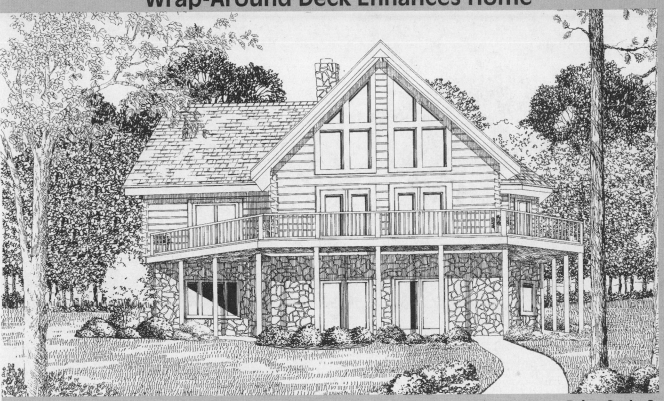

Log Home Plans

2,137 total square feet of living area

Price Code C

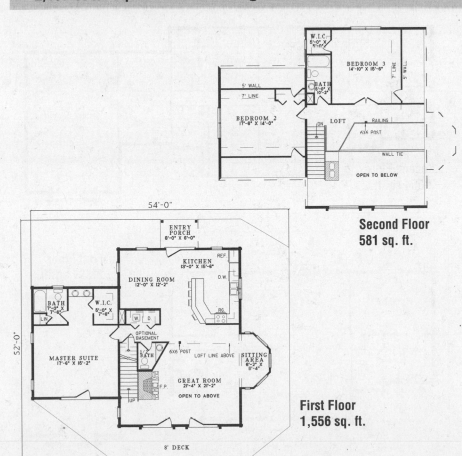

Second Floor
581 sq. ft.

First Floor
1,556 sq. ft.

Special features

- Bay windowed sitting area is a cheerful nook located near main living areas
- Large counter creates plenty of dining area for a large crowd
- Private loft area on the second floor overlooks to the great room below
- 3 bedrooms, 2 1/2 baths
- Crawl space foundation

Luxurious Log Home

4,885 total square feet of living area

Price Code G

Special features

- Office includes cozy corner fireplace ideal for privacy
- Master bath is very special with whirlpool tub in a box bay window
- Second floor includes three bedrooms, a loft area and plenty of room for future expansion
- 4 bedrooms, 4 1/2 baths, 3-car side entry garage
- Crawl space foundation

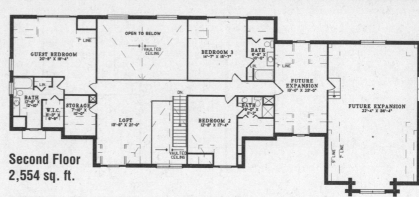

Second Floor
2,554 sq. ft.

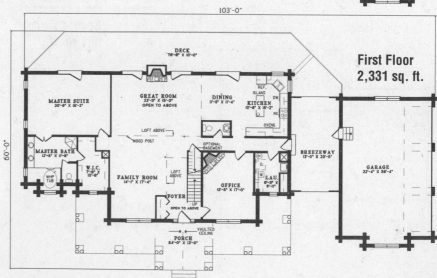

First Floor
2,331 sq. ft.

Lovely Log Home Living

Plan #703-JB-1018

Second Floor - 612 sq. ft.

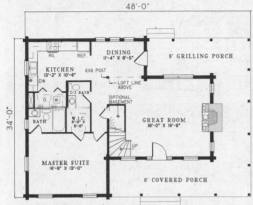

First Floor - 1,072 sq. ft.

1,684 total square feet of living area　　**Price Code B**

Special features

- Sunny dining room features rustic beams overhead and access to a grilling porch
- Both secondary bedrooms are private and share a bath
- Convenient laundry closet in kitchen
- 3 bedrooms, 2 1/2 baths
- Crawl space foundation

Open Areas Great For Gathering

Plan #703-JB-1015

Second Floor 605 sq. ft.

First Floor 1,120 sq. ft.

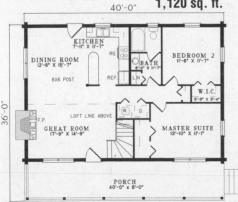

1,725 total square feet of living area　　**Price Code B**

Special features

- Beamed ceiling in great room adds a rustic feel especially with two-story ceiling and fireplace
- Sloped ceiling in second floor loft creates the feeling of a cozy nook
- Large counter space in kitchen creates plenty of seating for dining
- 3 bedrooms, 2 baths
- Crawl space foundation

Cozy Log Home Has A Terrific Interior

1,940 total square feet of living area

Price Code C

**Second Floor
653 sq. ft.**

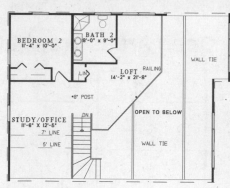

BEDROOM 2
11'-4" x 10'-0"

BATH 2
9'-0" x 9'-0"

WALL TIE

LOFT
14'-2" x 21'-8"

RAILING

LIN

•8" POST

OPEN TO BELOW

STUDY/OFFICE
11'-6" x 12'-5"

DN

7' LINE

5' LINE

WALL TIE

Special features

- Large second floor loft overlooks to living room below
- Private study/office tucked away from gathering places
- Enormous kitchen has space for dining, storage and food preparation
- 2 bedrooms, 2 baths
- Crawl space foundation

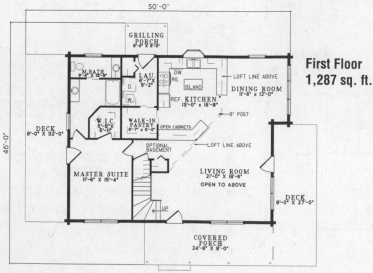

50'-0"

GRILLING
PORCH
6'-0" x 6'-0"

M. BATH
9'-1" x 8'-5"

LAU.
6'-7" x 9'-2"

D.W.
RG.

DINING ROOM
11'-6" x 12'-0"

**First Floor
1,287 sq. ft.**

ISLAND

REF.

KITCHEN
13'-0" x 15'-8"

LOFT LINE ABOVE

D.

W.

WALK-IN
PANTRY
6'-7" x 6'-1"

OPEN CABINETS

8" POST

W.I.C.
5'-8" x 5'-11"

46'-0"

DECK
8'-0" X 32'-0"

OPTIONAL
BASEMENT

LOFT LINE ABOVE

MASTER SUITE
11'-6" x 15'-4"

LIVING ROOM
21'-0" x 18'-6"

OPEN TO ABOVE

DECK
8'-0" X 27'-0"

UP

COVERED
PORCH
24'-6" x 8'-0"

TO ORDER BLUEPRINTS USE THE FORM ON PAGE 15 OR CALL TOLL-FREE 1-877-671-6036
View thousands more home plans online at www.familyhandyman.com/homeplans

Plan #703-JB-1014

Windows Flank Massive Stone Fireplace

Log Home Plans

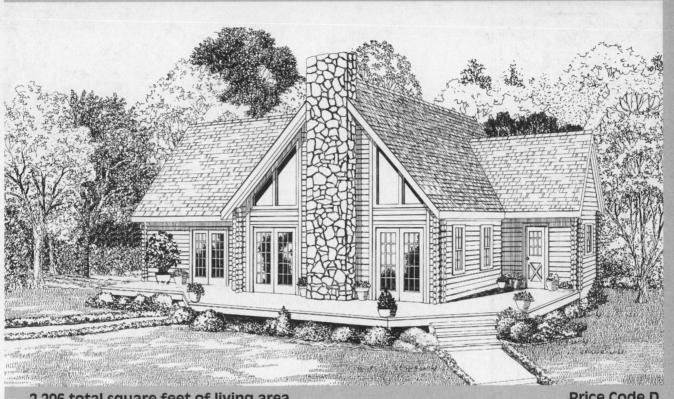

2,206 total square feet of living area

Price Code D

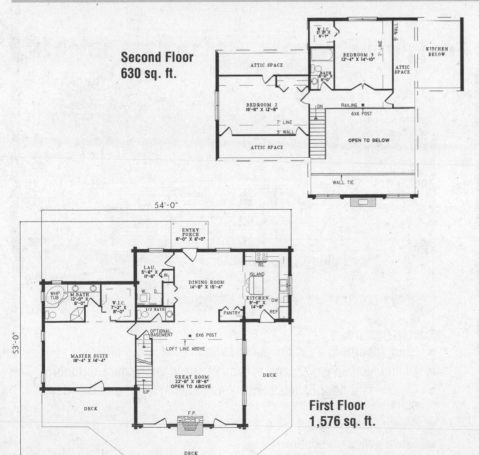

**Second Floor
630 sq. ft.**

- ATTIC SPACE
- BEDROOM 2 19'-6" X 12'-8"
- 7' LINE
- 5' WALL
- ATTIC SPACE
- DN
- RAILING
- 6X6 POST
- OPEN TO BELOW
- WALL TIE
- BEDROOM 3 12'-4" X 14'-10"
- 5' WALL
- 7' LINE
- ATTIC SPACE
- KITCHEN BELOW

54'-0"
53'-0"

- ENTRY PORCH 8'-0" X 6'-0"
- LAU. 5'-6" X 11'-6"
- DINING ROOM 14'-8" X 15'-4"
- ISLAND
- KITCHEN 9'-6" X 14'-8"
- DW
- REF.
- PANTRY
- WHP TUB
- M.BATH 12'-0" X 8'-0"
- W.I.C. 7'-2" X 8'-0"
- 1/2 BATH
- OPTIONAL BASEMENT
- LOFT LINE ABOVE
- 6X6 POST
- MASTER SUITE 18'-4" X 14'-4"
- GREAT ROOM 22'-8" X 18'-6" OPEN TO ABOVE
- UP
- DECK
- DECK
- F.P.
- DECK

**First Floor
1,576 sq. ft.**

Special features

- Enormous dining room is the center of activity with views into the great room
- Private master suite has a large walk-in closet, luxurious bath and direct access to the deck
- Two-story kitchen is incredibly spacious
- 3 bedrooms, 2 1/2 baths
- Crawl space foundation

Unbelievable Window And Beams — Plan #703-JB-1028

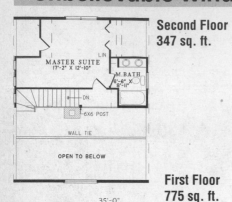

Second Floor
347 sq. ft.

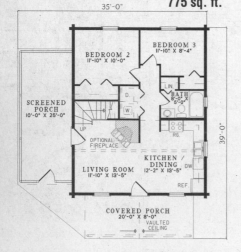

First Floor
775 sq. ft.

1,122 total square feet of living area — **Price Code AA**

Special features

- A large screened porch spans the length of the home for more casual area to enjoy the outdoors
- Cozy, yet comfortable indoor living areas
- Second floor master suite has access to additional storage and a private bath
- 3 bedrooms, 2 baths
- Crawl space foundation

Rustic Home Ideal For Family Living — Plan #703-JB-1023

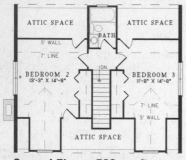

Second Floor - 596 sq. ft.

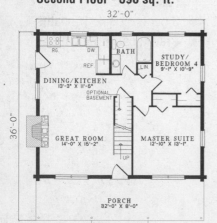

First Floor - 896 sq. ft.

1,492 total square feet of living area — **Price Code A**

Special features

- Study/bedroom #4 is private enough to be a home office
- Dining/kitchen enjoys lots of cabinet space and access outdoors
- Central first floor bath is convenient to living areas and the master suite
- 4 bedrooms, 2 baths
- Crawl space foundation

TO ORDER BLUEPRINTS USE THE FORM ON PAGE 15 OR CALL TOLL-FREE 1-877-671-6036

Traditional Log Home Feel To This Design

Log Home Plans

3,098 total square feet of living area

Price Code E

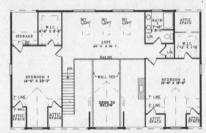

Second Floor
1,228 sq. ft.

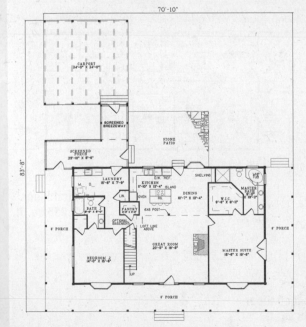

First Floor
1,870 sq. ft.

Special features

- Screened breezeway and porch add living areas in an outdoor setting
- Large second floor loft is brightened by a trio of skylights and overlooks to great room below
- Kitchen, dining and great rooms combine creating an area for entertaining and gathering
- 4 bedrooms, 3 baths, 2-car carport
- Crawl space foundation

Covered Porches Surround Home

2,821 total square feet of living area

Price Code E

Special features

- Cheerful sun room has double-door entry of dining area
- A garage vestibule connects to a large mudroom
- Enormous second floor loft could easily convert to a casual family room
- 2 bedrooms, 2 baths, 2-car side entry garage
- Crawl space foundation

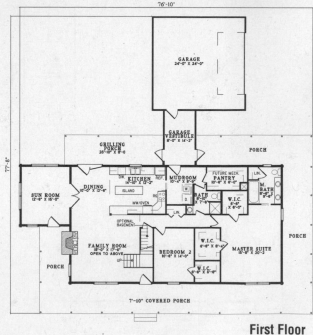

First Floor
2,056 sq. ft.

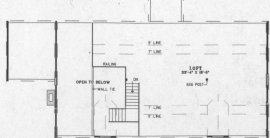

Second Floor
765 sq. ft.

TO ORDER BLUEPRINTS USE THE FORM ON PAGE 15 OR CALL TOLL-FREE 1-877-671-6036

View thousands more home plans online at www.familyhandyman.com/homeplans